Social Theory for English for Academic Purposes

New Perspectives for English for Academic Purposes
Series editors: Alex Ding, Ian Bruce and Melinda Whong

This series sets the agenda for studies in English for Academic Purposes (EAP) by opening up research and scholarship to new domains, ideas and perspectives as well as giving a platform to emerging and established practitioners and researchers in the field.

The volumes in this series are innovative in that they broaden the scope of theoretical and practical interests in EAP by focusing on neglected or new areas of interest, to provide the EAP community with a deeper understanding of some of the key issues in teaching EAP across the world and in diverse contexts.

Also available in this series
What Is Good Academic Writing? edited by Melinda Whong and Jeanne Godfrey
Pedagogies in English for Academic Purposes, edited by Carole MacDiarmid and Jennifer J. MacDonald
Contextualizing English for Academic Purposes in Higher Education, edited by Ian Bruce and Bee Bond

Forthcoming in the series
Practitioner Agency and Identity in English for Academic Purposes, edited by Alex Ding and Laetitia Monbec
Linguistic Approaches in English for Academic Purposes, edited by Milada Walková

Social Theory for English for Academic Purposes

Foundations and Perspectives

edited by

Alex Ding and Michelle Evans

BLOOMSBURY ACADEMIC
LONDON • NEW YORK • OXFORD • NEW DELHI • SYDNEY

BLOOMSBURY ACADEMIC
Bloomsbury Publishing Plc
50 Bedford Square, London, WC1B 3DP, UK
1385 Broadway, New York, NY 10018, USA
29 Earlsfort Terrace, Dublin 2, Ireland

BLOOMSBURY, BLOOMSBURY ACADEMIC and the Diana logo are trademarks of Bloomsbury Publishing Plc

First published in Great Britain 2022
Paperback edition published 2024

Copyright © Alex Ding and Michelle Evans and contributors, 2022

Alex Ding and Michelle Evans and contributors have asserted their right under the Copyright, Designs and Patents Act, 1988, to be identified as Author of this work.

For legal purposes the Acknowledgements on p. xv constitute an extension of this copyright page.

Series Design by Charlotte James
Cover image © Tuomas Lehtinen/Getty Images

All rights reserved. No part of this publication may be reproduced or transmitted in any form or by any means, electronic or mechanical, including photocopying, recording, or any information storage or retrieval system, without prior permission in writing from the publishers.

Bloomsbury Publishing Plc does not have any control over, or responsibility for, any third-party websites referred to or in this book. All internet addresses given in this book were correct at the time of going to press. The author and publisher regret any inconvenience caused if addresses have changed or sites have ceased to exist, but can accept no responsibility for any such changes.

A catalogue record for this book is available from the British Library.

A catalog record for this book is available from the Library of Congress.

ISBN: HB: 978-1-3502-2766-8
PB: 978-1-3502-2920-4
ePDF: 978-1-3502-3071-2
eBook: 978-1-3502-2918-1

Series: New Perspectives for English for Academic Purposes

Typeset by Integra Software Services Pvt. Ltd.

To find out more about our authors and books visit www.bloomsbury.com and sign up for our newsletters.

Contents

List of figures	vii
List of tables	ix
List of contributors	x
Foreword	xiii
Acknowledgements	xv

Introduction: A manifesto for social theory for
    EAP practitioners *Alex Ding*   1

Part One   Foundations   13

1. Genre: Some sociological foundations and implications
   Michelle Evans   15
2. Academic Literacies: Theorizing language as social practice
   Jackie Tuck   39
3. Systemic Functional Linguistics (SFL): A social theory of language
   J. R. Martin   59

Part Two   Perspectives   85

4. Legitimation Code Theory: Addressing fragmentation in EAP
   Steve Kirk   87
5. Social realism and genre theory: Knowledge-building in EAP
   Ian Bruce   113
6. Critical realism: What can it do for EAP?
   Julia Molinari   135
7. Bourdieu and field analysis: EAP and its practitioners
   Alex Ding   155
8. Ethnography: Expanding the boundaries in EAP
   Haynes Collins and Adrian Holliday   177

9 Feminism: Affordances and applications for EAP
   Yolanda Cerda   199

Afterword *Michelle Evans*   220

Index   227

Figures

1.1	Halliday (1978: 69), 'Schematic representation of language as social semiotic, and child's mode of access to it'	22
1.2	Genre Analysis Template	25
1.3	Adapted version of Miller (1984: 161), 'Proposed hierarchy of meaning, incorporating genre'	31
3.1	Projected law lecture infographic	61
3.2	Language strata	64
3.3	Language metafunctions	68
3.4	Language, register (field, tenor, mode) and genre	71
3.5	Cline of instantiation	72
3.6	Coupling of attitude and ideation	73
3.7	Imagic construal of types of misrepresentation	73
3.8	Temporal dimensions of language change (semogenesis)	75
3.9	Phases of pedagogic activity	75
3.10	Individuation (allocation and affiliation)	77
4.1	Signature semantic gravity wave in an EAP curriculum (adapted from Kirk 2018: 248)	95
4.2	Schematic semantic gravity wave across task sequences in an EAP lesson (adapted from Kirk 2018: 246)	96
4.3	Translation device enacting semantic gravity for talking about teaching	98
4.4	Conceptual class discussions represented for a teacher as a high semantic gravity flatline	99

4.5	Enhancing EAP teaching practices by 'waving'	100
4.6	A low semantic gravity flatline in EAP lesson design and enactment	100
4.7	Semantic gravity waving to connect practice tasks with wider course learning	101
4.8	Translation device enacting semantic gravity for planning conference talks	103
4.9	Semantic gravity wave profiling one section of a notional conference talk	104

Tables

3.1 Intermodal coupling (organized by metafunction)   74

3.2 Interlingual coupling (degrees of equivalence)   74

3.3 A teaching/learning cycle illustrated   76

5.1 The social genre/cognitive genre model   125

Contributors

Ian Bruce is Senior Lecturer in Applied Linguistics at the University of Waikato, Hamilton, New Zealand. His research involves the analysis of academic, professional and journalistic genres, and his publications are in the area of genre studies and academic writing. His most recent book is *Expressing Critical Thinking through Disciplinary Texts: Insights from Five Genre Studies* (Bloomsbury, 2020).

Yolanda Cerda is Executive Director of the Language Centre at the University of Leeds, UK. She is interested in feminist linguistics, feminism in education, intercultural communication, identities in education and language education in HEIs more broadly. She has taught and led EAP, language, language and culture and intercultural communication courses and modules at all levels at the University of Sussex, UK, and the University of London, UK. She has also lived and worked in education overseas in Spain and Egypt.

Haynes Collins is Director of Intercultural Studies in the School of Languages, Cultures and Societies at the University of Leeds, UK. His research falls broadly into the category of intercultural communication/studies, and he is specifically interested in how institutional and media discourses mobilize the concept of culture and interculturality to serve ideological agendas. His research interests also include ethnographic exploration of small culture formation in unique environments such as swimming pools. He teaches intercultural communication at undergraduate and postgraduate levels and is the programme manager for the MA in Professional Languages and Intercultural Studies (MAPLIS).

Alex Ding is Associate Professor of English for Academic Purposes at the University of Leeds, UK. He is also Director of Scholarship in the School of Languages, Cultures and Societies. His publications focus on EAP practitioners' education, development and scholarship, the social and political forces and structures that impact their working lives, and the associations that strive to represent their needs. He is co-author, with Ian Bruce, of *The English for Academic Purposes Practitioner Operating on the Edge of Academia* (2017).

He is series editor of the Bloomsbury series New Perspectives for English for Academic Purposes.

Michelle Evans is Lecturer in English for Academic Purposes at the University of Leeds, UK. With a background in the social sciences, she is interested in the Sociology of Education and approaches to genre analysis. Her research has drawn on genre and second language writing literature, and she continues to explore the role of social theory in genre traditions in EAP.

Adrian Holliday is Professor of Applied Linguistics and Intercultural Education at Canterbury Christ Church University, UK, where he supervises doctoral research in the critical sociology of language education and intercultural communication. The first half of his career was spent in Iran, Syria and Egypt as a curriculum developer.

Steve Kirk is Professor (Teaching) and Head of Academic Language and Communication at Durham Centre for Academic Development (DCAD), Durham University, UK. He has worked in EAP and ELT for over twenty years in a number of different roles, including as a director of EAP pre-sessional programmes and as director of Durham's former English Language Centre. Steve remains an EAP practitioner at heart and his professional and research interests lie primarily in EAP practitioner development, curriculum and pedagogies. His explorations in recent years have revolved mostly around Legitimation Code Theory (LCT) and its potential for enriching the theorizing and practice of EAP.

Jim Martin is Professor of Linguistics at the University of Sydney, Australia. His research interests include systemic theory, functional grammar, discourse semantics, register, genre, multimodality and positive discourse analysis (PDA), focusing on English, Tagalog, Korean and Spanish – with special reference to the transdisciplinary fields of clinical linguistics, educational linguistics, forensic linguistics and social semiotics. His recent publications include a book on Youth Justice Conferencing (*Discourse and Diversionary Justice*, 2018), with Michele Zappavigna; a collection of papers on language description (*Systemic Functional Language Description: Making Meaning Matter*, 2020) edited with Yaegan Doran and Giacomo Figueredo; a collection of papers on interpersonal grammar (*Interpersonal Grammar: Systemic Functional Theory and Description*, 2021) edited with Beatriz Quiroz and Giacomo Figueredo.

Julia Molinari is Lecturer in Professional Academic Communication in English (PACE) with the UK's Open University Graduate School for Research, Enterprise and Scholarship. Since 2008, her research and scholarship interests have brought into conversation the cognate fields of EAP, Applied Linguistics, Education, Philosophy and Sociology. Her fascination with academic communication culminated in a PhD (2019) on academic writing and a published monograph on *What Makes Writing Academic: Re-thinking Theory for Practice* (Bloomsbury, 2022). She has taught EAP, academic literacies and research writing at several universities in Italy and the UK.

Jackie Tuck is Senior Lecturer in English Language and Applied Linguistics at the Open University. She has worked for over thirty years as a teacher and lecturer in English Language, English Literature and Communication in a range of post-compulsory settings, including Higher, Further, Adult and Community Education, English as a Foreign Language and English for Academic Purposes. Her research brings together two broad fields of interest: on the one hand, the study of literacies from a critical perspective, as social practice, and, on the other, the role of language in higher education. She is particularly interested in throwing light on the complexity of 'hidden' literacy practices and events which play a huge but taken-for-granted role in higher education. To achieve this, she employs ethnographically oriented methodologies to explore lecturers' practices, including pedagogies around student writing.

Foreword

The new perspectives offered in this volume are fundamental in nature, interrogating the intellectual foundations of English for Academic Purposes (EAP). It feels fitting as the continuing global epidemic forces us to rethink some fundamental assumptions that this volume pushes us to ask ourselves about the very foundations upon which our work depends. In keeping with the spirit of the wider book series, *New Perspectives for EAP*, it does so in a way that remains firmly committed to the practitioner, in that it integrates theory with practice throughout. The contributors to this volume interrogate a range of social theories in terms of relevance and application to practice in EAP. While a focus on social theory is not new per se, the way in which a social theoretic approach has been pulled into questions of EAP practice is a new and welcome perspective, one we hope to see more of in future.

In the wider field of education, there is a considerable body of literature that has addressed the sociological dimensions of subject content, and of teaching and learning. However, in the sub-field of English language teaching and learning, and, in particular, in the area of EAP, there has been little focus on the sociological dimensions of the different aspects of practice and process. This volume pushes the boundaries at both ends of the theory and practice spectrum. There are relatively few attempts to bring a *sociological gaze* to EAP practice. While sociologists, such as Goffman, Bourdieu and Bernstein, are occasionally invoked in passing in some EAP literature, the level of engagement with sociological theories tends to be limited, and any connections made often minimal or undeveloped. That this volume addresses this explicitly can perhaps be seen as a sign of development and maturity in EAP as a discipline.

All of this may beg the question: why is it important to relate social theory to EAP? EAP is a complex, multifaceted field in terms of the knowledge base required. As noted by the editors of the first issue of the *Journal of EAP (JEAP)*, EAP embraces linguistic, cognitive and the social dimensions. Accepting that the EAP practitioner knowledge-base needs to be commensurable with wider understanding in the field, EAP practitioners tend to be well versed in the linguistic dimension, primarily of a discourse analysis orientation, while also having solid basis in cognitive learning theory for pedagogy. This volume tries to address the current imbalance in orientation, offering a social theory contribution to existing approaches in EAP. As shown in this volume, social theories provide a valuable tool to examine aspects of the target context for learning, a crucial part of needs analysis. Social theories also provide the basis for a reflexive self-examination by the practitioner. In this way, we offer this volume to complement current scholarly understanding of EAP.

Melinda Whong, on behalf of the Series Editors
January 2022

Acknowledgements

As the volume editors, we would like to thank all the contributors to the volume. All authors committed their time and attention to their chapter during some very challenging times throughout 2020–21. These have certainly been unsettling times, and individuals have faced considerable pressures at work and at home. In addition, in the process of creating the volume, the authors were invited to join online meetings to discuss their thinking and progress on their chapter. Most authors dedicated evenings or (very) early mornings to take part in the discussions. This commitment must be gratefully acknowledged. Towards the end of writing, as the final manuscript was being pulled together, the authors were asked to reflect on the processes they had engaged in to create their chapter. Many reflected on the role of these discussions. Further insights into this process and the authors' insights can be found in the Afterword.

We would like to thank colleagues at the University of Leeds, especially Bee Bond, Milada Walkova, Milena Marinkova and Geoffrey Nsanja, for their support. Thanks also go to John Swales and Karl Maton for their discussions and guidance in Chapter 1 on genre and Chapter 4 on Legitimation Code Theory.

We would like to single out Ian Bruce for special thanks. Ian has accompanied this book from when it was just a vague idea through to completion. He has been supportive, encouraging, insightful and generous in his time, feedback and discussion. Ian is an inspiration to those of us in the field who seek a more collegial and collaborative community.

Introduction: A manifesto for social theory for EAP practitioners

Alex Ding

A manifesto

This is not a conventional introduction, although it does perform the function of mapping out the scope and purposes of the volume as well as very briefly summarizing the chapters. The motivation for writing an unconventional introduction comes from several disparate sources. Experienced published colleagues have informed me that readers do not generally read (long) introductions, and this observation has given me licence to play with the genre of introduction to insert more polemical elements so that it resembles part introduction part manifesto in the hope it will be read. I have also allowed my own professional experiences to seep into this introduction as these experiences provide some of the motivations for wanting to publish a volume on social theory for EAP practitioners. The overall purpose of this introduction, and the volume, is rhetorical to argue that a sociological imagination or, more precisely, social theory should be a key element of the knowledge-base of EAP practitioners.

I want to scrupulously avoid the term 'social turn' in arguing for social theory for practitioners. 'Turn' in applied linguistics is so over-used that it loses impact. A cursory search of Google scholar reveals turn collocated (in applied linguistics) with emotional, multi/pluri/translingual, social, critical, ecological, political economy, complexity, material, discursive, creative, ethical, queer, decolonial, raciolinguistic and narrative. This carousel of competing turns in applied linguistics, on a generous reading, reveals tensions within fields which 'are not pathologies that distort a field, but intrinsic to the dynamics of knowledge production and the autonomy of its fields' (Moore, 2009: 123). A less charitable reaction is perhaps weariness where theoretical novelty and innovation appear frenetically, and cohesion is lost. It is not clear, always, whether 'turn' refers to a specific period and substantial body of work or a prospective pitch to create a new area of research. I am *not* arguing for a social turn in EAP. Instead, as Part One of this book shows, social theory has always been essential to key theories that inform EAP, namely genre theories, academic literacies and systemic functional linguistics. How social theory/ies operates within each of these three key EAP elements of the practitioner knowledge-base will be discussed later, but, for now, it is important to note simply that social theory operates quite differently within each and is explicit to varying degrees on how/why they draw on social theory.

Social theory provides 'the analytical and philosophical frameworks within which the social sciences can develop' (Turner, 2016: 1). Broadly speaking, social theory enables explanations of social phenomena and, as such, can inform as well as draw on all social sciences including, most obviously, sociology, but also anthropology, economics and political theory. And not just social sciences, Outhwaite (2015) argues for an approach to social theory which is 'promiscuous' or 'cosmopolitan' (2015: 121) that also draws widely on the humanities, especially philosophy. Turner (2016) and Callinicos (2007) both note the influence of literary theory and postmodernism on social theory. One should add that there is an ongoing re-assessment of social theory, through, for example, (re-)examinations of social theory and colonialism (Bhambra and Holmwood, 2021; Meghji, 2021), recognizing the South as (historically ignored) sources of social theory (Connell, 2007) as well as debates as to the nature of the complex and contested relationships between social theory and social justice and critique (Abraham, 2019). The 'founding fathers' classical tradition of social theory, via Weber, Marx and Durkheim, although still defended somewhat (cf. Turner, 2016; Callinicos, 2007), has, nonetheless, come under increasing scrutiny and critique.

One could characterize the current state of play in social theory as a 'boon' (Callinicos, 2007: xi) but also as 'fragmented' (Brezecry et al., 2017: 2), in 'crisis' (Turner, 2016: 5) and 'in decline' (Outhwaite, 2015: 122). These are hardly promising reasons to persuade practitioners to engage with social theory in EAP. It is important to note that these comments on the crisis of social theory come from within – from those who are social theorists/sociologists – and, as such, reflect a decline in the disciplinary status of sociology in universities where the 'space from which to theorise today is to a large extent more conflicted, ambiguous, and thus productive of massive ambivalence about what the project of social theory itself is' (Brezecry et al., 2017: 2). Indeed, Callinicos observes that 'social theory is often seen in contemporary intellectual debates as an outmoded form of understanding' (Brezecry et al., 2017: 1). Postmodernism has been influential in social theory, and its characteristics can be approximated as follows: antagonism to any meta-theory; promotion of various forms of relativism; sensitivity to and foregrounding of identities, difference and diversity; focus on contexts, discourses and practices; lack of faith in social progress; anthropomorphic understanding of knowledge; and deconstruction and dissolving of the self as an autonomous rational being. This has had a profound impact on social theory and an intellectual crisis of disillusionment (Turner, 2016: 5) has ensued. Also entailed in this has been a shift from 'sociology' to 'cultural studies' with a concomitant fragmentation of social theory into 'studies' (cultural, film, critical, race, queer, feminist, etc.). More broadly, neoliberalism has enabled a destruction of the social sphere where social institutions, community, public good and collective interests are under attack, and social theory either is reduced to *homo economicus* or fails to shape current socio-political issues.

Why, then, argue for social theory *for* practitioners? To answer this question, we need to have a closer look at EAP as a field of practice first. Ferguson was prescient in outlining the contours of the knowledge-base for EAP practitioners:

> Knowledge of disciplinary cultures and values; a form of knowledge which is essentially sociological or anthropological.
>
> Knowledge of the epistemological basis of different disciplines; a form of knowledge which is philosophical in nature.
>
> Knowledge of genre and discourse, which is mainly linguistic in nature.
>
> (Ferguson, 1997: 85)

Twenty years later, Ding and Bruce noted:

> Clear advances in EAP have been made in the third area (discourse and genre), some in the second area and little in the first. EAP practitioner identity and agency will, we believe, be greatly enhanced by developing a sociological understanding not only of the disciplines and departments, but of the university and those forces, values, discourses and policies that shape academia and EAP.
>
> (Ding and Bruce, 2017: 207)

I would still fully endorse this plea and argue that the development of the knowledge-base *for* practitioners has been lop sided with a clear focus on genre and discourse to the partial detriment of the two other pillars of the knowledge-base. However, this plea needs some adjustments and prompted some of the motivations for initiating, co-editing and contributing to this volume.

Firstly, although Ian Bruce and I provided a detailed account of the impact of neoliberalism on EAP practitioners and thus implicitly tried to give some substance to our call for a 'sociological imagination' in EAP, it was, nonetheless, just one example that covers an important aspect of EAP but very far from its entirety, and using just one (critical realism) social theory from the very many on offer. Many more uses of social theory and theories are available, and this book is partly motivated to demonstrate a range of theories in a variety of domains of concern to practitioners.

Secondly, Ferguson's contours for the knowledge-base of EAP practitioners are outward-facing towards the texts, cultures, values, practices and epistemologies of academic disciplines. What needs to be added to this is an inward-facing orientation to the texts, cultures, values, practices and epistemologies of the field and discipline of EAP. Practitioners need to understand their own field as well as strive to understand the fields and disciplines of their students. This understanding of the field of EAP is reflexive and draws on Bourdieu's concept of reflexivity.

The purpose of reflexivity is to reveal limitations to field knowledge production in three key aspects, relating to social position, the field and the academic (scholastic in Bourdieu's vocabulary) point of view where 'the social and political unconscious [is] embedded in analytical tools and operations' (Bourdieu and Wacquant, 1992: 36). This form of reflexivity is primarily epistemic and cognitive, aimed at identifying and overcoming the social and political unconscious that undermines the objectivity of knowledge. The purpose of this reflexive revealing is not to encourage a critical disillusionment with knowledge, nor is it a negative debunking reflexivity to undermine knowledge and disciplines; rather, 'Bourdieu's reflexivity aims at increasing the scope and solidity of social scientific knowledge' (Bourdieu and Wacquant, 1992: 36). The task for reflexivity is to reveal limitations in order to increase social scientific knowledge through a collective rather than individual endeavour which unfolds through institutionalizing 'reflexivity in mechanisms of training, dialogue and critical evaluation' (Bourdieu and Wacquant, 1992: 40), meaning to install reflexivity as part of the socialization and practices of social scientists, to become part of the habitus of the social scientist, and part of the cognitive system of the social scientist. In doing so, what becomes transformed is not only the cognitive system of the social scientist, but also, more importantly, the transformation of the social organization of the field. In other words, a reflexive orientation must be built into the field *and* their agents, and this orientation must be especially attentive to and put to work against the doxas in the field: 'a set of fundamental beliefs which do even need to be asserted in the form of an explicit, self-conscious dogma' (Bourdieu, 2000: 16) and by doing so reflexively we can break with 'the enchanted circle of collective denial' (Bourdieu, 2000: 5).

Thirdly, a motivation for editing this book emerged from a casual conversation with my co-editor where we discussed the often-fleeting references to social theory and theorists in EAP publications. Fleeting because although referenced in an article or chapter, social theory/theorist often too rapidly fades from view. While Roberts, in discussing the relationship between social theory and sociolingusitics, suggests that social theory and theorists are perhaps 'used more to quote with than think with' (2001: 332), this seems rather cynical. Hyland and Jiang (2019), while discussing citation practices more generally, offer a different, more charitable explanation:

> Clearly writers are moving towards a rhetorical style which gives less prominence to other authors. This may reflect an increasing 'scientism' in the social science disciplines, but overall it allows writers to appropriate authors' contributions with more cursory acknowledgement of their originators than in the past. Cited authors are increasingly relegated to peripheral spaces in the text over time, thus allowing writers to introduce material which supports their ideas but does not foreground the originators.
>
> (Hyland and Jiang, 2019: 74)

Cursory acknowledgement and appropriation of social theory were borne out when, to my surprise, in another article by Hyland and Jiang (2021) in which they trace, over a forty-year period, changes in EAP research, Bourdieu appeared as the second most cited author in EAP research over the past twenty years. Hyland and Jiang's study is extensive, covering 12,600 EAP-related articles from forty Social Science Citation Index (SSCI) journals and uses sophisticated methods to ascertain the most influential authors in EAP. However, looking at citations of Bourdieu in the *Journal of English for Academic Purposes* proved interesting. Searching Bourdieu in JEAP's research articles produced twenty-five hits in all volumes and issues since 2002. By contrast, Swales is cited 324 times and Hyland 395. Furthermore, examining the twenty-five articles citing Bourdieu more closely revealed two articles where Bourdieu appeared as part of the data sources from informants, two articles where Bourdieu is only mentioned in a long list of 'scholars' or 'influences' with no reference to his work as such and one article where Bourdieu appears only in a footnote. Of the remaining twenty citations, only three articles at most engage with one or more of Bourdieu's concepts in a more substantial manner. The seventeen other articles engage with Bourdieu in the most perfunctory manner by, for example, citing a few words from Bourdieu (e.g. 'the power to impose reception') without further elaboration, comment or development. Other practices include simply mentioning a Bourdieusian concept, for example 'field', with no further discussion. Interestingly, two articles repeat the commonly misunderstood and misused trope attributed to Bourdieu that academic English is no one's mother tongue.

Bourdieu is cited 11 times in *English for Specific Purposes* (Hyland 275 times and Swales 408) and 10 times in the *Journal of Second Language Writing* compared to 121 for Swales and 153 for Hyland. In the 645 pages of the *Routledge Handbook of English for Academic Purposes* (Hyland and Shaw, 2016), Bourdieu is mentioned very briefly on just 2 instances.

Rather than suggesting that social theory is central to EAP – even within the narrower research field of EAP – social theory/theorists often appear only fleetingly and implicitly, part of an assumed shared hinterland of culture and knowledge. Rarely does social theory take centre stage in EAP, and even less so in ways that are orientated to practice and practitioners.

The arguments, so far, for this volume can be summed up as follows:

1. Rather than arguing for a 'social turn' in EAP we are advocating for an extension to the knowledge-base *for* practitioners that explicitly and systematically incorporates a 'sociological imagination' to better understand the contexts, practices, values, cultures and structural forces that shape academia.
2. To insist on a reflexive understanding of the field of EAP to identify and confront the ideological, structural and discursive forces that shape our field and us.
3. To bring to the fore and to assess the often tacit and under-examined social theories that lurk in the shadows of the ideational/discursive domain of EAP and, if remain unexamined, risk-committing practitioners unreflexively to ways of seeing the world.

Furthermore, and much more polemically, there is an ongoing, often repeated, very longstanding and ultimately sterile debate in language education around the relationship between theory and practice and researchers and teachers. Ding and Bruce (2017) made an extended case throughout to argue that practitioners need to engage with and contribute to research and scholarship to enhance their academic identity, agency, power and cultural capital within academia and to orientate their investigations to practitioner concerns, which include concerns well beyond the classroom and into domains such as social theory and politics. The future of EAP and its practitioners depends on developing an academic identity, one that contributes *fully* to academia and EAP, and the struggle is to create the conditions across the sector to enable this. A parallel and equally powerful struggle is within EAP, where there is considerable resistance to this argument and vision for the practitioner. This volume is a contribution to persuade the practitioner field to adopt and develop an academic profile and vision for practitioners.

Finally, a central issue in social theory, structure and agency will continue to play out in the lives of practitioners whether or not practitioners engage actively in exploring this. Surely it is far better for practitioners to seek to understand the complex ways of understanding how structure and agency are related in the hope that we have

> a small chance of knowing what game we play and of minimizing the ways in which we are manipulated by the forces of the field in which we evolve ... [Sociology] allows us to discern the sites where we do indeed enjoy a degree of freedom and those where we do not.
> (Bourdieu and Wacquant, 1992: 198–9)

And, to go further, through this understanding, we can seek to address the gap between the real and the ethically ideal.

Organization of this volume

Part One focuses on social theory within the existent knowledge-base of EAP: genre theories, academic literacies and systemic functional linguistics. The remit for the chapter authors was to bring to the fore how social theories underpin each of these areas. That was the only guideline we gave, and each author was free to respond to the task as they saw fit.

In the opening chapter, Michelle Evans revisits key concepts within genre traditions that have been influential in different EAP contexts. She reveals ways in which grand sociological paradigms and themes have informed the development of genre theories and pedagogies. She convincingly demonstrates that there is theoretical eclecticism across genre theories and importantly shows how intellectual heritage and ontological commitments are embedded within genre in EAP.

In Chapter 2, Jackie Tuck explores academic literacies and provides a welcome clarity for a much misused and misunderstood theoretical approach in EAP and beyond. Emphasizing the non-neutral nature of academic communication, the chapter evokes issues of power, identity, inequality and authority in addition to a historical account of academic literacies. Concepts which support a transformative agenda in academic communication between the classroom and wider contexts are discussed with a stress on how academic literacies remain open-ended in its pursuit of political and social transformation in academia.

The final chapter in this section, written by Jim Martin, focuses on systemic functional linguistics. Martin approaches the task of relating the social to SFL quite differently to the previous authors perhaps reflecting SFL's long and rich theoretical tradition within applied linguistics and EAP. Rather than invoke social theory per se, Martin positions SFL contribution in terms of a social perspective on language and attendant semiosis. Key concepts in SFL as a meaning-making resource are discussed, including stratification, metafunction, instantiation and semogenesis. Martin finishes with comments on implications of SFL for a social orientation for EAP.

Part Two is orientated to social theories that are, in our view, promising for informing EAP but have, in almost instances, yet to fully make their mark within EAP. This choice of chapters and social theories is somewhat subjective and contingent, and I will comment on this at the end of this introduction. All chapter authors were tasked with making the case for the affordances of their social theory for EAP practitioners and, again, were given free rein as to how to go about this.

Part Two opens with an account of Legitimation Code Theory (LCT) by Steve Kirk. Kirk argues that LCT offers a productive lens through which to grasp a more integrated understanding of EAP practices and the field. An illustration of this is given through a key LCT tool, semantic gravity.

Ian Bruce, in Chapter 5, looks at an antecedent of LCT, social realism, and proposes social realism as a basis for framing genre knowledge. He presents his social genre/cognitive genre model as a broad framework for operationalizing this knowledge. The final section of the chapter relates genre-based pedagogy and its unpacking of the complexity of academic writing to social realism.

In Chapter 6, Julia Molinari asks (and answers) what critical realism can do for EAP. Molinari presents critical realism in order to theoretically ground and explain transformation in the field of EAP and to contribute to a collective understanding of the transformative and generative affordances of theories of social change.

In Chapter 7, on Bourdieu, I take the underlying impetuous of Bourdieu's social theory to be making the sacred profane. The chapter weaves between discussions of Bourdieu's key concepts and analysis of the field of EAP, thinking with Bourdieu, to highlight the ways in which EAP, as a field of practice, is subjected to forces that shape but do not determine the legitimacy, capitals, agency and power of practitioners in higher education.

In Chapter 8, Haynes Collins and Adrian Holliday explore perhaps the most familiar approach or method to EAP in this section: ethnography. However, this chapter contains a perhaps much less familiar notion – creative non-fiction. As they demonstrate in their chapter, ethnography enables a reflexive and holistic lens for engaging with institutional knowledge production, academic practices and discourses as well as a catalyst for both EAP practitioners and students to denaturalize, question and challenge institutional practices.

The final chapter in Part Two is on feminism. Written by Yolanda Cerdá, this chapter advocates for feminism as a theoretical framework and lens through which to analyse the texts, praxis and conditions of the field of EAP. She explores how feminist research and praxis have documented ethical and innovative approaches to production and pedagogies of academic writing within EAP and in related disciplines.

This volume concludes with an afterword written by my co-editor in which she discusses the themes that emerge in the volume as well as gathering the reflections of chapter authors having gone through the process of thinking and writing about social theory for this publication.

Edited volumes usually provide some guidelines on how to read it. I suspect readers will jump in and read whatever chapter(s) appeals the most and possibly get round to reading the less immediately appealing. We hope that you will read all of them though.

The publication is not a handbook nor a textbook, nor a coherent and compatible set of theories, but an invitation to practitioners (and researchers) to reflect on (1) how social theories are already implicit or explicit within more familiar theories operationalized within EAP and (2) how – possibly less familiar – social theories can be usefully put to work in EAP.

A good social theory is 'persuasive, plausible and parsimonious' (Turner, 2016: 5). A good critical social theory should show that 'things could be otherwise'. If, as a reader, and we fully expect this as editors, you find fault with our selection of social theories, finding them lacking or arbitrary, we implore you to make your case through scholarship and research and bring to attention to the EAP community those theories and ideas that merit attention and inclusion. There are many things we could have or would have liked to include. Of note, partly to provoke, we decided not to include critical EAP. One, because the literature and ideas that spurred EAP have fossilized and there has been little theoretical development of critical EAP for twenty years. Two, because CEAP no longer monopolizes the label critical in EAP. We would have liked to include a yet-to-be-written perspective that draws on Marxism and neo-Marxism and we also await the impact of decolonization on EAP.

A majority of the chapters have a strong critical underpinning – 'things could be otherwise' – and have, very differently with diverse epistemological and ontological underpinnings, all contributed to a vision of EAP that is, ultimately, concerned with narrowing the gap between the real and the ideal – that things could and should be otherwise for the field, its practitioners and their students.

References

Abraham, M. (2019), *Sociology and Social Justice*, London: Sage Publications.
Bhambra, G. K. and J. Holmwood (2021), *Colonialism and Modern Social Theory*, Cambridge: Polity Press.
Bourdieu, P. (2000), *Pascalian Meditations*, Cambridge: Polity Press.
Bourdieu, P. and L. J. D. Wacquant (1992), *An Invitation to Reflexive Sociology*, Cambridge: Polity Press.
Brezecry, C. E., M. Krausse and I. A. Reed (2017), 'Introduction', in C. E. Brezecry, M. Krausse and I. A. Reed (eds), *Social Theory Now*, 1–17, Chicago: University of Chicago Press.
Callinicos, A. (2007), *Social Theory: A Historical Introduction*, Cambridge: Polity Press.
Connell, R. (2020), *Southern Theory: The Global Dynamics of Knowledge in Social Science*. Routledge.
Ding, A. and I. Bruce (2017), *The English for Academic Purposes Practitioner: Operating on the Edge of Academia*, Basingstoke: Palgrave.
Ferguson, G. (1997), 'Teacher Education and LSP: The Role of Specialized Knowledge', in R. Howard and G. Brown (eds), *Teacher Education for Languages for Specific Purposes*, 80–9, Clevedon: Multilingual Matters.
Hyland, K. and F. Jiang (2019), 'Points of Reference: Changing Patterns of Academic Citation', *Applied Linguistics*, 40 (1): 64–85.
Hyland, K. and F. K. Jiang (2021), 'A Bibliometric Study of EAP Research: Who Is Doing What, Where and When?' *Journal of English for Academic Purposes*, 49: 100929.
Hyland, K. and P. Shaw, eds (2016), *The Routledge Handbook of English for Academic Purposes*, Abingdon: Routledge.
Meghji, A. (2021), *Decolonizing Sociology: An Introduction*, Cambridge: Polity Press.

Moore, R. (2009), *Towards the Sociology of Truth*, London: Continuum.
Outhwaite, W. (2015), *Social Theory*, London: Profile Books.
Roberts, C. (2001), '"Critical" Social Theory: Good to Think with or Something More?' in N. Coupland, S. Sarangi, and C. N. Candlin (eds), *Sociolinguistics and Social Theory*, 323–33, Harlow: Pearson.
Turner, B. S., ed. (2016), 'Introduction: A New Agenda for Social Theory?' in B. S. Turner (ed.), *The New Blackwell Companion to Social Theory*, 1–16, Chichester: John Wiley & Sons.

Part One

Foundations

1

Genre: Some sociological foundations and implications

Michelle Evans

Revisiting genre

Given its position in the 'foundations' section of this volume, this chapter revisits aspects of the multi-paradigmatic nature of sociology and genre traditions that have been influential in different EAP contexts, showing how these influences continue to impact on our understanding of genre and genre pedagogies. The content is informed by two literature reviewing strategies. The first involved a type of archaeological and intertextual tracing of the sociological heritage of key propositions in seminal texts within three genre traditions. This includes the work of Swales, Bhatia, Bakhtin, Halliday, Firth, Malinowski, Martin, Miller, Burke, Bitzer and Mead. The second approach revisited the sociological, anthropological and sociolinguistic influences on key concepts (*function, structure, system, context, culture, purpose, role* and *social action*). Some genre-based teaching materials related to different genre approaches were also reviewed alongside the themes and concepts being explored in the literature.

Hyon's (1996) comparative account of the three major genre traditions has been the preferred way of framing genre theory and pedagogies as they have developed in different contexts. Other useful introductions using this framing can be found in Wan Fakhruddin and Hassan (2015), Hyland (2004), Shaw (2016) and Bawarshi and Reiff (2010). Within these, Swales' ESP-based approach is compared to Sydney School genre pedagogy, which draws on Halliday's and Martin's Systemic Functional Linguistics (SFL). These are compared to the New Rhetoric tradition or North American genre studies related more closely to the Composition-based approach popularized by Miller and Devitt. Bawarshi and Reiff (2010) also include French, Swiss and Brazilian approaches. This chapter does not provide another overview of these main genre strands or more recent syntheses. Instead, some of the sociological concepts and themes within the traditions will structure the discussion.

While the pedagogical applications of genre theories are significant in EAP contexts, they can present theoretical and practice-based challenges. Genre approaches and associated discourse analyses can be used effectively by students to investigate (textually and ethnographically) the role of lexico-grammatical features selected to achieve rhetorical purposes within socially recognizable or conventionalized and purposeful texts within contexts or as contexts (Hyon, 2018). Yet there is variation in the extent to which these levels or features are systematically connected in genre-based pedagogies with the risk of text deconstruction that results in de-contextualized or over-simplified analysis of language features that can appear disconnected to rhetorical functions and purposes of whole texts and sub-genres. Other related and recurring questions or sticking points tend to revolve around the risk of conceptualizations of genre becoming a reduced version (of what key contributors intended) when they are perceived instrumentally or *used for* learning purposes. Other sticking points may be more inherent in the theoretical orientation itself.

In genre-based research articles, theoretical discussion can often be limited to a polite nod to a seminal text or contributor (as noted in Hyland and Jiang, 2021 and Riazi et al., 2020) with less opportunity to explore how ontological and conceptual commitments embedded in the chosen theoretical framework may be playing a role in the issues being addressed. This chapter offers some examples of how sociological paradigms, themes and concepts can be used to review discussions about genre-based pedagogies. At the risk of conflating challenges at this juncture, many of these recurring discussions focus on how to facilitate genre-awareness with students that allows for:

- enhanced understanding of the multi-functionality of genres in relation to social purposes and individual intentions at varying levels of analysis;
- analysis beyond the text and across genre sets, networks and systems in ways that explore relationships between formal features and lexico-grammatical choices, discourse, context, social actions and readers/ speakers;
- insights into the role of genre in maintaining social stability while also creating social and academic change, locally and internationally; and
- an understanding of explanations (beyond descriptions) of academic practices, conventions and constraints that may be or may not be treated as ideological alongside potential for genuine recontextualization, individual agency, choice and challenge.

Discrepancies in deciding how to define and classify genres and whether to proactively *teach* or allow students to *acquire* the types of knowledge that constitute genres are integrated in these points.

It is not possible to attend to all these challenges here, and, based on the analysis I have undertaken, the main sections of this chapter review questions about (a) the role of social purpose and individual motives, (b) the ways in which context is understood and (c) the extent to which genre pedagogies connect the layers of meaning between context, rhetorical functions and lexico-grammatical choices. These themed sections of the chapter offer a synthesis and analysis of selected aspects of seminal texts that focus on how these matters were addressed in genre traditions and some implications for today. Given word constraints and the scope of the chapter, some references to practice-based questions or challenges are offered for exemplification purposes but these could be expanded in further discussions. Before discussing these matters, the next section firstly introduces three major sociological traditions that highlight the relevance of key sociological concepts for Higher Education (HE), EAP and perceptions of genre. These establish some conceptual threads throughout the rest of the chapter.

Sociological paradigms, concepts and genre

Despite critiques of the relevance of traditional or 'grand' sociological paradigms, in comparison to later postmodern views (Eckberg and Hill, 1979; Skinner, 1985; Torres and Mitchell, 1998), this chapter shows how aspects of these are embedded in our work with genre. Paradigms are understood here as serving '*to define what should be studied, what questions should be asked, how they should be asked, and what rules should be followed in interpreting the answer obtained*' (Ritzer, 1975: 157); they provide macro-, meso- and micro-analytical lenses that help us to conceptualize social phenomenon in relation to (a) structural functions of institutions, including the role of these in maintaining social cohesion and stability and creating social change; (b) the role of power, inequality and hierarchy in the social world and the impact this has on groups and individuals and (c) the ways in which individuals interact with one another to create social reality symbolically and through social action (Hollis, 1994).

Ritzer (1975) categorizes sociological traditions as either 'social fact' or 'social definition' paradigms. (Structural) functionalism, as exemplified by Durkheim and Merton, and conflict-based traditions stemming from Marxist orientations study social facts as structures and institutions with coercive power over individuals, whereas social action-based traditions, exemplified by Weber, Mead and Shutz (including social action theory, symbolic interactionism and phenomenology), use social analyses that view humans as active creators of their own social realities rather than deterministically influenced by social facts (that includes norms, values, beliefs and social structures). Orientations within this latter paradigm are more open to investigating mental processes of individual actors, despite methodological issues attempting to do so. These claims are perhaps essentialist, but there are two important points that relate to genre traditions in EAP. One is the relative emphasis they have placed on analyses of social structure in relation to individual thinking and social actions within context. The second involves the practice of 'paradigmatic reconciliation' (Ritzer, 1975: 165) or bridging activities that is also evident in genre traditions. These will be discussed to some extent in this chapter following some examples of how these paradigms and levels of analysis can be seen in genre-related matters.

If genres are 'abstract, socially recognised ways of using language' (Hyland, 2002: 114) that are essential for communities to function, then genre must be an insightful way of understanding how these social structural realities influence and are influenced by shared and contested values, beliefs and actions of individuals and groups. Within this, macro-, meso- and micro-analyses do feature in discussions about the nature of and changes within Higher Education, EAP and genre-based pedagogies. At a global level, Bazerman et al. (2009) suggest humanity will struggle to remain connected and coordinated in the context of new technologies, new media and new social and economic arrangements. Apparently, achieving global wellbeing relies on every citizen developing communicative competence in *'genres of power and cooperation'* (Bazerman et al., 2009: xiv). Moving to a national and institutional level of analysis, we can explore the effect that immigration regulations have on types of assessment on pre-sessional courses in UK institutions – institutions that are almost wholly dependent on maintaining their licences to sponsor migrant students. At an institutional to individual level, we can also assess how inclusive education policies inform approaches to tutor feedback and then undertake further micro-analyses of how students engage with specific aspects of this feedback, for example.

These paradigms frame discourse on power, hierarchy and conflict. Decisions to take an ideological stance (or not) have had implications for EAP practice, including genre-based learning and teaching (Bastian, 2017; Benesch, 2009; Lillis and Scott, 2007). The virtue of EAP practitioners has been signalled in claims that our practice prioritizes student empowerment over profit-making (Hamp-Lyons, 2011). Yet for some time it has also been acknowledged that some genres (that may be deemed to be empowering or consensus-building by some) can contribute further to inequality, injustice and exploitation (Cope and Kalantzis, 1993). One can consider Threadgold's view (cited in Bawarshi and Reiff, 2010: 106) that what we really need to know is why certain genres are 'highly valued and others marginalised' over time. We can question the extent to which we agree on the need to understand *'how institutions and institutionalized power relationships and knowledges are both constructed by and impose constraints on (and restrict access to) possible situation types and genres'* (Bawarshi and Reiff, 2010: 106).

These questions also relate to the role of genre in maintaining social stability, social cohesion or the status quo (at institutional, disciplinary, national and international levels) while also being fundamental in social change in academic disciplines, in HE and beyond (Berkenkotter and Huckin, 1995; Valle, 1999 in Hyland, 2002). This does not depend solely on policy-linked genres but on all interactions and texts created by students, academics and professional colleagues functioning in particular roles and in relation to others. Hence, another thread of enquiry relates to the role of genre in identity (trans)formation of students and academics, as well as group affiliation within academic discourse communities. These sociological themes and approaches to analysis then are embedded in the full range of genre-related literature. Some of the ways in which these paradigms and concepts have influenced the development of genre theories will now be outlined.

Paradigmatic synthesis or theoretical eclecticism

While Hyon (1996) notes lines of delineation between genre traditions (including different disciplinary traditions, different emphases on text and context and different pedagogies), she and others also highlight more nuanced features and overlap (Devitt, 2004; Hyland, 2004; Johns et al., 2006). The theoretical eclecticism involved in the evolution of genre theories may not be problematic for some. Freadman (2012) suggests the instrumental or pedagogical pragmatism is most important and an attempt to arrive at a general theory of genre could undermine this. Others continue to address problems of construct validity when trying to account for genre as it is construed within these traditions (Bruce, 2008; this volume).

In terms of this blurring and borrowing of influences, Swales (1990: 4) saw opportunities to *cross-fertilize* ESP with the US, composition-based, 'Writing across the Curriculum' movement designed for 'L1 users' due to shared interests in '*student assessment, training instructors in discourse analyses, ethnography and methodology*' (1990: 4). Bhatia (1993) also discussed Miller's research and attended to contextual and functional issues in his definitions of texts and aims for genre pedagogy. Miller's (1984) use of Halliday's view of situation types was fundamental in her argument on the nature of exigence and motives within her model of genre. Bawarshi and Reiff (2010) and Motta-Roth and Haberle (2015) noted evidence of effective synthesis of rhetorical, sociological and linguistic traditions in the Brazilian genre approach. Before this, Hamp-Lyons (2011: 99) noted that Swales' (2000) work signalled a move (no pun intended) towards more 'socially-oriented educational theory and research' which was perceived to be closer to the Hallidayan 'genre literacy' of Cope and Kalantzis (1993) and Christie and Martin (2007). Swales (2004) also testifies to the significant influence of Bakhtin (1981, 1986). More recently, Martin (2020: 217) suggests that it is possible to bridge SFLs' concept of genre with the notion of action within Cultural Historical Activity Theory (CHAT). The importance of this suggestion will be outlined in the final section of the chapter.

To demonstrate one example of earlier theoretical syntheses, the types of 'skill and strategy studies' that led to the value Swales (1990: 14) placed on situation-specific practices and processes included Bazerman (1985) and Huckin's (1987) studies of reading approaches used by different groups of scientists and the suggestion that how people read texts could lead to changes in those texts over time. Looking more closely at Bazerman's (1985: 6) take on the 'constructivist character on reading', we find the influence of cognitive approaches but also Bruce's (1981) social interaction model of reading: one that sets out dimensions of analysis of social interactions with a particular emphasis on rhetorical relations. Readers are signposted to Goffman's *Strategic Interaction* (1969). This contribution utilized game theory to examine the use of moves and counter-moves within various examples of verbal interactions. Another example of this unpacking stems from Miller's application of Burke's (1954, 1967) work which, in turn, relied on George Herbert Mead's sociological interpretation of the *self* (in *Mind, Self and Society,* 1934) and the 'sociality of action and thought as the internalisation of objective relationships' (1967: 360). These unpicking exercises thus led directly to the heart of micro-sociology and the symbolic interactionist paradigm, but the same process has revealed the influence of functionalist and conflict-based traditions too.

What is most important perhaps is the extent to which these influences are used, for what purposes and the extent to which individuals are aware of these commitments. Given the diversity of influences in the genre traditions noted, this reviewing exercise was not completed entirely, and a larger, more systematic approach could reveal new insights. Of particular interest would be a mapping of the relative weight of influences of each paradigm used directly or explicitly in discussions relating to an ontology of genre. This chapter draws on just some examples and will now turn to the influence of (structural) functionalism.

Structural functionalism and purpose

Despite being criticized on many grounds (Burger, 1977; Nash, 1997), the contributions of sociological functionalists have been influential in the three genre traditions noted. Points of agreement and disagreement remain evident in aspects of genre approaches today. One point of departure was the decision to take a social rather than psychological analysis of language and genre. Swales (1990: 35) uses Malinowski's (1960) work on folklore genres to show the value of paying attention to 'how a community views itself and classifies genres' and maintains social groups. Parsons and Malinowski influenced the work of Firth and Halliday. Parsons viewed language as essential for the functioning of society and a key part of culture. Here, language is a type of instrumental knowledge developed through a socially structured learning process in relation to others – a process that is part of an action system of social relations which is orderly and imposes conventional, shared meanings on situations (Parsons, 1964). Here, individual needs and motivations integrate with normative cultural standards.

Taking a Durkheimian perspective, Halliday's (1978) analysis of language (Figure 1.1) prioritizes function over structure to explain how individuals become capable of meaning-making within society comprised of social relations that define the social roles they take on via language and together form a 'personality'. So, we can learn something about language and about the individual development of personality via *the social* rather than relying only on the psychological or mental processes (Halliday, 1978). The 'linguistic system and social structure are integral parts of the social system' and transmission of culture is dependent on language (Halliday, 1978: 68).

For Halliday and Firth, language is to be studied as behaviour (rather than taking Parson's view of language as instrumental knowledge) via a social rather than a psychological or psycholinguistic perspective (of the type that Halliday felt

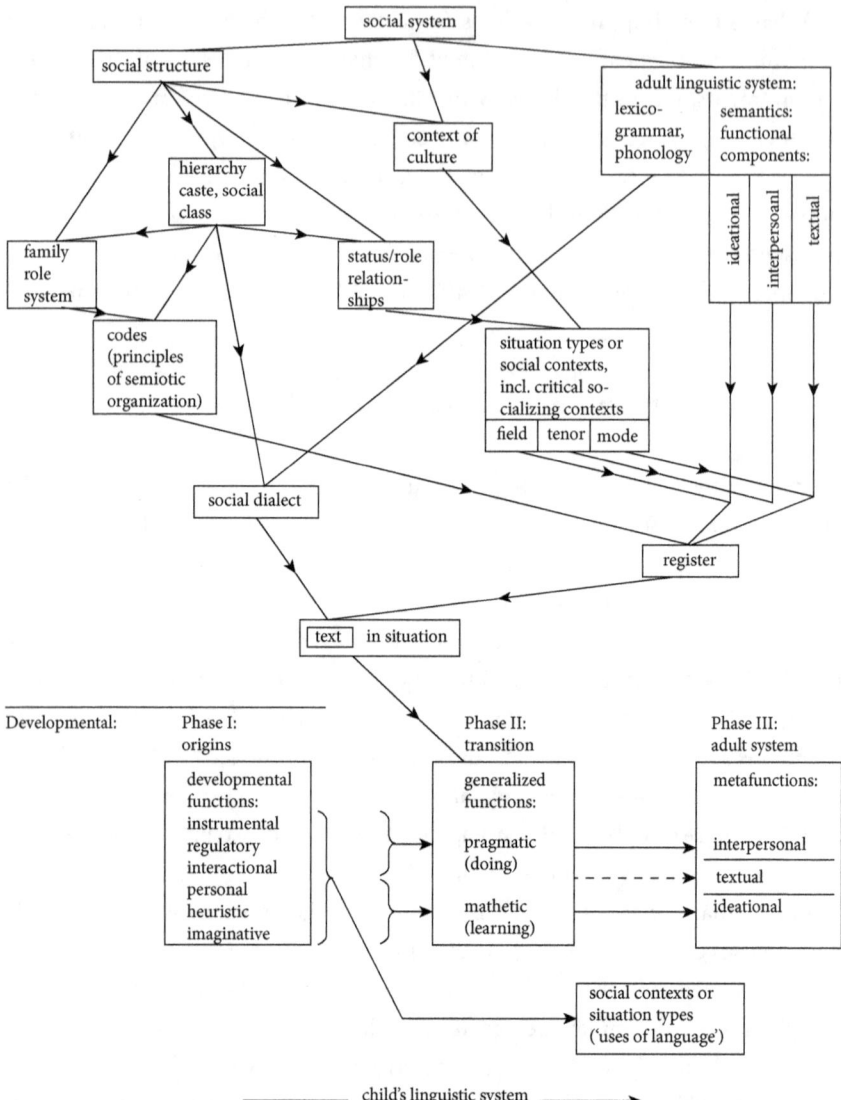

Figure 1.1 Halliday (1978: 69), 'Schematic representation of language as social semiotic, and child's mode of access to it.'

features in Malinowski's (1960) and Bühler's (1934) work)). Martin (1992: 503) agrees the purposes of genres are interpreted socially rather than psychosocially; again, there is less interest in the speaker's or writer's intentions but rather a [social] view of genre as *'goal-oriented and purposeful activity'* (Martin, 1984: 25; Coffin and Donohue, 2012). More recently, Martin (2020: 230) addresses *'the feeling that a social semiotic theory of language is in some sense lacking if it* is not positioned as part of a theory of mind' by reminding us that Halliday and others regard semiosis and cognition as 'alternative conceptions of meaning, not supplementary ones' and suggests that richer models of semiosis that interface with those of neurobiology may offer new contributions. For the point here however, the recurring issue of how to reliably understand and explore the social purposes and individual goals or motivations of those creating genres still exists.

Swales and Bhatia also had somewhat opposing views on the value of exploring individual motivations or goals in genre-based approaches. For Bhatia (1993: 13), Swales 'underplays psychological aspects'; he notes how members of discourse communities do have private intentions and they exploit constraints imposed by genres to achieve these intentions 'within the framework of socially recognised purpose(s)'. In his revisit of the concept of communicative purpose, while Swales (2004) acknowledged that private intentions may well exist, it is debatable whether these should be investigated.

> *Although we do not precisely find 'private intentions' here, we certainly recognize that certain players may know 'the rules of the game' and have longer-term perspectives on underlying strategies and institutional dispositions. In consequence, we are no longer looking at a simple enumerable list or 'set' of communicative purposes, but at a complexly layered one, wherein some purposes are not likely to be officially 'acknowledged' by the institution, even if they may be 'recognized' particularly in off-record situations by some of its expert members.*

At the same time, Askehave and Swales (2000) and others have shown how difficult it is to investigate, determine and agree on the 'real' communicative purposes of texts (even when these are self-stated) to the extent that communicative purpose should not really be used in isolation for classification purposes. Identifying general or all-encompassing communicative purposes (like saying the purpose of a research article is to share empirical findings) does not do justice to the 'underlying intentions behind' a genre (Askehave and Swales, 2000: 204).

This issue is evident in Miller's (1984) discussion of genre incorporating Burke's (1973) *motive* and Bitzer's (1968) *exigence*. While Burke (1967) was clear that literary criticism did not depend on knowing details of a writer's circumstances or psychology (and that analyses only of structure were useful in their own ways), insights of this kind could contribute a great deal to understanding a text. In order to create a *rhetorically sound definition* of genre, i.e. one that focuses on the action rather the form or substance only, Miller (1984: 151) had to bridge conceptual tensions between Burke's focus on motive in the situation of context (motives which are found within or created by situations and situations perceived in terms of motives (Miller, 1984: 154)) and Bitzer's exigence (which involves a type of reaction or response in comparable or recurrent situations that involve objects, events and people). This required a rejection of Bitzer's ontological premise that situations are real, objective or external to the individual (in the way a Durkheimian social fact might be perhaps) because what is recurring is not the material (people, objects and events) nor is it the subjective perceptions of these (which are also more unique). Instead, recurrence is intersubjective, and situations are social constructs given definition by the meaning by our interpretation of them. For Miller (1984: 175), situations (including the 'indeterminate material environment') must be determined or interpreted before we can act; so, it is how we construe the situations that recur rather than the situation itself. Miller uses the social construct argument to claim that Bitzer's exigence is a form of *social* knowledge rather than being located in private perception; it puts individual intentions into a socially recognizable form. Drawing next on Burke's motive, these are social rather than private or idiosyncratic; they are linguistically derived and come from joint or shared rhetorical actions and socialization.

Burke (1967) uses Malinowski's context of situation to explain how the material interests (of private or class structure) which influence our thinking and ways of communicating are defended or are supported (symbolically) in what we say and how we say it. These form our roles and personalities as we 'symbolically enrol ourselves with the promise that this symbolic enrolment would culminate in objective, material fulfilment' (Burke, 1967: 112). This process involves internalizing the external in taking on these ways of thinking and communicating (Burke credits Mead for this phrase) but also an externalizing or impersonalizing the internal, private intentions to meet the expectations of readers and the accepted motivations of the 'general scientific *Weltanschauung*' (Burke, 1954: 24).

Using these insights to review the student activity shown in Figure 1.2, we can reflect on the extent to which our approaches allow students to explore shared social purposes of genres and/or the personal goals or private intentions of writers and readers in a discourse community. When working with a research article, for example, a student response might be limited to '*the author's purpose is to share their research findings*'. This could be compared to an extended investigation, for example, into the legitimizing role of research and wider social functions of empirical contributions in the field; or discussion about the relative kudos awarded for different types of publications (such as research reports) and how this might impact on an authors' career progression in the faculty and the

Genre Analysis Template

Once you are clear about the genre of any text (both spoken and written), you should find that you are much more able to understand the purpose of the author, and therefore the language they choose to use.

Below is a template to use to help you analyse the genre of any text you are working with. This will also provide you with examples of language and organisational structures that you could use in your own writing.

Purpose: Why has the author chosen to write this text?
Audience: What kind of people do you thinks will be reading the text?
Context: What is the main point the writer is trying to make? where can you find this? How does it connect to the title of the piece?
Structure: What is the function or purpose of each paragraph? How does each paragraph connect to the next one? Give examples of the langrage used to show this.
Appearance: What does the text look like? Are there any pictures/graphics? How is it organised on the page?
Language: Is this formal or informal? Are sentences simple or complex? What tense is used most frequently? Write down some examlples.
Vocabulary: Are there any words or phrases that are commonly used in a specific genre? Or That link the wiring to particular subject? Would most people know the majority of the words used or are some only used by experts in the area being discussed?
Argument and writer's voice: How is the argument constructed? Are the cliams valid? Are there any clues which shown the values, thoughts and biases of the author? Is the argument credible? If so, why?

Figure 1.2 Genre Analysis Template. The origin of the template is unconfirmed. It was developed and revised over time by EAP practitioners in at least two universities in the UK.

field. Depending on the practitioner's discipline-specific knowledge, they might realize an authors' intention to extend or challenge dominant epistemologies and the implications this could have on readers and further research in the field. By exploring 'purpose' in this way, it is possible to see how 'private and public areas of a symbolic act at once overlap and diverge' (Burke, 1967: 11). Trying to unveil 'what the author was about when he produced the text' (Harris, cited in Widdowson, 2004: 22) is not methodologically unproblematic however, and relies on a more explicit examination of context. Another challenge, of course, is how these purposes are achieved textually and linguistically throughout the text. These issues are revisited in the final section.

At this transition, one can appreciate how the use of textography and other ethnographic approaches can extend students' understanding of purposes and contexts (Bhatia, 1993; Hyland, 2006; Hyon, 2018; Lillis, 2008; Nesi and Gardner, 2012; Swales, 1998, 2004, 2019; Paltridge and Starfield, 2016). Students and EAP practitioners can deploy a range of methods to 'gain insight into […] conventions of disciplinary conduct and reach some understanding of their [tutors/colleagues] broad discoursal aspirations' (Hyon 2018: 85). Although students might find more tensions and discrepancies than consensus, the process can enhance their understanding of the layered and complex purposes of texts they are reading and creating.

Revisiting language in context

Halliday, Firth, Miller and Swales comment on the limitations of generative grammar and other *formal* linguistic or descriptive text analyses in explaining the functional meaning-making across levels of language in a given context. This necessitated, in all genre traditions, the development of a social model of context that could explain the complex, yet relatively predictable, relationship between language choices (at varying levels of text) and the context in which decisions are made, interpreted or evaluated. Malinowski's context of situation and context of culture are fundamental in all models of context but the divergent development of these concepts for linguistic (and pedagogical) purposes has been critiqued (Lyons, 1966; Widdowson, 2004). Some of the issues raised are reviewed in this section.

While the relationships between context, social and communicative purpose(s), rhetorical functions and lexico-grammatical features are made in genre traditions, these are not theoretically unproblematic and there is a risk of disconnect in the relations between levels of language and context in genre-based pedagogy (Flowerdew, 1993). Although there is evidence of the variety of ways in which EAP practitioners do use genre theory effectively today, the extent to which these lead to descriptions of rather than explanations for the existence of rhetorical functions and whole genres is still a discussion point; as is the extent to which these features are understood in the broader sociocultural context (Paltridge, 2019). In the example in Figure 1.2, it is possible that the 'Language' box could become a decontextualized descriptive activity if not linked to larger units of meaning within the text and beyond.

This section revisits some ways in which these tensions were addressed within genre traditions and, in doing so, came to rely on the social for analyses of discourse that endeavour to show the social reality of contexts that language within texts keys into (Widdowson, 2004: 9). These tensions embed debates about the relationship between action and structure and between mind and society from different disciplinary perspectives. To begin, the issue of agreeing a concept of context is reviewed followed by an outline of ways in which language in context has been modelled.

Genres have been interpreted within contexts or as contexts. We can see differences in Blommaert's (2005: 251) definition of context as 'the totality of conditions under which discourse is being produced, circulated and interpreted' to Van Dijk's (2009) account of context, 'not as social situations, but as mental models or representations that individuals use to define a situation that, in turn, influence or are influenced by discourse'. This latter view, again, emphasizes the influence of the psychological and the role of knowledge (not just behaviour) in language choice and decision making. Context is also seen as a combination of situation or aspects of the physical place together with non-linguistic factors, events and sociocognitive knowledge (Bhatia, 1993; Hyland, 2004). Although the immediate context might be regarded as *'the university, and the need to prepare students for study at university'* (Hyland, 2004: 77), other relevant features of sociocultural context and schematic knowledge include no less than 'the institutions in which genres are used; the meanings that genres has for those who use it; intertextuality and what elements are borrowed or anticipated from other texts; the degree of formality, authority, intimacy, and other interpersonal aspects [...] who typically uses the genre and who they use it with; the kinds of purposes that the genre is used to accomplish' (Hyland, 2004: 77).

Drawing on Van Dijk (1997), Askehave and Swales (2001) left context as a *'black box'* that analysts can decide what to include based on what they think is relevant. In Devitt et al.'s (2004) rhetorical approach, aspects of academic *scenes* include an understanding of the objectives of universities generally, as well as understanding smaller scenes like individual schools, disciplines and courses in which individuals communicate around some shared objectives. Each of these numerous scenes has numerous situations which are the rhetorical interactions that involve people, purposes and settings. Within this approach, genres are defined as the 'typical rhetorical ways of responding to a situation that repeatedly occurs within a scene' (Devitt et al., 2004: 192). From here, teaching approaches explore the content, rhetorical appeals (i.e. logos, pathos and ethos), structure, format, sentences and words in key genres.

Depending on the conceptual framework and texts used then, insightful aspects of context can range from the microscopic (e.g. using the situation to interpret the meaning of intonation) to more macroscopic phenomena such as features of social structures and institutions as *far up* as the global economy (Saint-Georges, 2013). Taking Widdowson's (2004) development of Hymes (1974) account of context, if context is understood as a dynamic socio-psychological construct dependent on culturally shared and negotiated schematic knowledge, and if EAP practitioners do not have subject-specific schematic knowledge (and are not members of the academic discourse community or familiar with the wider context of a disciplinary culture), then identifying meaningful features and functions in texts without facilitation of those in the field can be difficult (Paltridge and Starfield in Hyland, 2016).

Having briefly reintroduced some of the conceptual challenges of context, the next step is to revisit some of the decisions made to explore the relationship between context and lexico-grammatical forms and functions of texts (in a 'context-first' approach) and vice versa (in a 'text-first' approach). Widdowson (2004) possibly captures the main issue when he explains how the categorizations and divisions within models separate language in artificial ways rather than fully explaining the co-occurrence and complex relationships. Referring to systemic functional grammar specifically, 'the potential that the grammar seeks to capture is misrepresented by the very process of accounting for it' (Widdowson, 2004: 26).

Continuing with SFL, Martin (2014, 2016) summarizes the intellectual influence of Saussure, Firth, Hjelmslev, Lamb and Gleason on Halliday's appreciation of form over substance but also notes Halliday's point of departure in viewing language as *system* (following Firth) that prioritizes the paradigmatic relations at each level of meaning (phonological, grammatical and semantic) rather than foregrounding language as *structure* which relates to the syntagmatic form of organization. Although syntagmatic descriptions are fundamental, it is the system networks of SFL that move it away from lists of rules and give it its systemic and functional capabilities (Martin, 2016).

In this model 'the social context (or situation) is a temporary construct or instantiation of meanings from the social system' (Halliday, 1978: 189). Context is the highest (language eternal) stratum understood as field (of social process, i.e. what is going on), tenor (of social relationships, i.e. who are taking part) and mode (of symbolic interaction, i.e. how are meanings exchanged) (Hasan, 2009: 170). Language internal stratum includes semantics, lexicogrammar, phonology and phonetics. The context, meaning and wording come together in language use via realization. The task of accounting for how meaning 'realises an aspect of the social system and, secondly, how it is in turn realised in the lexicogrammatical system' however was not unchallenging (Halliday, 1978: 41). Nevertheless, realization was used to unpick how extrinsic functions of language influence grammatical functions, 'in the sense of roles' (Halliday, 1978: 47). These extrinsic, abstract metafunctions (ideational, interpersonal and textual) form the basis of the organization of the entire linguistic system (Halliday, 1978: 47). Halliday (1978: 50) and others warn against undermining the simultaneous mapping of all functions by prioritizing some functions over others, i.e. psycholinguists (taking intra-organism view of semantics) might favour the ideational function and sociolinguistics might favour the interpersonal function.

As highlighted at the beginning of this section, critiques of Firth's and Halliday's use of Malinowski's context of situation, in this early model, identify problems in reducing it to deconstructed categories (i.e. 'relevant features of participants', including verbal and non-verbal action; 'relevant objects' and 'effect of verbal action' (Firth, 1967 cited in Widdowson, 2004: 39)) and for separating linguistic events into different levels or 'component parts' (i.e. phonological, syntactic, etc.). Again, deciding what is *relevant* requires more unpacking, as does the impact of sociocultural and political pre-conceptions of individuals involved (Hasan, 2009; Widdowson, 2019). While Firth (1950) consciously departed from Saussure's concept of *parole* (and was unconvinced by his Durkheimian structuralism ideology and ontological premises), using Firth's schema to identify the relations between the syntactic and features of the context of situation was problematic; it tended to discuss one of these categories in isolation rather in relation (Hasan, 2009). Firth's perceptions of context undermined concepts of context as a cognitive construct or a socio-psychological one in which individuals identify what is schematically relevant (Widdowson, 2004). More recently, Bruce's (2008, 2015: 163) model of social and cognitive genres aims to 'operationalise both the socially constructed and the more general, rhetorical and linguistic elements of genre knowledge'.

Furthermore, SFL's encoding of the three metafunctions as theme, mood and transitivity (or field, tenor, mode) that co-exist in a clause was said to undermine the opportunity for 'inter-systemic connections' (Widdowson, 2004: 29). It was also unclear how the textual function works with the other functions and it did not explain functional or pragmatic language *use* partly because the semantic and the functional are conflated (Widdowson, 2004: 29). Halliday's original two levels of analysis (i.e. linguistic analysis of text and evaluating or interpreting text) did not help to explain relations between sentences and larger linguistic units and tended to dissociate text from the 'contextual conditions which make it a text in the first place' (Widdowson, 2004: 23). Perhaps in response to some of these issues, Martin (2006) and Halliday (2008) (and others, i.e. Hasan and Matthiessen) continued to explore patterns of meaning across metafunctions and strata via *instantiation* in relation to *realization*. Note that Martin (2020) does study co-text – analysis of discourse semantics within and between clauses that may not be grammatically related to one another.

Martin's modified stratified model of context (as register and genre) partly came about in response to tensions trying to map purpose (as a variable of context) to the metafunctions. In this model the highest level is ideology which refers to the 'assumptions that a social interactants bring with them to their texts' (Eggins and Martin, 1997: 237). Context is a higher stratum of meaning (at the level of context of culture), rather than extra-linguistic phenomenon (Martin, 1992, 2016), and genres coordinate choices across field, tenor and mode. More recent studies of multimodality however indicate an ongoing theoretical challenge in understanding the instantiation process when features of different modalities are amalgamated (Martin, 2016). The modelling challenge here is informed by Halliday's reworking of Saussure's *language* and *parole* as a cline rather than an opposition. Again, this involves questions as to how to relate the concept of instantiation (the relation of system to text) to the strata and metafunctions. Furthermore, Martin (2020: 229) has since suggested that Cultural Historical Activity Theory (CHAT) use of activity theory, which is 'culturally positioned and historically contextualized', can help SFL to tap into the importance of 'what lies beyond the scope of linguistic analysis' and can help to overcome the risk of underplaying persons, i.e. who we are impacts on what we mean and vice versa. It is evident then that there are significant features of the intellectual heritage and theoretical premises that continue to be developed.

Miller (1984) also used hierarchical models to explain relations between form, substance and context and the way these are seen to acquire meaning at various levels. Again, understanding the real meaning of genre was deemed to require a fusion of 'substantive, stylistic (including form) and situational elements' (Campbell and Jamieson, cited in Miller, 1984: 153). Burke's *substance* here is the semantic value of discourse or those aspects that come from shared ideas, concepts and attitudes, whereas *form* is the way this is symbolized and guides the reader sequentially to steer their navigation and response. This, together with influence from Searle's Speech Act Theory, led to Miller's original hierarchies of meaning in which substance and form were positioned within the higher level of context or 'forms of life' (using a Wittgenstein description of context). Genre is form at a particular level and also serves as the substance of forms at higher levels. Figure 1.3 shows Miller's original take on the relationship between specific lived experiences and culture. Each of the levels in the diagram has a triple nature so 'each level is interpretable in its pragmatic aspect as action, in its syntactic aspect as form and in its semantic aspect as the substance for the next higher level of meaning' (Miller, 1994: 68)

In this model, context allows us to interpret the fusion of substance and form in a meaningful way. In a similar vein to Martin (1992), Miller noted that context itself could be hierarchical and so the three levels of meaning were relative and hierarchical rather than absolute. However, Miller (1994) revisited the way in which genre had been positioned as existing somewhere in between the micro-level and macro-level analysis. At the lower levels it was possible to demonstrate the three levels via pragmatic linguistics and conversational analysis, but it was not possible to do the same for the levels above genre (Miller, 1994: 70). Miller (1994: 59) continues

Proposed Hierarchy

Human Nature

Culture

Form of Life

Genre

Episode or Strategy

Speech Act

Locution

Language

Experience

Figure 1.3 Adapted version of Miller (1984: 161), 'Proposed hierarchy of meaning, incorporating genre.'

to ask how we can account for the relationship between the micro-discursive levels (e.g. speech acts, moves, episodic encounters) in relation to the culture (e.g. the scientific community) and how 'the macro-levels (genre, forms of life, culture, etc.) contextualize the micro-levels' (p. 59).

Returning to the sociological themes at the beginning of this chapter, Miller (1994) identifies this problem as being embedded in the recurring question of 'micro vs macro-sociological analysis, subject vs society, action vs institution, innovation vs regularity, subjectivism vs objectivism, private vs public and cognitive vs social'. She turns to Gidden's Structuration Theory and the instantiation of structure, which has a dual nature in providing the framework for social practice which then, in turn, reconstitutes and reproduces social practice. Here, genre is *a mid-level structuration nexus between mind and society. [… .] and the practical need to marshal linguistic resources for the sake of social action connects the micro and macro levels*' (Miller, 1994: 71).

The extent to which EAP practitioners can facilitate exploration of this marshalling process in a systematic way or theoretically informed way (using SFL, New Rhetoric or ESP traditions) continues to require navigation of the types of conceptual challenges revisited above. Appreciating the theoretical complexity and acknowledging ways in which influential contributors have also grappled with these issues can enhance understanding of genre and language use in context. Many practice-based publications (Brisk, 2015; Bruce, 2008; Hyland, 2004; Rose, 2008; Rose and Martin, 2012; Swales and Feak, 2012) offer useful ways of exploring features of context, purpose and discourse. These, together with conceptual discussions, can inform endeavours to reflect on procedures for deciding which features of text are more functionally salient than others, which aspects of context are most relevant to which features of text and how changes in textual and contextual factors can impact on interpretation of texts (Widdowson, 2004). These discussions might also mitigate against the danger of reifying text descriptions and making oversimplified claims drawn from texts collected from a single institution or department (Coffin and Donohue, 2012).

This chapter has reviewed some ways in which influential genre traditions have drawn on different sociological paradigms for different purposes. It has indicated how fundamental sociological themes and concepts are embedded in discussions about genre theory and pedagogies and it has demonstrated some of the contemporary implications of decision making at the ontological and conceptual level. A further unpicking of the theoretical eclecticism could offer new insights into the impact of intellectual influences and developments on EAP practice today. In terms of extending EAP practitioners' knowledge base, understanding the underpinning premises and theoretical basis of teaching opportunities and challenges can enhance practice in a way that reflects the complexity of working with the concepts we draw on. The discussion here was limited to that of *genre, context, purpose, function, system* and *structure* but there is much scope to extend this analytical approach by revisiting other influential theories and concepts.

References

Askehave, I. and J. M. Swales (2001), 'Genre Identification and Communicative Purpose: A Problem and a Possible Solution', *Applied Linguistics*, 22 (2): 195–212.

Bakhtin, M. M. (1981), *The Dialogic Imagination*, trans. C. Emerson and M. Holquist, Texas: University of Texas Press.

Bakhtin, M. M. (1986), 'The Problem of Speech Genres', in C. Emerson and M. Holquist (eds), *Speech Genres and Other Late Essays*, 60–102, Austin: University of Texas Press.

Bastian, H. (2017), 'Student Affective Responses to "Bringing the Funk" in the First-year Writing Classroom', *College Composition and Communication*, 69 (1): 6–34.

Bawarshi, A. and M. J. Reiff (2010), *Genre: An Introduction to History, Theory, Research, and Pedagogy*, West Lafayette, IN: Parlor Press LLC.

Bazerman, C. (1985), 'Physicists Reading Physics', *Written Communication*, 2 (1): 3–23.

Bazerman, C., A. Bonini, and D. Figueiredo (2009), *Genre in a Changing World*, Fort Collins, CO: The WAC Clearinghouse and Parlor Press.

Benesch, S. (2009), *Critical English for Academic Purposes: Theory, Politics and Practice*, Mahwah, NJ: Erlbaum.

Berkenkotter, C. and T. Huckin (1995), *Genre Knowledge in Disciplinary Communication*, Hillsdale, NJ: Lawrence Erlbaum.

Bhatia, V. K. (1993), *Analysing Genre: Language Use in Professional Settings*, London: Longman.

Bitzer, L. F. (1968), 'The Rhetorical Situation', *Philosophy and Rhetoric Quarterly*, 7: 31–40.

Blommaert, J. (2005), *Discourse*, Cambridge: Cambridge University Press.

Brisk, M. (2015), *Engaging Students in Academic Literacies*, New York: Routledge.

Bruce, I. (2008), *Academic Writing and Genre*, London: Continuum.

Bruce, I. (2015), 'Use of Cognitive Genres as Textual Norms in Academic English Prose: University Essays in English Literature and Sociology', *Bulletin suisse de linguistique appliquée*, Centre de linguistique appliquée Université de Neuchâtel No spécial: 161–75.

Bruce, B. (1981), 'A Social Interaction Model of Reading', Research Report 218, Center for the Study of Reading. University of Illinois: Urbana.

Burke, K. (1954), *Permanence and Change*, California: Hermes Publications.
Burke, K. (1967), *The Philosophy of Literary Form*, Baton Rouge: Louisiana State University Press.
Burke, K. (1973), 'The Rhetorical Situation', in L. Thayer (ed.), *Communication: Ethical and Moral Issues*, 263–75, New York: Gordon and Breach.
Burger, T. (1977), 'Talcott Parsons, the Problem of Order in Society, and the Program of an Analytical Sociology', *American Journal of Sociology*, 83 (2): 320–39.
Coffin, A. and J. P. Donohue (2012), 'Academic Literacies and Systemic Functional Linguistics: How Do They Relate?' *Journal of English for Academic Purposes*, 11 (1): 64–75.
Cope, B. and M. Kalantzis (1993), *The Powers of Literacy: A Genre Approach to Teaching Writing*, Pittsburgh: University of Pittsburgh Press.
Christie, F. and J. R. Martin, eds (2007), *Language, Knowledge and Pedagogy: Functional Linguistic and Sociological Perspectives*, London/New York: Continuum.
Devitt, A., M. J. Reiff and A. Bawarshi (2004), *Scenes of Writing: Strategies for Composing with Genres*, New York: Pearson Education.
Devitt, A. (2004), *Writing Genre*, Carbondale: Southern Illinois University Press.
Eckberg, D. and L. Hill (1979), 'The Paradigm Concept and Sociology: A Critical Review', *American Sociology Review*, 44: 925–37.
Eggins, S. and J. R. Martin (1997), 'Genres and Registers of Discourse', in T. A. van Dijk. (ed.), *Discourse as Structure and Process: Discourse Studies: A Multidisciplinary Introduction*, 230–56, London: Sage Publications.
Firth, J. R. (1950), 'Personality and Language in Society', *The Sociological Review*, a42 (1): 37–52.
Flowerdew, J. (1993), 'An Educational, or Process, Approach to the Teaching of Professional Genres', *ELT Journal*, 47 (4): 305–16.
Freadman, A. (2012), 'The Traps and Trappings of Genre Theory', *Applied Linguistics*, 33 (5): 544–63.
Goffman, I. (1969), *Strategic Interaction*, Pennsylvania: University of Pennsylvania Press.
Halliday, M. A. K. (1978), *Language as Social Semiotic: The Social Interpretation of Language and Meaning*, Baltimore, MD: University Park Press.
Halliday, M. A. K. (2008), 'Working the Meaning: Towards an Appliable Linguistics', in J. Webster (ed.), *Meaning in Context: Strategies for Implementing Intelligent Applications of Language Studies*, 7–23, London: Continuum.
Hamp-Lyons, L. (2011), 'English for Academic Purposes', in E. Hinkel (ed.), *Handbook of Research in Second Language Teaching and Learning*, 89–105, New York: Routledge.
Hasan, R. (2009), 'The Place of Context in a Systemic Functional Model', in J. Webster and M. A. K. Halliday (eds), *Continuum Companion to Systemic Functional Linguistics*, 166–89, London: Continuum.
Hollis, M. (1994), *The Philosophy of Social Science: An Introduction*, Cambridge: Cambridge University Press.

Huckin, P. (1987), 'Surprise Value in Scientific Discourse', Paper presented at the CCC Convention, Atlanta, Georgia.

Hyland, K. (2002), 'Language, Context and Literacy', *Annual Review of Applied Linguistics*, 2: 113–35.

Hyland, K. (2004), *Genre and Second Language Writing*, Michigan: University of Michigan Press.

Hyland, K. (2006), *English for Academic Purposes: An Advanced Resource Book*, London: Routledge.

Hyland, K. and F. Jiang (2021), 'A Bibliometric Study of EAP Research: Who Is Doing What, Where and When?' *Journal of English for Academic Purposes*, 49: 100929.

Hymes, D. H. (1974), *Foundations of Sociolinguistics: An Ethnographic Approach*, Pittsburgh: University of Pennsylvania Press.

Hyon, S. (1996), 'Genre in Three Traditions: Implications for ESL', *TESOL Quarterly*, 30 (4): 693–722.

Hyon, S. (2018), *Genre and English for Specific Purposes*, Abingdon: Routledge.

Johns, A. M., A. Bawarshi, R. M. Coe, K. Hyland, B. Paltridge, M. R. Reiff and C. Tardy (2006), 'Crossing the Boundaries of Genre Studies: Commentaries by Experts', *Journal of Second Language Writing*, 15: 234–49.

Lillis, T. (2008), 'Ethnography as Method, Methodology, and "Deep Theorizing": Closing the Gap between Text and Context in Academic Writing Research', *Written Communication*, 25 (3): 353–88.

Lillis, T. M. and M. Scott (2007), 'Defining Academic Literacies Research: Issues of Epistemology, Ideology and Strategy', *Journal of Applied Linguistics*, 4: 5–32.

Lyons, J. (1966), 'Firth's Theory of "Meaning"', in C. E. Bazell, J. C. Catford, M. A. K. Halliday and R. H. Robins (eds), *In Memory of J. R. Firth*, London: Longman.

Malinowski, B. (1960), *A Scientific Theory of Culture and Other Essays*, New York: Oxford University Press.

Martin, J. R. (1984), 'Language, Register and Genre', in F. Christie (ed.), *Children Writing: Reader*, 21–30, Geelong, VIC: Deakin University Press.

Martin, J. R. (1992), *English Text: System and Structure*, Amsterdam: John Benjamin's Publishing Company.

Martin, J. R. (2006), 'Genre, Ideology and Intertextuality: A Systemic Functional Perspective', *Linguistics and the Human Sciences*, 2 (2), 275–98.

Martin, J. R. (2014), 'Evolving Systemic Functional Linguistics: Beyond the Clause', *Functional Linguistics*, 1 (3): 1–24.

Martin, J. R. (2016), 'Meaning Matters: A Short History of Systemic Functional Linguistics', *Word*, 62 (1): 35–58.

Martin, J. R. (2020), 'Genre and Activity: A Potential Site for Dialogue between Systemic Functional Linguistics (SFL) and Cultural Historical Activity Theory', *Mind, Culture, and Activity*, 27 (3): 216–32.

Mead, G. H. (1934), *Mind, Self, and Society*, Chicago: University of Chicago Press.

Miller, C. (1984), 'Genre as Social Action', *Quarterly Journal of Speech*, 70: 151–67.

Miller, C. (1994), 'Rhetorical Community: The Cultural Basis of Genre', in A. Freedman and P. Medway (eds), *Genre and the New Rhetoric*, 57–66, Bristol: Taylor and Francis.

Motta-Roth, D. and V. Heberle (2015), 'A Short Cartography of Genre Studies in Brazil', *Journal of English for Academic Purposes*, 19: 22–31.

Nash, J. (1997), 'When Isms Become Wasms', *Critique of Anthroppology*, 17 (1): 11–32.

Nesi, H. and S. Gardner (2012), *Genres across the Disciplines: Student Writing in Higher Education*, Cambridge: Cambridge University Press.

Paltridge, B. (2019), 'Focusing on Language in Second Language Writing Classrooms: Rethinking the Approach', *Journal of Second Language Writing*, 46: 100680.

Paltridge, B. and S. Starfield (2016), 'English for Specific Purposes', in E. Hinkel. (ed.), *Handbook of Research in Second Language Teaching and Learning*, 56–67, New York: Routledge.

Parsons, T. (1964), *Social Structure and Personality*, New York: The Free Press of Glencoe.

Riazi, A. M., H. Ghanbar and I. Fazel (2020), 'The Contexts, Theoretical and Methodological Orientation of EAP Research: Evidence from Empirical Articles Published in the Journal of English for Academic Purposes', *Journal of English for Academic Purposes*, 48: 100925.

Ritzer, G. (1975), *Sociology: A Multiple Paradigm Science*. Boston, MA: Allyn and Bacon.

Rose, D. (2008), 'Writing as Linguistic Mastery: The Development of Genre-based Literacy Pedagogy', in D. Myhill, D. Beard, M. Nystrand and J. Riley (eds), *Handbook of Writing Development*, 151–66, London: Sage Publications.

Rose, D. and J. Martin (2012), *Learning to Write, Reading to Learn: Genre, Knowledge and Pedagogy in the Sydney School*, Sheffield: Equinox.

Saint-Georges, I. (2013), 'Context in the Analysis of Discourse', in C. A. Chapelle (ed.), *The Encyclopedia of Applied Linguistics*, London: Blackwell Publishing Ltd.

Shaw, P. (2016), 'Genre Analysis', in K. Hyland and P. Shaw (eds), *The Routledge Handbook of English for Academic Purposes*, 243–55, London: Routledge.

Skinner, Q. (1985), *The Return of Grand Theory in the Human Sciences*, Cambridge: Cambridge University Press.

Swales, J. (1990), *Genre Analysis: English in Academic and Research Settings*, Cambridge: Cambridge University Press.

Swales, J. (1998), *Other Floors, Other Voices: A Textography of a Small University Building*. Mahwah, NJ: Lawrence Erlbaum.

Swales, J. (2004), *Research Genres: Explorations and Applications*, Cambridge: Cambridge University Press.

Swales, J. (2019), 'The Futures of EAP Genre Studies: A Personal Viewpoint', *Journal of English for Academic Purposes*, 38: 75–82.

Swales, J. (2000), 'Languages for Specific Purposes', *Annual Review of Applied Linguistics*, 20: 59–76.

Swales, J. and C. Feak (2012), *Academic Writing for Graduate Students*, Ann Arbor: The University of Michigan Press.

Torres, C. A. and T. R. Mitchell (1998), *Sociology of Education: Emerging Perspectives*, Albany: State University of New York Press.

Van Dijk, T. A. (1997), 'Discourse as Interaction in Society', in T. A. van Dijk (ed.), *Discourse as Social Interaction*, 1–37, London: Sage Publications.

Van Dijk, T. A. (2009), *Society and Discourse: How Social Contexts Influence Text and Talk*, Cambridge: Cambridge University Press.

Wan Fakhruddin, W. F. W. and H. Hassan (2015), 'A Review of Genre Approaches within Linguistic Traditions', *LSP International Journal*, 2 (2): 58–68.

Widdowson, H. G. (2004), *Text, Context and Pretext: Critical Issues in Discourse Analysis*, Oxford: Blackwell Publishing.

Widdowson, H. (2019), 'Disciplinarity and Disparity in Applied Linguistics', in C. Wright., L. Harvey and J. Simpson (eds), *Voices and Practices in Applied Linguistics: Diversifying a Discipline*, 33–50, York: White Rose University Press.

2

Academic Literacies: Theorizing language as social practice

Jackie Tuck

What is meant by Academic Literacies?

The term 'academic literacies' is some way off having a shared or settled meaning (Lillis, 2019; Lillis and Scott, 2007). The plural phrase is often used descriptively by academic language specialists to acknowledge that academic reading and writing vary according to contextual factors, particularly discipline. Important though this insight is, the notion of 'disciplinary plurality' does not fully 'convey the theoretical nuance of academic literacies as a research paradigm' (Turner, 2012: 18). The term has also, in some contexts, come to replace 'skills' or is even 'used to mask ... "decontextualised" approaches' (Boughey and McKenna, 2016: 5). This chapter aims to give an account of Academic Literacies[1] as a distinctive theoretical paradigm, including some of its nuances, with the aim of proving useful to those working in EAP teaching, programme delivery and research. As a starting point, I use Lillis's (2019: 4) brief working definition of the field as 'a critical and social practice perspective on writing and reading in the academy' and begin to unpack this further. I then give a short historical account of Academic Literacies and of how it has been taken up in a range of language-specialist fields, in higher education more broadly and in EAP, sometimes problematically. The central section of the chapter focuses in turn on the concepts of 'the social', 'practice' and being 'critical' as they relate to Academic Literacies. I then consider selected examples of critical theoretical concepts which have been used in

[1] To distinguish the 'critical, social practice' meaning from the more general, descriptive meaning of the term, I use capitals A and L for the former. However, this convention is not always used, and there is no intention to suggest that Academic Literacies represents a neatly bounded, discrete field; the reality is a much messier series of influences, debates and overlaps. Some key foundational work does not use the term at all (e.g. Ivanič, 1998; Thesen, 1997). It is sometimes abbreviated to 'Ac Lits' (e.g. McGrath and Kaufhold, 2016).

Academic Literacies to facilitate analysis of literacy practices in the academy. I conclude with reflection on the nature of Academic Literacies as paradigm in which theory and practice are closely bound up with one another in a creative dialogue which leaves open the possibility of continual questioning and change.

> ## A reflection on positioning
>
> *By virtue of this chapter's literal position in the first section of the current volume, 'Academic Literacies' is metaphorically positioned as an established theory in EAP (see introduction: 8). This contextualization of Academic Literacies as foundational is a positive indication of its influence on EAP practitioners and researchers and more broadly in higher education, particularly in geopolitical locations such as the UK, Europe, South Africa and Australia, over three decades. Academic Literacies has indeed often been referred to as 'influential' (Canton et al., 2018; Wingate, 2012) and even as 'dominant' (Wingate and Tribble, 2012). Classic Academic Literacies texts, especially Lea and Street (1998), remain widely cited in journals such as JEAP, JESP, Studies in HE and Teaching in HE.*
>
> *However, the idea that Academic Literacies is 'established' in the context of EAP sits uncomfortably with me as I draft this chapter. It could be argued that both at a theoretical level and 'on the ground' in EAP classrooms, programmes and teacher development, the field remains very much marginal and radically at odds with entrenched conceptualizations of language which help to position much EAP, like other language-focused provision, as a service at the academic margins (Ding and Bruce, 2017; Turner, 2004, 2012). My experience of struggles to apply an Academic Literacies approach to curriculum development and tuition strategy in my own institutional contexts reinforces my sense that Academic Literacies places me on the margins, asking 'awkward' questions. Perhaps this is a question of 'field' as well as individual identity and temperament. What I mean by that is that the Academic Literacies practitioner's 'comfort zone' (whatever their institutional location) **is** the margin and that marginality is a key resource for their practice because it is predicated on critique, reflexivity and the continual negotiation of tensions. The practice of Academic Literacies still often means working within the 'cracks' in institutional walls rather than being part of the foundations (Street in Street et al., 2015: 389). This boundary positioning is a consequence of the field's theoretical character, which I argue in this chapter is more helpfully understood as a commitment to theoriz**ing** rather than as a settled theory of how things are, could or should be as a disposition to questioning rather than something which provides 'answers'.*

Street (in Blommaert et al., 2007) identifies two key dimensions of Academic Literacies as a critical and social practice perspective. First, it takes an empirically driven view of what academic reading and writing[2] are and how they are practised at university. Rather than starting with a priori understandings of expectations surrounding texts or practices, Academic Literacies teacher-researchers see these as open questions to be empirically explored (e.g. Lillis et al., 2015), sometimes by students themselves (e.g. Scalone and Street, 2006). This includes an interest in the perspectives of writers and readers in any given context, as well as textual analysis where relevant. Accordingly, pedagogies influenced by this approach focus less on inducting students and evaluating their texts against presumed norms and more on processes of critical enquiry about conventions and requirements in any given context – what they are, why they may exist, how they vary, which are most valued, with what consequences and for whom. Secondly, 'Academic Literacies' indicates a shift *towards* an understanding that academic reading and writing are intricately linked to issues of identity, power and authority, and that they are not only 'situated' in contexts at different scales (disciplines, levels of study, departments, institutions, national policies, global publication regimes) but fundamentally ideological and contested. This shifts us *away* from the pervasive 'common sense' understanding that academic reading and writing are primarily psychological competencies which university students should transfer from schooling and take onward to employment as a portable (albeit expanded) package of discrete skills. This theoretical move has clear implications for pedagogy as it foregrounds the need for all students, whatever their language background, to be *taught* the norms and expectations which prevail in their new academic contexts, explicitly and implicitly through socialization. It rejects a 'deficit' positioning of students and is closely linked with discourses of equity, access and widening participation in the 'mass' university (Boughey and McKenna, 2016; Ivanič and Lea, 2006; Lillis, 2019). In this respect, the Academic Literacies commitment to dismantling the 'institutional practice of mystery' (Lillis, 2001) has much in common with SFL and genre pedagogies which seek to empower students by giving them access to powerful discourses 'which are not equally distributed in society' (Coffin and Donohue, 2012: 72). However, Academic Literacies requires a *further* critical pedagogic shift which is particularly important in the context of EAP, where the need for explicit teaching is a given, *raison d'être* of the field. That is, instead

---

[2] I use 'reading' and 'writing' here in the broadest sense, to include texts of all kinds including visual modes and particular types of 'literate' oracy.

of focusing on supporting learners to be continually adaptive to norms as these change from one context to another, 'agility and responsiveness [are seen] as the responsibility of academic communities and gatekeepers' (Lillis and Tuck, 2016: 37), thus addressing *institutional* value systems and practices in which the understandings and practices of individual students and teachers are enmeshed.

Academic Literacies in the wider landscape of language and higher education

The history/ies of Academic Literacies as a field have been traced in some detail elsewhere (e.g. Lillis, 2019; Lillis and Tuck, 2016; Lillis and Scott, 2007) so here I confine myself to a few key points. Academic Literacies is often traced to Lea and Street's much cited 1998 paper in *Studies in Higher Education*. Their pioneering study's chief contribution was to bring the theoretical and empirical perspective of the New Literacy Studies (NLS) – a field influenced by anthropology in which language and literacy are conceptualized as a social practice – to bear on the question of university students' writing. The authors used Street's theorization (1984) of writing and reading as fundamentally sociocultural and ideological rather than decontextualized and 'autonomous'. They showed how the latter conceptualization, in the context of university literacies, was closely linked to a 'deficit' framing of students as lacking the required language, literacy skills or even intellectual ability to succeed. This theorization was closely tied to an ethnographic research methodology. Lea and Street's (1998) succinct three-part 'model' for thinking about academic reading and writing (as skills, socialization and literacies) has been widely used, adapted and interpreted in higher education research, language development and in EAP specifically. However, the framework has sometimes been used in isolation or as a set of instructions rather than as a thinking tool for navigating complex practices and contexts.

Significantly, Academic Literacies as a field also grew out of the work of other teacher-practitioners and applied linguists, particularly that of Ivanič (1998) and Lillis (2001), but also of EAP practitioners such as Turner (2004, 2012) and by those working in other language specialisms within and outside the disciplines in UK universities (e.g. see Lea and Stierer, 2000). These disparate UK origins are often overlooked, as is the leading early contribution of South African scholars such as Thesen (1997) and Leibowitz (2000). These early 'Academic Literacies' conversations played a vital role in bringing knowledge from diverse fields to bear on the questions of students' writing. For example, scholars drew on emancipatory adult education and adult literacy work in the UK (e.g. Gardener, 1992, Barton and Hamilton, 1998), and on diverse traditions within US-based writing research (e.g. Bartholomae, 1985; Bazerman, 1988). The two key points here are (a) that if we focus too exclusively on Lea and Street (1998), we risk dehistoricizing Academic Literacies and missing out on the rich intellectual soil in which it grew and (b) that as a field Academic Literacies has always acted as a kind of 'land bridge' facilitating the gradual spread of ideas between different knowledge communities: a trait which potentially applies to its role in EAP.

Since the earlier days of Academic Literacies in the 1990s, scholars in the field have been in dialogue with a range of overlapping academic language specialisms including Second Language Writing (e.g. Tang, 2014); Writing Centres (e.g. Cain, 2011; Hutchings, 2006); university writing development and academic support (e.g. Mitchell, 2010; Hill et al., 2010); research writing (e.g. Lillis and Curry, 2010; Thesen, 2014); English as a Medium of Instruction in Europe (e.g. Kaufhold, 2017); 'Didactiques' in French-medium higher education (e.g. Brereton et al., 2009); in Spanish-medium (e.g. Carlino, 2013) and Portuguese-medium systems (e.g. Castanheira et al., 2015) as well as in EAP. Work in Academic Literacies has also had some impact more generally in the field of learning development in higher education, for example Mann (2008), Haggis (2003), Jacobs (2005), Kendall and French (2018), Hilsdon et al. (2019).[3] Another key strand of influence is where Academic Literacies has been applied by disciplinary specialists in collaboration with language practitioners (e.g. Bhagatt and O'Neill (2009) in Art and Design; Gimenez (2012) in nursing; Lillis and Rai (2011) in social work education; McGrath and Kaufhold (2016) in anthropology). The chapter next turns more specifically to focus on connections and conversations between Academic Literacies and EAP specifically.

Academic Literacies and/in EAP

As previously noted, some researchers who broadly locate themselves 'in' EAP have been highly influential in the development of Academic Literacies. Turner (2004, 2011, 2012, 2018) and Wingate (e.g. 2012) have been particularly influential in bringing these fields into productive and critical dialogue with one another (see also Harwood and Hadley, 2004; Street and Leung, 2009;

---

[3] Papers in the 2019 Special Issue of *Journal of Learning Development in Higher Education* give a good flavour of this influence.

McGrath and Kaufhold, 2016; Murray, 2016). Both arose from 'practitioner-led' concerns and share an interest in helping students and academics 'to succeed as writers and communicators in the increasingly globalized, English-dominant academy' (Lillis and Tuck, 2016: 36) by surfacing tacit conventions and expectations and by carrying out empirical work to establish what forms and practices are valued in any particular (especially disciplinary) context. There are also resonances between Academic Literacies and 'critical' EAP, leading to shared areas of interest such as the consequences of practices for academic text producers, a questioning of unidirectional novice/expert trajectories and investigating occluded, ethically complex practices such as proofreading (e.g. Turner, 2012 and Harwood et al., 2012).

Despite these areas of common ground, there are key differences in emphasis deriving from the different histories and institutional locations of the two fields. Analysis of participants' texts is not always central in Academic Literacies research (e.g. Ivanič et al., 2009; Lea and Stierer, 2011). This reflects Academic Literacies' primary interest in text producers (though not to the exclusion of the text) in contrast to 'mainstream' EAP's primary interest in texts (Coffin and Donohue, 2012; Lillis and Scott, 2007).[4] Work in multilingual contexts (e.g. Thesen and van Pletzen, 2006; Preece, 2009; Lillis and Curry, 2010) has helped to keep language(s) on the Academic Literacies agenda, theorized as an ideologically loaded, stratified[5] 'practice-resource' (Lillis, 2014: 158) for meaning-making in academic writing. The field was founded on empirical work in which intersectional issues of class, race and monolingualism were acknowledged as part of students' complex experiences of marginalization in relation to academic language norms (e.g. Lillis, 2001). Nonetheless, the tendency of early Academic Literacies' research to focus on 'non-traditional' students (Lea, 2004) has meant that it is more often associated with widening participation than internationalization agendas. As a result, it has sometimes been perceived as backgrounding 'EAL' issues (see Street and Leung, 2009: 308) which may be one reason for the sometimes limited porosity of the boundary between the two fields.

Sometimes these fields have been seen as conflicting or incompatible (a point made by McGrath and Kaufhold, 2016). The focus on 'transformation' in Academic Literacies has consciously been framed as providing a useful

---

[4] An interest broadly represented by chapters by Evans and Martin in this volume. This is not to suggest that these are non-social theories of language/text. EAP also often incorporates research in other traditions such as ethnography (see Holliday and Collins, this volume).
[5] Meaning that not all languages/varieties are accorded equal value or status.

counterpoint to what has been characterized as EAP's orientation towards given academic norms (Lillis and Scott, 2007; see response by Wingate and Tribble, 2012). On the other hand, Academic Literacies has been criticized for lacking a writing pedagogy and because 'its preferences for issues such as identity, power relations and institutional practices over text seems [*sic*] to be at conflict with students' preferences' (Wingate, 2012: abstract). Although the Academic Literacies approach does provide a strong basis on which to critique mystifying academic textual norms and practices, it has the 'capacity to include' pragmatic work at skills and socializing levels and does not insist on working 'only oppositionally' (Turner, 2012: 18). This is important because misunderstandings about the potential role of Academic Literacies in EAP practice have sometimes derived from an oversimplified notion that it is 'theory-driven' and research-based on the one hand, with 'practice' and teachers positioned on the other. Academic Literacies has therefore sometimes been experienced by EAP teachers as being 'brought in' by outsiders with little understanding of the realities of practice or constraints in context. Despite efforts to stress the practitioner-led character of the field and the need for interdependence and dialogue between theory and practice for their mutual flourishing (Lillis et al., 2015; Turner, 2012), Academic Literacies is sometimes resisted on misconceived grounds that it requires an 'all or nothing' (and rather teacher-centred) commitment to throwing caution and academic textual conventions to the wind.

A theory of/perspective on academic writing and reading as social

Academic Literacies has at its core the theory that language and literacy are intrinsically social; hence, any form of communication is situated in and shaped by specific sociocultural contexts. This view of literacy 'has been grounded in and propelled by situated, ethnographic studies of the use of written language that have emphasized the particularity of what people in concert do with each other, and what they are doing with and through written language' (Bloome et al., 2019: 15). A key reason why Lea and Street's work in the UK in the 1990s made an impact was that it explicitly departed from the then dominant tradition of phenomenographic research on the 'experience of learning' (e.g. Marton et al., 1997) which, they argued, derived from a psychological and individualistic model of learning. A social perspective on literacy was particularly radical in a university context because of the dominance of the twin ideologies of (a) academic reading and writing as individual but disembodied pursuits, involving transferable skills and (b) academic language as a neutral and transparent 'conduit' for ideas (Turner, 2011, 2018), both of which in effect *deny* the intrinsic role of the social, material and political context in shaping any act of communication and its uptake by others.

An 'autonomous' ideology of academic literacy, also captured as 'essayist' literacy (Lillis, 2001, 2011), has implications both for texts and for text producers which are of interest in the context of EAP. An essayist text characteristically exhibits 'textual unity' (one central theme and a linear argument); is 'neutral' and 'objective'; uses formal, standard, language and is monolingual (English in many contexts). Lillis (2011, and 2021) has exemplified ways in which academic texts might push against such conventions, exposing their social and historical origins and thus rendering them more open to critique and change. These articles make visible the multiple voices of academic knowledge-making processes which are so often flattened into a monolingual textual product. English (2011), Hamilton and Pitt (2009) and others have explored how teachers (within and outside subject disciplines) can experiment with genre in ways which disrupt the monologic authority of essayist writing to productive effect. Turner (2011, 2018) unpacks the historical and philosophical origins of the autonomous view of language in the academy which goes hand in hand with essayist literacy and points to a 'smooth read' ideology in which language is ideally a transparent carrier for content. The ideal student writer adeptly removes 'self' and process from the text, meets tacit but variable expectations and creates an uninterrupted reading experience for the teacher/assessor. Writers of any language background who do not achieve this are at risk of marginalization and failure: EAL or 'international' students who do not use written language in recognizably Anglophone 'centre' ways are potentially seen as deficient in thinking skills and knowledge as well as language. Thus where an essayist model dominates, the diverse linguistic and cultural resources which students bring to their studies are backgrounded, and students labelled as functionally 'illiterate' in the context of academic study (in English). The 'language as conduit' ideology leads to the positioning of work with such students as superficial fixing, tidying, polishing, mopping, patching, medicating – metaphors which belie the intellectually complex work of student writers and their teachers who in turn *share the stigma* (Tuck, 2018; Turner, 2011). Such a view requires acknowledgement that language and literacy in the academic world are far from neutral activities and are historically and culturally produced, powerful mechanisms for generating or perpetuating inequality.

A theory of/perspective on academic writing and reading as social practice

A notion of language as social, however, does not on its own distinguish Academic Literacies from other 'foundational' paradigms such as Swalesian or Hallidayan Sydney School genre approaches. Indeed, these different traditions share early roots in early-twentieth-century anthropological studies. One key difference lies in the concept of *practice*, particularly 'literacy practice', owed to work in what was later labelled as the New Literacy Studies. The notion of literacy practice[s] (equivalent to 'literacy understood as social practice' and signalled by the plural form 'literacies') shifts the focus to what people do with written language in the material and social world, how they feel about what they do and what it means to and for them and for others. This does not preclude a 'functional' approach to language and literacy, but it does suggest that the functions served by written language cannot be treated as given but are an 'open question … the thing to be ethnographically determined' (Blommaert, 2007: 687) and may vary amongst participants (for example, between tutors and students, as Lea and Street (1998) discovered).

The term 'practice' in the context of reading and writing is 'both usefully and problematically elastic' (Lillis, 2014: 84). At one level, as indicated above, it simply denotes an interest in what people do (with written language) in their day-to-day activities, researched through ethnographic methods such as participant observation, field notes, interviews and participant diaries. Much early research in NLS focused on such activities in the context of particular communities (e.g. Heath, 1983; Street, 1984). Later this approach was extended to research in particular domains including universities (see Lillis (2014) for an account). Crucially, at another level, 'practice' also refers to the fact that such daily activities become routinized 'hardened into a … relative permanency' (Shay, 2008: 160) through repetition. Even though each event is slightly different, practices can be inferred through the detailed study of a series of observable events, and via insiders' accounts of their own histories and future imaginaries of these events. This leads to a third implication of a focus on 'practice' which is that not only do single concrete instantiations of what people do with texts add up over time to more abstract 'practices', the practical understandings that people bring with them from one event about what they are doing and why then shape the next event. In other words, 'practice' at a theoretical level signals a dynamic relationship between 'on the ground' activity and more settled social patterns and structures.

'Practice' steers us away from a 'container' model of context. Instead, it suggests a complex, networked and mutually shaping relationship between what individuals and groups do, institutional and local community systems and values, and wider social structures. The precise nature of this relationship between the 'micro' and 'meso' and 'macro' levels is much debated by practice theorists. However, what most theories have in common is that they attempt to resolve 'false antimonies' (Shay, 2008: 160) between individuals and society and so between 'agency' (whether this means capacity to act intentionally or is conceived of in terms of more general capability) and 'structure'. This is important in the context of student writing and reading practices in academia because if this dynamism is acknowledged it allows scope for writer agency and change. This might mean doing something different – even if just a bit different – where this suits the writer's own purposes at any one time, or consciously choosing to do 'the usual' as one option out of others, even in contexts which might otherwise seem highly constraining. This scope for agency also extends to their teachers whether within disciplinary or 'language' roles. It allows room for 'critical hope' (Bozalek et al., 2014; Tuck, 2018) without underestimating the power of valued norms to privilege some writers over others.

A critical theory of/perspective on academic writing and reading as social practice

The mention of the word 'power' leads me to a third key theoretical element which is that Academic Literacies researchers consistently see the 'social structures' constituted by practices in broadly critical terms. This means recognizing that the 'social' is fundamentally stratified and unequal. This applies to material inequalities between social groups and to other kinds of capital (social, cultural, linguistic, symbolic) at their disposal. Such inequalities cannot be understood without recognizing the role of power relations. A literacies theoretical approach insists that the exercise of power in various forms underpins literacy practices at every level, whether it is visibly exercised (e.g. through institutional policies, rules, penalties and rewards and in education, tests and curricula) or ideologically hidden (e.g. through discourses which define language and literacy narrowly in ways which marginalize some writers, communities and communicative resources). This includes the practice of research (including literacies research) and teaching (including EAP). The ethnographic sensibilities of Academic Literacies tend to mean that researchers work with 'bottom up' models of power. For example Turner (2011: 46) draws on Foucault's notion of the 'capillary effects of power' and others have drawn extensively on Bourdieu's notion that power operates through individual habitus (e.g. Lillis, 2001). However, researchers have also drawn on more 'top down' analyses of power such as that deployed in some versions of Critical Discourse Analysis (e.g. Fairclough, 1989 used by Lea and Street (1998) and by Ivanič (1998)), Bernstein's sociology of knowledge (Coleman, 2012) or Wallerstein's centre/periphery framing (Lillis and Curry, 2010).

The field's critical positioning is most clearly seen in the commitment to 'transformation', articulated amongst others by Lillis and Scott (2007) and Lillis et al. (2015: 3–22). The focus on transformation in Academic Literacies has been criticized (e.g. Henderson, 2020) as a form of imposition or pre-determined idea of what students 'should' want to do with their academic writing. However, there does not need to be an a priori end point of transformation – as Mitchell (2015: 17) puts it, 'any transformative goal is never finalized; being socially, politically, ideologically constructed, what counts as "good" or "better" is always rightly the object of further scrutiny'. The educators' role is therefore to enable students to exercise their agency in ways of their own choosing while fully recognizing that students' starting points are fundamentally unequal, allowing different degrees of agency within the educational status quo. Moreover, Academic Literacies involves an inclusive commitment to increasing opportunities for agency for writers *at whatever stage of their journey*, from 'basic writers' and adult literacy learners to doctoral student writers (see Wingate, 2012: 34 for a counter-argument). This represents a major pedagogic challenge, of course, but a vital one from a critical perspective – otherwise there is a danger that possibilities for 'transformation' may be reserved for students already in, or who have navigated their way to, a relatively privileged position in the academy, from which an investment in norms is maximized and their ability to imagine alternatives and to experiment (even in small ways) may be minimized. Students may be resistant to countenancing the possibility of something more personally alive and meaningful in their academic writing for a range of reasons. However, the messy reality is that writing norms are always already continually in flux, and thus our agency as writers in either reproducing or reworking academic literacies is not optional – any act of writing involves choices at different levels. Moreover, a critical, transformative approach asks us to creatively re-imagine writing and so at one level is about the possibilities of play (Creme, 2008; Mitchell, 2010) even when doing the serious work of academic writing. Moreover, not all such play will necessarily result in risky, transgressive 'final' texts.

Critical theory and Academic Literacies

It is at this third level, of the 'critical', that work in Academic Literacies is most varied and eclectic. Researchers and practitioners have found different ways of thinking about the nature of social stratification and inequality and about power in their contexts, guided by their empirical focus and by key problems or issues (Turner, 2012). They choose concepts to work with in a pragmatic way, asking 'how does this concept help us to understand the issue at hand'? and 'how might this understanding help us to intervene transformationally in a given scenario'? In the section which follows, I discuss three examples of how Academic Literacies scholars have drawn on critical concepts to extend and explain their empirical observations and to develop imaginaries about how things might be made different (and better). I also make tentative connections between these explorations and potential issues dilemmas facing EAP practitioners.

Critical discourse analysis. A number of key early studies in Academic Literacies combined ethnographic methodologies with discourse analysis using SFL-based Critical Discourse Analysis (CDA, e.g. Fairclough, 1989). Ivanič (1998) drew extensively on CDA to analyse student writers' presentations of self in their academic writing. Lea (1994) and Lea and Street (1998) analysed documents and feedback comments written by tutors on undergraduate assignments along lines influenced by CDA. For example, they comment on the use of 'categorical modality' in feedback, using this analysis as the basis for imagining a 'more provisional and mitigated' modality which could signal and enact less hierarchical pedagogic relationships. More recently, I have argued that feedback is no more fixed and its functions no more transparently readable than any other genre and that ethnographic perspectives of feedback writers are an essential to understanding the complexities of academic writing assessment practices (Tuck, 2018). Lillis (2008) has argued for the use of more context-sensitive analytic categories such as 'orientation' for exploring the uptake and evaluation of academic texts. These approaches provide rich ongoing potential lines of enquiry for EAP practitioners as they explore how best to engage with students' writing.

Habitus. Bourdieu's ideas have been taken up in different ways by scholars in Academic Literacies. One particularly powerful notion is that of *habitus* which Blommaert (2018: 94) describes as a 'nexus' concept 'in which different scale levels of social behaviour are shown to be dialectically connected'. *Habitus* links individual behaviours, language, dispositions and practices with social structures precisely because these ways of being are habitual, embodied, unconsciously reproduced and closely linked to a person's sense of identity and belonging (or non-belonging). Habitus can be negotiated and challenged at any given moment, but this does not detract from its reproductive function (2018: 94) and from the fact that certain forms of habitus, including ways of using written language, are valued in the academy over others. This concept therefore helps to explain the challenges for students who arrive at university without the requisite valued cultural, social and linguistic capital to thrive as they are – faced not only by the need to re-learn taken-for-granted practices 'from scratch' but also with challenges to their very identity. For example, Lillis (2001) traces how the 'non-traditional' students in her study, including some using multiple languages on a daily basis, wrestled with the conflicting desires both to conform to expectations of their writing and to be 'themselves', i.e. to write in ways which had personal meaning for them and did not leave them feeling inadequate or excluded. These ideas also have potentially fruitful application in the context of EAP both for 'domestic' and 'international' students.

Recontextualization. The ideas of educational sociologist Bernstein have also been used in conjunction with academic literacies approaches. Coleman (e.g. 2012) draws on Bernstein's notion of recontextualization to throw light on the specific ways in which knowledge construction processes in specific vocational curriculum areas result in the privileging of some academic literacy practices over others. In this way she attempts to address a potential weakness in the Academic Literacies' 'bottom up' ethnographic approach as a means of capturing how institutional contexts and structural factors impinge on students' literacy practices. This empirical focus on curriculum was insightful in the context of South Africa where entrenched historical divisions between vocational and academic provision are bound up with unequal outcomes for different population groups in the post-Apartheid HE landscape. Coleman's work provides a good example of the way in which Academic Literacies researchers have reached out to structurally oriented, realist social theory and combined it with context-sensitive and interpretivist paradigms of literacy practices research.

A number of other theoretical approaches have been used generatively by researchers who are also actively working with Academic Literacies. For example, Actor Network Theory and related sociomaterial theories were fruitful for Ivanič et al. (2009) in their study of students' writing practices in UK Further Education and influenced Tusting et al.'s (2019) investigation of UK academics' writing practices. English's work on re-genring (2011) makes use of social semiotic and multimodal theory combined with an academic literacies perspective to explore new possibilities for student 'writing' beyond the verbal mode (see also Kiteley, 2018; Parkin, 2009). Other theoretical connections have been made, although there is no scope to explore these here, reflecting the somewhat 'polyvalent' nature of Academic Literacies as an approach.

Academic Literacies and reflexivity

One important way in which Academic Literacies has contributed and has potential to contribute more to EAP is through its commitment to reflexivity. Its foundation on ethnographic empirical principles means that the researcher's own positioning in the field always has to be taken into account, profoundly informing data analysis. Within 'criticality' we must therefore include 'self-criticality' – an approach which aligns happily with traditions of reflexive practice in higher education (e.g. Thesen and Coleman, 2018), EAP (e.g. Cadman, 2005) and in education more generally (Schön, 1983). For Academic Literacies this means an expanded focus not only on the learner but on the teacher and on academics' own writing, e.g. see Lillis and Curry (2010). Street and Leung (2009: 304–5) describe how an ethnographic perspective on writers can spiral round to an ethnographic perspective on language programmes and pedagogies themselves. In the context of EAP, Turner (2012) demonstrates the potential of Academic Literacies to be a 'strong and capacious' theoretical framework for 'thinking outside the classroom about the problems arising from EAP's socio-political position' (2012: 18). In this respect, Academic Literacies has played a valuable role in helping to legitimize conversations about the role of politics and power in EAP, contributing indirectly to recent analyses of the EAP sector and its current challenges (e.g. Ding and Bruce, 2017).

The practice of theorizing/theorizing of practice

A lack of identifiable monolithic social theoretical underpinning – beyond the commitment to an understanding of language and literacy as social practice and critical interest in transformation – could be seen as one disadvantage of Academic Literacies. It may be one reason why the term has a tendency to become all things to all people and why the field can seem 'established' to some/in some moments but still feel marginal and struggling to/in others. A coherent theoretical identity can lend an attractive intellectual legitimacy which might help to raise the status and profile of EAP activities within institutions. Another issue worth raising here is the question of ontological and epistemological consistency. For example, the interpretivist epistemological approach of ethnography does not, for some, sit unproblematically alongside realist structural explanations of sociological theory and therefore they find such fusions clunky and unhelpful. Others are more comfortable with the need for a 'compound' theoretical eye and have argued for the generative nature of theoretical ambiguity and contradiction (Thesen and Coleman, 2018).

On the whole, the eclecticism and reflexivity of Academic Literacies, along with the dynamism of its core understanding of language, have meant that as a field it is open and resilient, able to work with fundamental changes in contemporary academic communication (see for example Avila-Reyes et al. (2021) on researching literacy during the pandemic). It has been reimagined by Blommaert and Horner (2017) in terms of a mobilities sociolinguistics paradigm for a superdiverse and hypermobile world in which complex and shifting language repertoires are the norm, not the exception. Academic Literacies is also theoretically well equipped to embrace developments in social semiotic theory, e.g. recognizing multiple modes of academic meaning-making in which written language is one resource amongst many (e.g. English, 2011). These developments have influenced EAP directly (e.g. Leung et al., 2016; Archer and Breuer, 2016) but Academic Literacies can play a potentially useful role in sensitizing EAP researcher-practitioners to such developments. The firm ethnographic commitment to an 'insistence on complexity and human sense-making in context' (Thesen and Coleman, 2018: 130) means a reflexive, questioning relationship with theory, a commitment to theory 'as a verb' rather than as a 'vehicle for differentiation, othering and separation' (Thesen and Coleman, 2018: 131). The most fundamental theoretical commitment of Academic Literacies, therefore, is to 'provisionality' (Street and Leung, 2009: 310). Academic Literacies seeks to sustain a space for critique and for dialogue outside our conceptual 'comfort zones' (Lillis, 2019) and to continue to open empirical exploration of what it means to do academic writing and reading in specific contexts. Ultimately, therefore, the question of Academic Literacies' potential theoretical contribution to EAP is an open, pragmatic but principled one which will be answered collectively and through collaboration.

References

Archer, A. and E. Breuer (2016), *Multimodality in Higher Education*, Leiden: Brill.

Ávila Reyes, N., L. Calle-Arango and E. Léniz (2021), 'Researching in Times of Pandemic and Social Unrest: A Flexible Mindset for an Enriched View on Literacy', *International Studies in Sociology of Education*, DOI: 10.1080/09620214.2021.1927142.

Bartholomae, D. (1985), 'Inventing the University', in M. Rose (ed.), *When a Writer Cannot Write: Studies in Writer's Block and Other Composing-process Problems*, 134–65, New York: The Guildford Press.

Barton, D. and M. Hamilton (1998), *Local Literacies: Reading and Writing in One Community*, London: Routledge.

Bazerman, C. (1988), *Shaping Written Knowledge: The Genre and Activity of the Experimental Article in Science*, Madison, WI: University of Wisconsin Press.

Bhagat, D. and P. O'Neill (2009), 'Writing Design: A Collaboration between the WriteNow CETL and The Sir John Cass Department of Art, Media and Design', *Art, Design and Communication in Higher Education*, 8 (2): 177–82.

Blommaert, J. (2018), *Dialogues with Ethnography*, Bristol: Multilingual Matters.

Blommaert, J. (2007), 'On Scope and Depth in Linguistic Ethnography', *Journal of Sociolinguistics*, 11 (5): 682–8.

Blommaert, J. and B. Horner (2017), 'Mobility and Academic Literacies: An Epistolary Conversation', *London Review of Education*, 15 (1): 2–20.

Blommaert, J., B. Street, and J. Turner (2007), 'Academic Literacies: What Have We Achieved and Where to from Here?' *Journal of Applied Linguistics and Professional Practice*, 4 (1): 137–48.

Bloome, D., J. Kalman and M. Seymour (2019), 'Fashioning Literacy as Social', in D. Bloome et al. (eds), *Re-theorizing Literacy Practices: Complex Social and Cultural Contexts*, 15–29, New York, Abingdon: Routledge.

Boughey, C. and S. McKenna (2016), 'Academic Literacy and the Decontextualized Learner', *Critical Studies in Teaching and Learning*, 4 (2): 1–9.

Bozalek, V., B. Leibowitz, R. Carolissen, M. Boler (2014), *Discerning Critical Hope in Educational Practices*, London and New York: Routledge.

Brereton, J., C. Donahue, C. Gannett, T. Lillis and M. Scott (2009), 'Le socioculturel et la didactique de l'écrit dans le superieur aux Etats-Unis et en Grande Bretagne: Cadres comparitifs et influences françaises', in I. Delcambre and Y. Reuters (eds), *Didactique du Français: le socioculturel en question*, 151–69, Villeneuve d'Ascq: Université de Lille.

Cadman, K. (2005), 'Towards a "Pedagogy of Connection" in Critical Research Education: A REAL Story', *Journal of English for Academic Purposes*, 4 (4): 353–67.

Cain, K. S. (2011), 'From Comfort Zone to Contact Zone: Lessons from a Belfast Writing Centre', *Arts and Humanities in Higher Education*, 10 (1): 67–83.

Canton, U., M. Govan, and D. Zahn (2018), 'Rethinking Academic Literacies: A Conceptual Development based on Teaching Practice', *Teaching in Higher Education*, 23 (6): 668–84.

Carlino, P. (2013), 'Alfabetización académica diez años despuez', *RMIE*, 18 (57): 355–81.

Castanheira, M. L., B. V. Street and G. T. Carvalho (2015), 'Navigating across Academic Contexts: Campo and Angolan Students in a Brazilian University', *Pedagogies*, 10 (1): 70–85.

Coffin, C. and J. P. Donohue (2012), 'Academic Literacies and Systemic Functional Linguistics: How do they Relate?', *Journal of English for Academic Purposes*, 11 (1): 64–75. DOI: 10.1016/j.jeap.2011.11.004.

Coleman, L. (2012), 'Incorporating the Notion of Recontextualization in Academic Literacies Research: The Case of a South African Vocational Web Design and Development Course', *Higher Education Research and Development*, 31 (3): 325–38.

Creme, P. (2008), 'A Space for Academic Play', *Arts and Humanities in Higher Education*, 7 (1): 49–64.

Ding, A. and I. Bruce (2017), *The English for Academic Purposes Practitioner: Operating on the Edge of Academia*, London: Palgrave.

English, F. (2011), *Student Writing and Genre*, London: Continuum.

Fairclough, N. (1989), *Language and Power*, London: Longman.

Gardener, S. (1992), *The Long Word Club*, Bradford: RaPAL.

Gimenez, J. (2012), 'Disciplinary Epistemologies, Generic Attributes and Undergraduate Academic Writing in Nursing and Midwifery', *Higher Education*, 63 (4): 401–19.

Haggis, T. (2003), 'Constructing Images of Ourselves? A Critical Investigation into "Approaches to Learning" Research in Higher Education', *British Educational Research Journal*, 29 (1): 89–104.

Hamilton, M. and K. Pitt (2009), 'Creativity in Academic Writing: Escaping from the Straitjacket of Genre?' in A. Carter, T. Lillis and S. Parkin (eds), *Why Writing Matters*, 61–79, Amsterdam: John Benjamins.

Harwood, N., L. Austin and R. Macaulay (2012), 'Cleaner, Helper, Teacher? The Role of Proofreaders of Student Writing', *Studies in Higher Education*, 37 (5): 569–84.

Harwood, N. and G. Hadley (2004), 'Demystifying Institutional Practices: Critical Pragmatism and the Teaching of Academic Writing', *English for Specific Purposes*, 23: 355–77.

Heath, S. B. (1983), *Ways with Words: Language, Life and Work in Communities and Classrooms*, Cambridge: CUP.

Henderson, J. (2020), 'Styling Writing and Being Styled in University Literacy Practices', *Teaching in Higher Education*, 25 (1): 1–17.

Hill, P., A. Tinker, and S. Catterall (2010), 'From Deficiency to Development: The Evolution of Academic Skills Provision at One UK University', *Journal of Learning Development in Higher Education* (2). https://doi.org/10.47408/jldhe.v0i2.54.

Hilsdon, J., C. Malone and A. Syska (2019), 'Academic Literacies Twenty Years on: A Community-sourced Literature Review', *Journal of Learning Development in Higher Education* (15). November 2019. DOI: 10.47408/jldhe.v0i15.567.

Hutchings, C. (2006), 'Reaching Students: Lessons from a Writing Centre', *Higher Education Research and Development*, 25 (3): 247–61.

Ivanič, R. (1998), *Writing and Identity: The Discoursal Construction of Identity in Academic Writing*, Amsterdam: John Benjamins.

Ivanič, R. and Teaching Learning Research Programme (2009), *Improving Learning in College: Rethinking Literacies across the Curriculum*, London: Routledge.

Ivanič, R. and M. R. Lea (2006), 'New Contexts, New Challenges: The Teaching of Writing in UK Higher Education', in L. Ganobcsik-Williams (ed.), *Teaching Academic Writing in UK Higher Education*, 6–15, Basingstoke: Palgrave Macmillan.

Jacobs, C. (2005), 'On Being an Insider on the Outside: New Spaces for Integrating Academic Literacies', *Teaching in Higher Education*, 10 (4): 475–87.

Kaufhold, K. (2017), 'Tracing Interacting Literacy Practices in Master's Dissertation Writing', *London Review of Education*, 15 (1): 73. DOI: 10.18546/LRE.15.1.07.

Kendall, A. and A. French (2018), 'Re-thinking Employability with a Literacies Lens', *Higher Education, Skills and Work-Based Learning*, 8 (2): 164–78.

Kiteley, R. (2018), 'How Can I Make This Work? Genre Affordances, Agency and Identity in a Doctoral Research Journey', *Journal of Writing in Creative Practice*, 11 (1): 121–38.

Lea, M. (1994), '"I Thought I Could Write Before I Came Here": Student Writing in Higher Education', in G. Gibbs (ed.), *Improving Student Learning: Theory and Practice*, 216–26, Oxford: OSCD.

Lea, M. (2004), 'Academic Literacies: A Pedagogy for Course Design', *Studies in Higher Education*, 29 (6): 739–56.

Lea, M. and B. Stierer (2000), *Student Writing in Higher Education: New Contexts*, Buckingham: Society for Research into Higher Education.

Lea, M. and B. Stierer (2011), 'Changing Academic Identities in Changing Academic Workplaces: Learning from Academics' Everyday Professional Writing Practices', *Teaching in Higher Education*, 16 (6): 605–16.

Lea, M. and B. Street (1998), 'Student Writing in Higher Education: An Academic Literacies Approach', *Studies in Higher Education*, 23 (2): 157–72.

Leibowitz, B. (2000), 'The Importance of Writing and Teaching Writing in the Academy', in B. Leibowitz and Y. Mohamed (eds), *Routes to Writing in Southern Africa*, 15–42, Cape Town: Silk Road International.

Leung, C., J. Lewkowicz and J. Jenkins (2016), 'English for Academic Purposes: A Need for Remodelling', *Englishes in Practice*, 3 (3): 55–73.

Lillis, T. (2001), *Student Writing: Access, Regulation, Desire*, London: Routledge.

Lillis, T. (2008), 'Ethnography as Method, Methodology and Deep Theorising: Closing the Gap between Text and Context in Academic Writing research', *Written Communication*, 25 (3): 353–88.

Lillis, T. (2011), 'Legitimizing Dialogue as Textual and Ideological Goal in Academic Writing for Assessment and Publication', *Arts and Humanities in Higher Education*, 10 (4): 401–32.

Lillis, T. (2014), *The Sociolinguistics of Writing*, Edinburgh: Edinburgh University Press.

Lillis, T. (2019), '"Academic Literacies": Sustaining a Critical Space on Writing in Academia', *Journal of Learning Development in Higher Education* (15).

Lillis, T. (2021), '¿Academic Literacies: Intereses Locales, Preocupaciones Globales? Academic Literacies: Local Interests, Global Concerns?' in N. Avila-Reyes (ed.), *Multilingual Contributions to Writing Research: Towards an Equal Academic Exchange*, 35–59, Fort Collins/Anderson: WAC Clearinghouse/Parlor Press.

Lillis, T. and M. J. Curry (2010), *Academic Writing in a Global Context: The Politics and Practices of Publishing in English*, London: Routledge.

Lillis, T., K. Harrington, M. Lea and S. Mitchell (2015), *Working with Academic Literacies: Case Studies towards Transformative Practice*, 15–17, Fort Collins/Anderson: WAC Clearinghouse/Parlor Press.

Lillis, T. and L. Rai (2011), 'A Case-study of Research-based Collaboration around Writing in Social Work', *Across the Disciplines: A Journal of Language, Learning and Academic Writing*, 8 (3). DOI: 10.37514/ATD-J.2011.8.3.12

Lillis, T. and M. Scott (2007), 'Defining Academic Literacies Research: Issues of Epistemology, Ideology and Strategy', *Journal of Applied Linguistics*, 4 (1): 5–32.

Lillis, T. and J. Tuck (2016), 'Academic Literacies: A Critical Lens on Writing and Reading in the Academy', in K. Hyland and P. Shaw (eds), *The Routledge Handbook of English for Academic Purposes,* 30–43, London: Routledge.

Mann, S. J. (2008), *Study, Power and the University*, Maidenhead: Open University Press/McGraw Hill.

Marton, F., D. Hounsell and N. Entwistle (1997), *The Experience of Learning*, Edinburgh: Scottish Academic Press.

McGrath, L. and K. Kaufhold (2016), 'English for Specific Purposes and Academic Literacies: Eclecticism in Academic Writing Pedagogy', *Teaching in Higher Education*, 21 (8): 933–47.

Mitchell, S. (2010), 'Now You Don't See It; Now You Do: Writing Made Visible in the University', *Arts and Humanities in Higher Education*, 9 (2): 133–48.

Mitchell, S. (2015), 'Editors' Introduction', in T. Lillis, K. Harrington, M. Lea and S. Mitchell (eds), *Working with Academic Literacies: Case Studies towards Transformative Practice*, 15–17, Fort Collins/Anderson: WAC Clearinghouse/Parlor Press.

Murray, N. (2016), 'An Academic Literacies Argument for Decentralizing EAP Provision', *ELT Journal*, 70 (4): 435–43.

Parkin, S. (2009), 'Ivanič and the Concept of "Wrighting"', in A. Carter, T. Lillis and S. Parkin (eds), *Why Writing Matters*, 27–43, Amsterdam: John Benjamins.

Preece, S. (2009), *Posh Talk: Language and Identity in Higher Education*, Basingstoke: Palgrave Macmillan.

Scalone, P. and B. Street (2006), 'An Academic Language Development Programme (Widening Participation)', in C. Leung and J. Jenkins (eds), *Reconfiguring Europe: The Contribution of Applied Linguistics*, 123–37, London: Equinox Publishing Group.

Schön, D. (1983), *The Reflective Practitioner: How Professionals Think in Action*, London: Temple Smith.

Shay, S. (2008), 'Researching Assessment as Social Practice: Implications for Research Methodology', *International Journal of Educational Research*, 47 (3): 159–64.

Street, B. (1984), *Literacy in Theory and Practice*, Cambridge: Cambridge University Press.

Street, B., M. Lea and T. Lillis (2015), 'Revisiting the Question of Transformation in Academic Literacies: The Ethnographic Imperative', in T. Lillis, K. Harrington, M. Lea and S. Mitchell (eds), *Working with Academic Literacies: Case Studies towards Transformative Practice*, 383–90, Fort Collins/Anderson: WAC Clearinghouse/Parlor Press.

Street, B. and C. Leung (2009), 'Sociolinguistics, Language Teaching and New Literacy Studies', in N. H. Hornberger and S. L. Mackay (eds), *Sociolinguistics and Language Education*, 290–316, Clevedon: Multilingual Matters.

Tang, R. (2014), *Academic Writing in a Second or Foreign Language: Issues and Challenges Facing ESL/EFL Academic Writers in Higher Education Contexts*, London: Bloomsbury.

Thesen, L. (1997), 'Voices, Discourse and Transition: In Search of New Categories in EAP', *TESOL Quarterly*, 31 (3): 487–511.

Thesen, L. (2014), 'Risk as Productive: Working with Dilemmas in the Writing of Research', in T. Thesen and L. Cooper (eds), *Risk in Academic Writing: Postgraduate Students, Their Teachers and the Making of Knowledge*, 1–24, Bristol: Multilingual Matters.

Thesen, L. and L. Coleman (2018), 'Theory as a Verb: Working with Dilemmas in Educational Development', *SOTL in the South*, 2 (1): 129–35.

Thesen, L. and E. van Pletzen (2006), *Academic Literacy and the Languages of Change*, London/New York: Continuum.

Tuck, J. (2018), *Academics Engaging with Student Writing: Working at the Higher Education Textface*, London: Routledge.

Turner, J. (2004), 'Language as Academic Purpose', *Journal of English for Academic Purposes*, 3 (2): 95–109.

Turner, J. (2011), *Language and the Academy: Cultural Reflexivity and Intercultural Dynamics*, Bristol: Multilingual Matters.

Turner, J. (2012), 'Academic Literacies: Providing a Space for the Socio-political Dynamics of EAP', *Journal of English for Academic Purposes*, 11 (1): 17–25.

Turner, J. (2018), *On Writtenness: The Cultural Politics of Academic Writing*, London: Bloomsbury.

Tusting, K., S. McCulloch, I. Bhatt, M. Hamilton and D. Barton (2019), *Academics Writing*, London: Routledge.

Wingate, U. (2012), 'Using Academic Literacies and Genre-based Models for Academic Writing Instruction: A "Literacy" Journey', *Journal of English for Academic Purposes*, 11 (1): 26–37.

Wingate, U. and C. Tribble (2012), 'The Best of Both Worlds? Towards an English for Academic Purposes/Academic Literacies Writing Pedagogy', *Studies in Higher Education*, 37 (4): 481–95.

Systemic Functional Linguistics (SFL): A social theory of language

J. R. Martin

Language as social semiotic

As reflected in the title of Halliday's well-known *Language as Social Semiotic* (1978), SFL is widely recognized as a social theory of language. But what exactly does this mean? How can a theory of language claim to adopt a social perspective on language – including its phonological, lexicogrammatical and discourse semantic systems – however richly described? In this chapter I'll pursue this theme, writing as a linguist with a longstanding interest in language education (Rose and Martin, 2012). I begin with Systemic Functional Linguistics' multi-functional perspective on meaning before moving on to its model of context (as register and genre). I next bring uses of language into the picture, focusing on text as the instantiation of language resources. And I continue this reflection by bringing in users of language, reviewing recent work on individuation and its concern with how linguistic resources and their uptake are distributed across members of communities. For a complementary perspective on SFL and EAP by an educational linguist with several decades of experience as an EAP teacher, curriculum designer and researcher, see Hood (2016).

By way of contextualizing this review, it is important to note that throughout its history Systemic Functional Linguistics (hereafter SFL) has evolved as an appliable linguistics (Halliday, 2008a), developing theory and description in relation to applications – a dialectic of theory and practice unfolding through interventions in educational linguistics, clinical linguistics, forensic linguistics and beyond (Caldwell et al., 2022; Martin 1998). This has brought considerable pressure to bear on the model as far as developing descriptions of different languages is concerned (Mwinlaaru and Xuan, 2016), as applications arise for speakers of diverse tongues. And it has also fostered descriptions of multimodal texts, where language cooperates with attendant modalities of communication (e.g. paralanguage, image, music, dance, architecture and so on) to make meaning (O'Halloran et al., 2019). Accordingly, given its current stage of development, it might make more sense to talk about Systemic Functional Semiotics since the theory along with its descriptions and applications model cultures holistically as social semiosis. For sake of familiarity, however, I'll stick with the familiar SFL acronym here.

Text as semantic choice in social contexts

One of the key papers in Halliday (1978) is the source of the title for this section (originally published as Halliday, 1977). In this paper he illustrates his conception of language as social semiosis through analysis of a fable by James Thurber (namely *The lover and his lass*). The presentation involves an outline of the evolving model of language Halliday and his colleagues had designed to account for language as a meaning-making resource (with some illustrative analysis). And it introduced a model of social context resonating with this resource that could be explicitly related to the semantic choices that characterize coherent text. I'll follow this programme in broad outline here, updating SFL's mapping of language resources and elaborating its modelling of social context. In doing so I will privilege the register of SFL reviewed in Martin (2014, 2016); for a glimpse of alternative registers, see Bartlett and O'Grady (2017) and Thompson et al. (2019).

For purposes of illustration below I draw on a text introduced in Hood and Maggiora (2016), redeployed here with the authors' permission (see also Martin, 2020, 2021). Its spoken verbiage opens as follows:

> Right ladies and gentlemen, where's all our friends from the other night? Once was enough? Call it quits? Hah, anyway, glad you're here. So we're looking at misrepresentation, which is a Common Law doctrine. So what we've been doing is going through these essential elements here. We have our different types of misrepresentation. This is important because, depending on what type it is, will be your solution. And so fraudulent, negligent, innocent. We'll come to that later tonight.

Where are we? How do we know? The first of these questions invites some common-sense inferencing. The beginning of a law lecture perhaps. Probably in a commonwealth university. In the evening. Focusing on misrepresentation. The second question is harder to answer. What exactly is our evidence? How does language do it? And as the text continues, we realize there is more than spoken language going on.

> We started off looking at the elements of misrepresentation. These ones up here, a statement that is not a puff or a hyperbole and is not a term of the contract necessarily. So that's what we've been doing. So the recap, just going through what we've looked at.

'Up here' refers to an infographic, projected on a screen positioned above and behind the lecturer at the front of the lecture theatre. This image is presented in Figure 3.1; it enables the lecturer to orient students to what's already been covered in the course and what's about to come. So our text is in fact a multimodal one, in which language and image play complementary roles.

> So misrepresentation, we are at that middle juncture, a representation that is false. So it's not a term of the contract but can if it meets the indicia of that, but it's certainly not a puff. Is it all coming flooding back to you? Yes? Well you want to do the same lecture again?

What kind of model of language and attendant semiosis deals effectively with a multimodal text of this kind? What kind of model of context, including

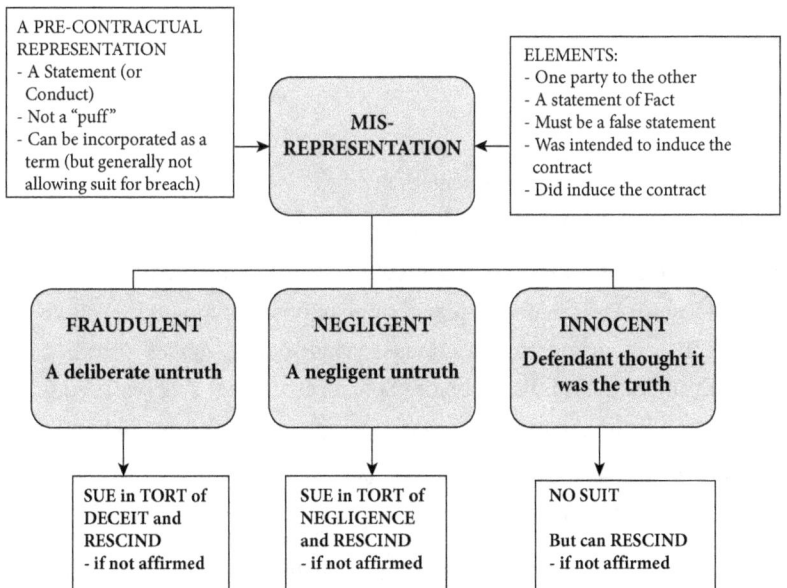

Figure 3.1 Projected law lecture infographic.

consideration of both uses and users of language, deals with the social process unfolding here? SFL's response to these challenges, and the social nature of this response, are reviewed below.

Semantic choice

As far as language is concerned, SFL's response to these challenges has been to develop a theory that models language as a resource for meaning. This involves taking into account the contributions of both different levels of language (phonology, lexicogrammar and discourse semantics) and of different kinds of meaning (ideational, interpersonal and textual).

In SFL each level of language is referred to as a stratum. With respect to phonology (Halliday and Greaves, 2008), our lecturer for example begins on a falling tone (addressing his students), follows on with three rising tones (enacting uncertainty) and continues with falling tones (asserting where things are at). The double slash ('//') below marks a tone group boundary; '1' marks a falling tone and '2' a rising one. The movement of the tones contrasts information that is settled with information that is not. At stake here are the sounds of language, and how they contribute to the meanings of spoken language.

>//1 Right ladies and gentlemen,
>//2 Uh where's all our friends from the other night?
>//2 Once was enough?
>//2 Call it quits?
>//1 Hah,
>//1 anyway glad you're here.
>//1 So we're looking at misrepresentation,
>//1 which is a Common Law doctrine.

Turning to lexicogrammar (Halliday, 1985 and subsequent editions), there are structural resources that cooperate with tone to position moves in dialogue. Our lecturer includes two interrogative clauses in his opening moves – one beginning with *where* and both with Finite before Subject structure (*'s all our friends* and *is it* below). This is the grammar's unmarked way of seeking information.

>'**where's all our friends** from the other night?
>**Is it** all coming flooding back to you?'

These contrast with his other clauses, which are declarative (sometimes elliptically so) – each with Subject before Finite structure (e.g. *we're* and *we'll* below). This is English grammar's unmarked way of giving information.

> 'So **we're** looking at misrepresentation,
> **We'll** come to that later tonight.'

At stake here is the distinctive grammatical structure of English clauses, groups/phrases and words, which so often differs considerably from that in the languages of students in EAP classrooms (Caffarel et al. (2004); Doran et al. (2021a, b, 2022a, b); Martin et al. (2021) provide a glimpse of the variation in play).

Moving on to discourse semantics (Martin, 1992; Martin and Rose, 2007), and moving beyond the clause, our lecturer deploys one (albeit monologic) question–answer pair. At this stage of the lecture the students do not in fact respond verbally to any of the lecturer's moves, and he has to make his own reply.

/2 Well you want to do the same lecture again?
//2 – Yes?

The lecturer tracks the legal concept of misrepresentation with two anaphoric demonstratives (*this, that*) and one pronoun (*it*).

> We have our different types of misrepresentation. ←**This** is important because, depending on what type ←**it** is, will be your solution. And so fraudulent, negligent, innocent. We'll come to ←**that** later tonight.

And he marks links in his presentation as it unfolds – rhetorically between sentences (*so, so, and so, so, so, so, so, well* ... in bold below) and logically between clauses within them (*because, and, but, if, but* ... in italics below).

> Right ladies and gentlemen, where's all our friends from the other night? Once was enough? Call it quits? Hah, anyway, glad you're here. **So** we're looking at misrepresentation, which is a Common Law doctrine. **So** what we've been doing is going through these essential elements here. We have our different types of misrepresentation. This is important *because*, depending on what type it is, will be your solution. **And so** fraudulent, negligent, innocent. We'll come to that later tonight. We started off looking at the elements of misrepresentation. These ones up here, a statement that is not a puff or a hyperbole *and* is not a term of the contract necessarily. **So** that's what we've been doing. **So** the recap, just going through what we've looked at ... **So** misrepresentation, we are at that middle juncture, a representation that is false. **So** it's not a term of the contract *but* can *if* it meets the indicia of that, *but* it's certainly not a puff. Is it all coming flooding back to you? Yes? **Well** you want to do the same lecture again?

At stake here is the 'coherence' of discourse, as speakers negotiate moves in dialogue – introducing and tracking entities and logically connecting states and goings on.

These different strata of language are outlined in Figure 3.2. In the image, the circles reflect the fact that language is an evolving system, not a designed one; and their co-tangential organization reflects their organization as a hierarchy of realization – with discourse semantic patterns realized by patterns of lexicogrammatical ones and lexicogrammar realized by patterns of phonological ones. Critically, as we have illustrated, all strata make a contribution to meaning.

The significance of stratification for EAP is twofold. For one thing, it encourages the field to focus on texts as the basic unit of meaning on which control of academic discourse depends. For another, it makes room for description of the elaborated meaning potential that makes academic discourse academic. This has to do with what is referred to as grammatical metaphor (introduced in Halliday, 1985) – i.e. SFL's interpretation of congruent and metaphorical relations across strata. We have already met an example of this alternation. The lecturer realizes his opening question through an interrogative clause with rising intonation. In this case the choices on each stratum match (i.e. discourse semantic question, lexicogrammatical interrogative, phonological rising tone). The lecturer follows up immediately with another question. But this time round there is a mismatch – we have a questioning move realized by

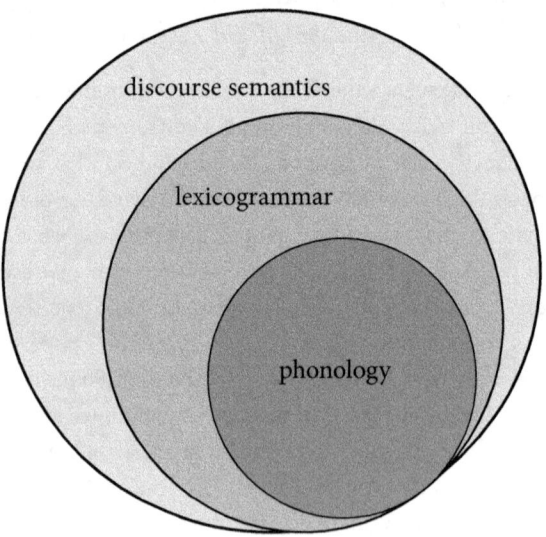

Figure 3.2 Language strata.

a declarative clause realized with rising intonation. Where the first question registers ignorance, the second encodes speculation. They both invite an answer, but the second, in addition, circumscribes an expected one.

//2 Uh where's all our friends from the other night?
//2 Once was enough?

Another example arises later on when the lecturer mentions someone's decision to enter into a contract. In this case a discourse semantic happening (i.e. someone deciding to enter into a contract) is realized as a nominal group (*that person's decision to enter into a contract*) rather than a clause (*that person decided to enter into a contract*). The lecturer's metaphorical realization and then its congruent unpacking are presented below (highlighted in bold).

> And we looked at the general entitlement to remain silent, even if there's a factor that will influence **that person's decision to enter into a contract**, say with you.

> And we looked at the general entitlement to remain silent, even if there's a factor that will influence **that person to decide to enter into a contract**, say with you.

Mismatches of this kind are a fundamental feature of academic discourse (Halliday, 2004; Halliday and Martin, 1993; Hao, 2020; Martin, 2008a) for various reasons. For one thing, the nominalizations involved are the source of a great deal of the technical nomenclature construing taxonomies of items in academic discourse (e.g. the legal terms in early phases of our lecture – *misrepresentation, statement, representation, contract, puff, rescission, remedy, tort of deceit, tort of negligence, tort of innocence, exceptions, half-truth, active concealment*). For another the grammatical metaphors allow a discourse semantic figure to be reconstrued as if it was an entity. And once realized as a nominal group, the meaning potential afforded that structure opens up – we can appraise the figure (e.g. *a foolish decision*), we can nuance the way it was brought about (e.g. *encourage their decision, induce their decision, determine their decision, enforce their decision*) and we can move it around in the clause, adjusting information flow (cf. *that factor influenced his decision to enter into a contract* vs *his decision to enter into a contract was influenced by several factors*). The whole EAP project is in some sense dedicated to fostering an elaborated meaning potential of this order. Irwin and Liu (2019) for example focus on helping students pack and unpack technical nomenclature by way of proving their mastery of disciplinary concepts. Liardét (2016) nicely complements this work with her focus on grammatical metaphor in low- and high-performing student texts. SFL's model of stratification makes explicit what the meaning potential of academic discourse involves and lays the foundation for understanding why it matters and doing something about it.

Alongside stratification, modelling language as a resource for meaning involves recognition of different kinds of meaning – addressed in SFL from the perspective of the ideational, interpersonal and textual metafunctions. In basic terms, ideational meaning construes social activity (e.g. teaching law), interpersonal meaning enacts social relations (e.g. between lecturer and students) and textual meaning composes texts as digestible waves of information (e.g. a shift from cases to their adjudication). Our tour of meaning across strata above focused at first on interpersonal meaning – the realization of moves in discourse in the grammar of mood and phonological tone. To this picture we can add the negotiation of feelings (Martin and White, 2005), as the lecturer speculates about why students have not returned (implying they are fed up) and then expresses his positive reaction to those who have come along (inscribing his happiness).

//1 Right ladies and gentlemen,
//2 uh where's all our friends from the other night?
//2 **Once was enough?**
//2 Call it quits?
//1 Ah,
//1 anyway, **I'm glad you're here**.
//1 So we're looking at misrepresentation,
//1 which is a Common Law doctrine.

Then, in our discussion of grammatical metaphor we brought ideational meaning into the picture in order to focus on the stratal tension engendered as something happening is realized grammatically as if it were a thing:

And we looked at the general entitlement to remain silent, even if there's a factor that will influence **that person's decision to enter into a contract**, say with you.

This brought a range of entities into the picture, including people (*we, you; person*), legal abstractions (*entitlement, contract*) and one semiotic entity (*factor*). These entities played various roles in state and occurrence figures – describing entities or positing their existence (*to remain silent, there's a factor*) and construing behaviour (*we looked at the general entitlement ..., that will influence that's person's decision ..., to enter into a contract*).

The key point here is that language does both things at once – it enacts interpersonal meaning at the same time as it construes ideational meaning. Accordingly SFL does not privilege one kind of meaning over another. This holds true as well for textual meaning, since meanings deriving from the ideational and interpersonal metafunction have to be fit for purpose. This means arranging them so they organize a text as pulses of prominence, adjusting information flow to the modality of communication through which speaker/listeners or writer/readers are interacting. The basic strategy our lecturer adopts for this is to begin clauses with pronouns referring to information that is readily recoverable from the context or co-text and end clauses with the legal technicality that he expects his students to learn. This makes for a relatively light context-dependent point of departure for each message (its Theme in SFL terms) and relatively technical context-independent pulse of news at the end of each message (its New in SFL terms). This complementarity is highlighted below (with topical Themes in italics and News in bold); the ellipses afforded by the spoken discourse have been filled in in parentheses below.

> So *we're* looking at **misrepresentation**,
> *which* is **a Common Law doctrine**.
> So *what we've been doing* is going through **these essential elements here**.
> *We* have **our different types of misrepresentation**.
> *This* is **important**
> because, *depending on what type it is*, will be **your solution**.
> And so (*it* will be) **fraudulent, negligent, innocent**.
> *We*'ll come to **that later tonight**.
> *We* started off looking at **the elements of misrepresentation**.
> (*we* started off looking at) **These ones up here**,
> (*we* started off looking at) **a statement that is not a puff or a hyperbole and is not a term of the contract necessarily**.
> So *that's* **what we've been doing**.

These different functional components of languages are outlined in Figure 3.3. The yin/yang-derived motif has been designed to reflect the inherent complementarity of interpersonal, ideational and textual strands of meaning alongside the interlacing of their contributions to unfolding discourse.

The significance of metafunctional diversity in language for EAP has to do with drawing attention to ideational, interpersonal and textual dimensions of academic discourse – and so not privileging one kind of meaning over another. On the one hand, this means not focusing exclusively on ideational meaning (i.e. the content students are learning); and it entails not trivializing a focus

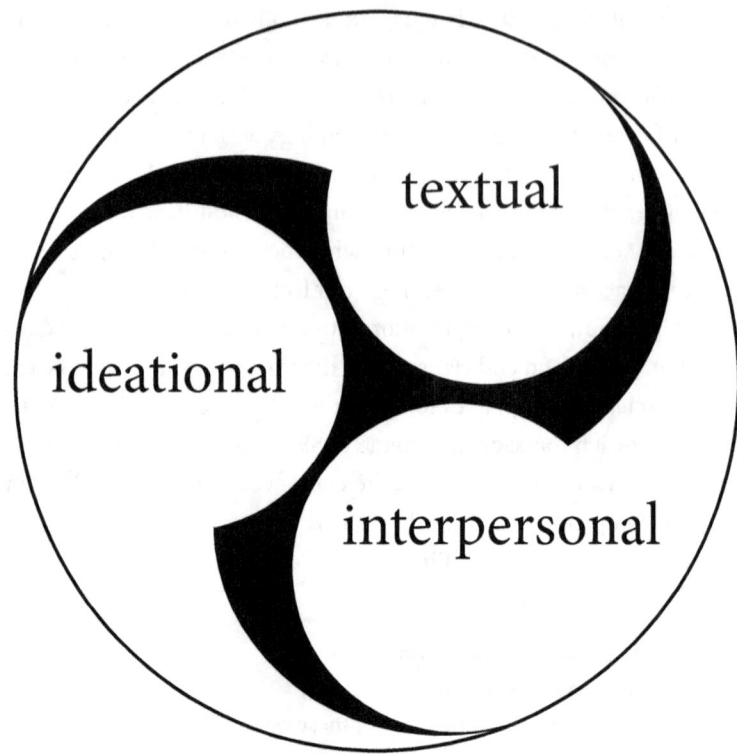

Figure 3.3 Language metafunctions.

of this kind by reducing it to the study of the distinctive technical lexis of a discipline. Mastery of interpersonal and technical dimensions of academic discourse is equally crucial. On the other hand, it signals that it is important not to privilege interpersonal and textual meaning by setting up generic EAP courses which don't involve disciplinary expertise, as if academic discourse can simply be generalized across disciplines. The academic discourses of science, social science and the humanities have evolved in very different directions in English over the past 400 years (Halliday, 2004; Wignell, 2007). They draw on grammatical metaphor in different ways to construe different kinds of knowledge – involving more and less technicality, more and less symbolism, more and less mathematics, different kinds of imaging and so on (Christie and Martin, 1997, 2007; Christie and Maton, 2011; Martin et al., 2020a; Maton et al., 2021). Some kind of embedded literacy programme is crucial if a balance is to be struck. Each metafunction matters, and how each matters depends on the discipline being taught. That said, we have to accept that embedded programmes are far from the norm. Monbec (2020) shows how stratification and metafunction can be harnessed to map the meaning that matters in an English for General Purposes programme – in work that usefully models how to recontextualize SFL technicality for EAP teaching practice in general terms.

Social context

Throughout its history SFL has had a productive collaboration with sociology – the code theories of Benrstein (1971, 2000) and Maton (2014) in particular. As explored in say Martin (2011) and Martin et al. (2020b), the success of this dialogue depends on a range of factors. The most relevant of these for purposes of this paper is that SFL has always been concerned with developing a linguistic model of social processes; it has never considered this the exclusive responsibility of social theorists. It is this stance which has made it possible for linguists and sociologists to share perspectives on issues of mutual concern and refocus theory and description in light of what the complementary perspectives call to mind.

In section 'Semantic choice' above we introduced SFL's model of intrinsic functionality – the metafunctional organization of linguistic resources as ideational, interpersonal and textual. SFL uses this intrinsic functionality to shape its model of extrinsic functionality – as field, tenor and mode. In general terms its model of language and social context suggest that ideational meaning by and large construes field, just as interpersonal meaning by and large enacts tenor, just as textual meaning by and large composes mode. Projected in these terms, field is a resource for construing phenomena as a set of activities oriented to some institutional purposes, including the items involved in these activities (organized by classification and composition) and any associated properties (Doran and Martin, 2021; Martin, 1992). Tenor is modelled as a resource for negotiating power and solidarity (the dimensions of equal/unequal status and close/distant contact in Poynton (1985)). And mode is modelled as a resource for managing context dependency (i.e. how much work language is doing alongside other modalities of communication and somatic behaviour and how dialogically that work is done (Martin, 2010a)).

It might seem that in a model of this kind the key 'social' variable is tenor since it is there that the hierarchical and horizontal dimensions of social relations are addressed. But we need to be careful here. Field is also strongly oriented to community. Doing things together (at home, at work, at play, wherever) involves communion with insiders (e.g. kith and kin, team members, co-workers, colleagues) and an inevitable concomitant separation from outsiders. The same can be said for mode. Communication is always ultimately a shared experience, whatever the mode – chatting, interviewing, texting, e-mailing, posting, blogging, vlogging, lecturing and so on. Field, tenor and mode (referred to collectively as register in Martin, 1992) are all concerned with the social nature of semiosis.

Alongside these three metafunctionally resonant register variables, Martin and his colleagues (e.g. Martin, 1992; Martin and Rose, 2008) work with an overarching level of social context they refer to as genre. The basic idea here is that a culture can be conceived as a system of 'text types' and that these genres coordinate choices in field with choices in tenor and with choices in mode. For practical purposes, genre in this model is often explained as a staged, goal-oriented social process. More technically speaking, its job is to outline the stages through which a text unfolds to realize say a story, a report, a procedure, an argument, a service encounter or an invitation, and to adjust specific choices for field, tenor and mode depending on the staging of the genre (cf. the shift from the everyday, friendly, dialogic nature of the first few moves of our lecture text to the more authoritative, relatively impersonal, monologic discourse which follows). Once again, as for field, tenor and mode, in SFL genre is part of a social model of context. It looks at how we do things together as we use language to live.

The stratified model of language and social context presented to this point in the paper is outlined in Figure 3.4. In a model of this kind, genre is realized through a pattern of register variables, which are in turn realized through a pattern of linguistic ones. In Hjelmslev's (1961) terms, SFL models context as a connotative semiotic realized through the denotative semiotic of language. Not having an expression plane of its own, genre and register piggy-back on language – skewing the probability of choices in discourse semantics, lexicogrammar and phonology to suit their goals. In this respect the Firthian heritage of SFL is very clear (Firth, 1968). Context is modelled as higher strata of meaning, not as an extra-linguistic phenomenon. Analysing genre and register accordingly becomes an integral aspect of any text analysis – always already ensuring the social is brought into the picture.

For an illustration of genre analysis see Martin (2020), which addresses the presentation of a precedent setting case as a story genre later on in the lecture. For discussion of field, tenor and mode shifting in the lecture and its pedagogic function, see Martin (2021). For a popular accessible introduction to this way of modelling social context, see Martin (2010a).

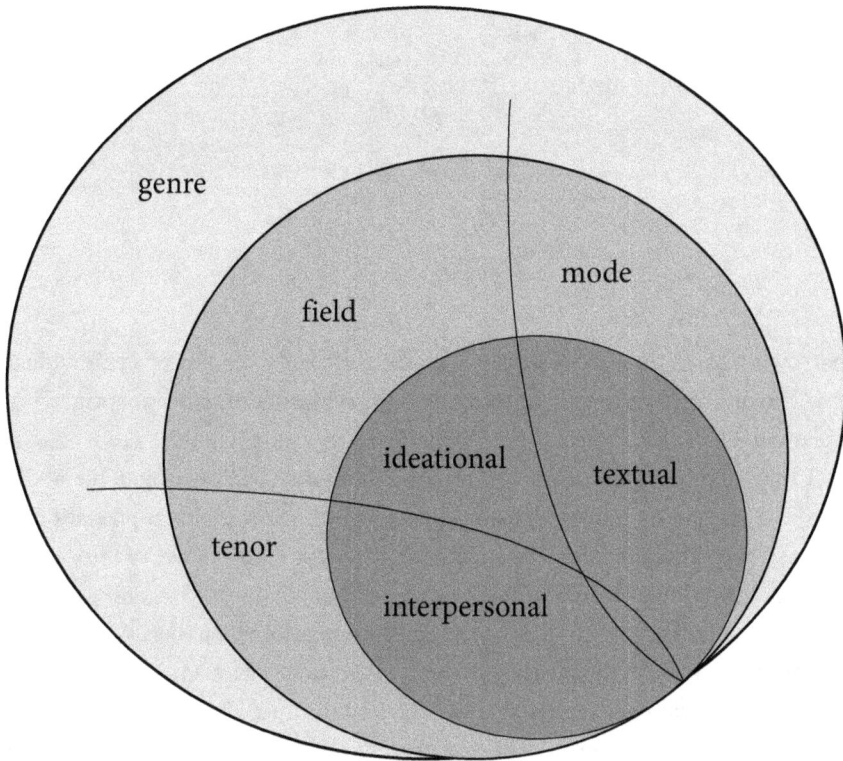

Figure 3.4 Language, register (field, tenor, mode) and genre.

Instantiation

In sections 'Semantic choice' and 'Social context' above we built a map of the meaning potential of language and context, as modelled in SFL. As consolidated in Figure 3.4, the overall picture is one of stratification (levels of abstraction) intersecting with metafunctions (kinds of meaning) – with genre playing an over-arching coordinating role. A model of this kind involves a mix of more and less categorical connections between categories, without ever prescribing how most meanings can be combined. In order to focus on how meanings are in fact combined SFL sets up a complementarity hierarchy alongside realization – namely instantiation (Halliday, 2008b, Chapter 3). Unlike realization, which is a hierarchy of abstraction, instantiation is a hierarchy of generalization. Its focus is on the instantiation of system in text – of the meaning potential of the system in instances of language use. A crude map of this hierarchy is presented in Figure 3.5. Looking down from the system end, we have a cline of specialization,

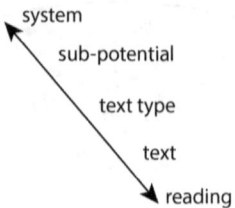

Figure 3.5 Cline of instantiation.

narrowing down from the system as a whole to a specific reading of an individual text; moving up from the reading end, we have a cline of generalization, amassing meanings across data and working towards the meaning potential as a whole.

Compared to stratification, instantiation is a much less developed hierarchy in SFL. Here we focus on dimensions of special relevance to our appreciation of SFL as a social theory of language. Potentially the most productive of these is the notion of coupling, which deals with recurrent combinations of meaning as texts unfold – including intramodal, intermodal and interlingual patterns.

Intramodal coupling picks up where realization leaves off – focusing on patterns of meaning across metafunctions and strata that the stratification hierarchy does not prescribe. This has proved especially productive in appraisal analysis (Martin and White, 2005), where the relation between an attitude and its trigger/target is crucial to the interpretation of a text. This coupling is explored in work on restorative justice (Martin and Zappavigna, 2016; Zappavigna and Martin, 2018a, b), on business discourse (Szenes, 2021, 2022) and critical reflection on social work and business in Szenes and Tilakaratna, (2021). The concept of coupling allows analysts to bring together interpersonal and ideational meanings as outlined in general and then specific terms in Figure 3.6 (drawing on an example from opening of our law lecture). These couplings of feeling and ideation are explored as invitations for interlocutors to bond by Knight (2010), a point we will take up in relation to the hierarchy of individuation below.

Intermodal coupling focuses on combinations of meaning from two or more modalities in multimodal texts. Our law lecture for example construes a taxonomy of types of misrepresentation in both verbiage and image. The relevant spoken verbiage is highlighted in bold below, and the parts of the infographic (Figure 3.1) that his verbiage couples with are isolated in Figure 3.7.

> We have our **different types of misrepresentation**. This is important because, depending on **what type** it is, will be your solution. And so **fraudulent, negligent, innocent**. We'll come to that later tonight.

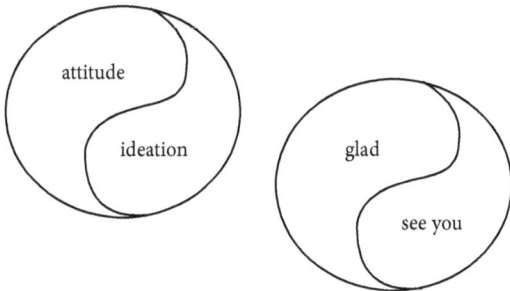

Figure 3.6 Coupling of attitude and ideation.

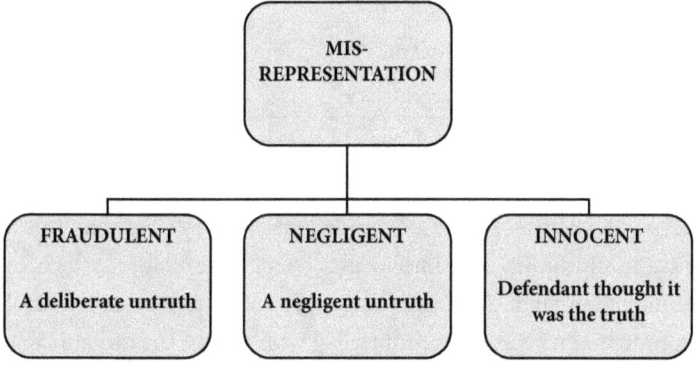

Figure 3.7 Imagic construal of types of misrepresentation.

Painter et al. (2013), in their work on children's picture books, suggest a metafunctionally organized model of convergence across the modalities of language and image – comprising ideational concurrence, interpersonal resonance and textual synchronicity. This model is outlined as Table 3.1, using Kress and van Leeuwen's (2021) terms for metafunctions in images. Intermodal convergence needs to be interpreted by degree, since the complementary affordances of different modalities make it unlikely that the meanings made will ever be exactly the same. And the model should not be interpreted as precluding the possibility of cross-coupling, across different metafunctions (when an image uses ideational resources to invoke an interpersonal evaluation for example). For an application of this model to the intermodal convergence of language and paralanguage, see Ngo et al. (2022).

Interlingual coupling focuses attention on multilingual texts, including the source and target texts involved in translating and interpretating and the field's abiding concern with 'equivalence' (Kim et al., 2021). de Souza (2013) introduces

Table 3.1 Intermodal coupling (organized by metafunction).

Verbiage	Convergence	Image
Ideational	*Concurrence*	Representation
Interpersonal	*Resonance*	Interaction/validity
Textual	*Synchronicity*	Composition

Table 3.2 Interlingual coupling (degrees of equivalence).

Source (L1)	'Equivalence'	Target (L2)
Ideational	*Concurrence*	Ideational
Interpersonal	*Resonance*	Interpersonal
Textual	*Synchronicity*	Textual

the concept of re-instantiation to model this process. For her this involves moving up the instantiation cline (a process of distantiation which opens up the meaning potential of the source language) until a point is reached where the meaning potential converges appropriately with that of the target language and then crossing over and moving back down the cline (a process of instantiation into the target language).

This re-instantiation process (Martin and Quiroz, 2021) is in many respects comparable to the process of moving from L1 to L2 in EAP classrooms as students shift from the spoken and/or written texts they control in their L1 to the academic texts they need to master in L2. Table 3.1 is re-worked as Table 3.2, allowing for degrees of interlingual 'equivalence' (without precluding the possibility of cross-coupling – e.g. a lexical metaphor invoking attitude in L1 rendered as an inscribed attitude in L2). de Souza makes the point (which is relevant to both her field of translation and EAP) that the process re-instantiation is always an ideologically invested one, a point we shed further light on in our discussion of individuation below.

As our process-oriented discussion of coupling reveals, the instantiation hierarchy involves a dynamic orientation to semiosis (complementing the synoptic perspective afforded by stratification). In SFL (e.g. Matthiessen and Halliday, 1999) semogenesis is usefully conceived in relation to three dimensions of time – logogenesis (as a text unfolds), ontogenesis (as language

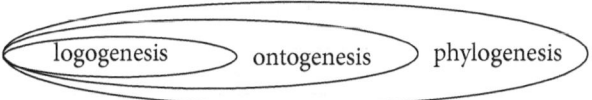

Figure 3.8 Temporal dimensions of language change (semogenesis).

Figure 3.9 Phases of pedagogic activity.

is learned) and phylogenesis (as language evolves). As crudely imaged in Figure 3.8, phylogenesis provides an epochal environment for ontogenesis, which in turn provides a generational environment for logogenesis, and conversely, logogenesis provides the instances enabling ontogenetic development, which in turn provides the repertoires engendering phylogenetic evolution.

The ways in which logogenesis feeds ontogenesis is of course the central concern of any language development programme, including EAP. In language in education programmes informed by SFL (e.g. Rose and Martin, 2012) teaching/learning activities are designed as cycles, each with a nuclear task. In effective pedagogy students are adequately prepared to succeed and supported where necessary by a move focusing their attention, and tasks are of course evaluated (positively since students have been primed for success) and elaborated (by way of reinforcing or extending the learnings to hand). A logogenetic process of this kind is outlined in Figure 3.9 (adapted from Rose, 2020). It designs pedagogic discourse as a social process – a reciprocity of teaching and learning in which dialogic logogenesis engenders ontogenesis.

Table 3.3 presents an illustration of this process from our law lecture. The focus in this instance is a compositional one – on the elements of a misrepresentation (see Figure 3.1). The lecturer is in fact taking a moment to review earlier work on rescission.

Table 3.3 A teaching/learning cycle illustrated.

Speaker	Activity	Discourse
Lecturer	Prepare	So we look at all these particular things, we go through all our elements; each element must be there to constitute a misrepresentation and to bring about a rescission.
	Focus	What was a rescission? Anyone recall?
Student	Task	- Returning parties to the position they were in beforehand.
Lecturer	Evaluate	- Yes, good.
	Elaborate	So both parties go back to their previous position. If you've paid money for goods, you get your money back, the proprietor gets his/her goods back. So that is the solution, on a contractual level. If someone has lied to you, deceived you, deliberately, then you also have a remedy in the tort of deceit. You're not allowed to lie to people, and if there are damages associated with that, the victim will be awarded those damages. If someone has been negligent in the statement they make to you, causing you to enter into a contract, then to lose, money in particular, you'll have a suit in the tort of negligence. If it is an innocent misrepresentation, in other words, it's neither negligent nor fraudulent, rescission of contract but no damages, no tort of innocence.

Individuation

In sections 'Semantic choice' and 'Social context' above we explored the meaning potential of language and context, as modelled in SFL. Then in section 'Instantiation' we opened up a complementary hierarchy, instantiation, to make room for exploring how this meaning potential is used. We now turn out attention to a third hierarchy, individuation, which allows us to bring users of language into the picture (Martin, 2006, 2010b).

Basically what we are concerned with here is the distribution of the meaning potential of a culture and its uptake by users. A crude map of this hierarchy is presented in Figure 3.10, scaled in terms of 'identities' of different orders – from the persona we enact in one or another of our coteries and on through our positioning by class, generation, gender, ethnicity and the like as we member

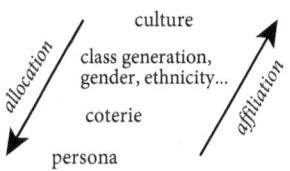

Figure 3.10 Individuation (allocation and affiliation).

the culture as a whole. In relation to this cline, allocation is concerned with how the meaning potential of the community as a whole is distributed, both in terms of what resources are made available and dispositions for how they are taken up. Bernstein (e.g. 2000) uses the metaphor of reservoir and repertoire for this perspective; Hasan (e.g. 2009) brings together papers documenting some of the implications of his code theory through her studies of semantic variation in relation to class and gender.

The affiliation perspective on the other hand is concerned with how allocated resources are taken up as interlocutors align. Inspired by the work of Stenglin (see her 2022 overview) and Knight (2010), promising research on bonding has emerged – a lot of it focused on the attitude/ideation couplings introduced in section 'Instantiation'. The basic idea here is that interlocutors negotiate alignment around these couplings, with shared couplings referred to as bonds. This creates the possibility of ultimately interpreting individuation as a hierarchy of bond complexes (Martin, 2008a, b, 2012). Zappavigna and Martin (2018a) develop these ideas in relation to Tann's work (2010, 2012) on identity and iconization by way of interpreting successful and less successful reaffiliation processes in Youth Justice Conferencing. This work draws in addition on Maton's Legitimation Code Theory (2014) – his specialization dimension in particular. Martin et al. (2010) make connections between SFL and LCT in relation to work on bonding and Maton's proposals for epistemological and axiological cosmologies.

As far as EAP is concerned, individuation opens up possibilities for thinking about pedagogy and curriculum from the perspective of belonging. Mastery of academic discourse involves a major reallocation of semiotic resources for all social subjects. And we have to be sensitive about how we open up this path. What some students experience as liberating in terms of the creation of new possibilities for affiliation other students may find alienating (as they experience perhaps a loss of connection with where they are coming from and some sense of 'imposter syndrome' in where they're going to). In order to deal effectively with such issues empathy is not enough. A requisite amount of attention has to be given to curriculum goals, including decisions about how to properly position the vernacular discourses students bring to class alongside the academic discourse EAP has evolved to proffer. And a requisite amount of attention has to be given to carefully designed pedagogy – including steps which properly value vernacular discourses at the same time as bridges are built between them and the academic discourses of the sciences, social sciences and the humanities. For overviews of very promising work on bilingual and multilingual language teaching in this regard, see Crane (2022), Kartika (2022) and Ramirez (2022).

Social linguistics and EAP

Bernstein (2000: 52) makes a useful distinction between singulars and regions as far as the classification of knowledge structures is concerned. Singulars he characterizes as disciplines such as physics, chemistry, history, economics, psychology and so on which have their own specialized discourse. Regions on the other hand recontextualize singulars into larger units which interface the production of knowledge with fields of practice – engineering, medicine, architecture, information science, business studies for example. The principles for recontextualization are crucial; it matters which singulars are selected and what knowledge within a singular is chosen and introduced. Seen in these terms EAP is of course a canonical region. As reflected in many chapters of this book, its draws on a wide range of singulars (including SFL) to inform its practice and could and will no doubt continue to draw on more. The special mission of this collection is to adjust EAP's recontextualizing principles so that social perspectives are foregrounded and brought to bear on EAP teaching/learning technologies.

It is instructive to speculate on the recontextualizing principles connecting SFL and EAP as these complementary knowledge structures have emerged since the 1970s. One key factor has surely been the ways in which SFL's model of language and social context has been able to clarify the ways in which academic discourse differs from discourse of other kinds. I am less confident that this difference has been appreciated as a registerial one (i.e. ways of meaning different things) rather than a dialectal one (i.e. different ways of meaning similar things). And I am less confident still that SFL work on ontogenesis and its implications for a language-based theory of learning (Halliday, 1993) have impacted on EAP curriculum and pedagogy (cf. Dreyfus et al., 2016) – in spite of exemplary practice such as that outlined in Monbec (2020). An eclectic approach, drawing on SFL influenced genre-based language programmes among many others, has tended to hold sway.

I won't jump up on my soap box here to try and prescribe how EAP should draw on SFL. But I hope the 'social' turn promoted by this volume encourages the region to look again at what it can recontextualize from SFL. As part of this process I do hope SFL's concern with a wide range of languages (e.g. Caffarel et al., 2004; Martin and Doran, 2015; Martin et al., 2020, 2021; Doran et al., 2021a, 2021b, 2022a, 2022b; Mwinlaaru and Xuan, 2016) and a wide range of modalities of communication (e.g. Kress and van Leeuwen, 2021; Painter et al., 2013; Ngo et al., 2022) nudge the region to recontextualize itself – shifting its gaze beyond English (to academic discourse in a range of world languages) and beyond language (to multimodal discourse involving a range of semiotic modes). What to call this new globalized region of practice is something we can let evolve. If going 'social' is the trigger, let it be.

References

Bartlett, T. and G. O'Grady, eds (2017), *The Routledge Handbook of Systemic Functional Linguistic*, London: Routledge.

Benrstein, B. (1971), *Class, Codes and Control, Volume 1 Theoretical Studies towards a Sociology of Language*, London: Routledge & Kegan Paul.

Bernstein, B. (2000), *Pedagogy, Symbolic Control and Identity: Theory, Research, Critique*, London: Rowman & Littlefield.

Caffarel, A., J. R. Martin and C. M. I. M. Matthiessen, eds (2004), *Language Typology: A Functional Perspective*, Amsterdam: Benjamins (Current Issues in Linguistic Theory).

Caldwell, D., J. Knox, and J. R. Martin, eds (2022), *Appliable Linguistics and Social Semiotics: Developing Theory from Practice* (Bloomsbury Studies in Systemic Functional Linguistics), London: Bloomsbury.

Christie, F. and J. R. Martin, eds (1997), *Genre and Institutions: Social Processes in the Workplace and School*, London: Cassell.

Christie, F. and J. R. Martin, eds (2007), *Language, Knowledge and Pedagogy: Functional Linguistic and Sociological Perspectives*, London: Continuum.

Christie, F. and K. Maton, eds (2011), *Disciplinarity: Functional Linguistics and Sociological Perspectives*, London: Continuum.

Crane, A. (2022), 'Revitalizing an Endangered Genre: Applying Genre Theory and the Teaching and Learning Cycle', in D. Caldwell, J. R. Martin and J. Knox (eds), *Appliable Linguistics and Social Semiotics: Developing Theory from Practice*, x–xx, London: Bloomsbury (Bloomsbury Studies in Systemic Functional Linguistics).

de Souza, Ladjane Maria Farias (2013), 'Interlingual Re-instantiation – A New Systemic Functional Perspective on Translation', *Text & Talk*, 33 (4–5): 575–94.

Doran, Y. J. and J. R. Martin (2021), 'Field Relations: Understanding Scientific Explanation', in K. Maton, J. R. Martin, and Y. J. Doran (eds), *Teaching Science: Knowledge, Language, Pedagogy*, 105–33, London: Routledge.

Doran, Y. J., J. R. Martin & D. Zhang, eds (2021a), *Word* (Special Issue 'The grammar of nominal groups: Systemic functional linguistics perspectives'. *Word* 67.3. 2021. 182pp.

Doran, Y. J., J. R. Martin & D. Zhang, eds (2021b), *Word* (Special Issue 'The grammar of nominal groups: Systemic functional linguistics perspectives'. *Word* 67.4. 2021.

Doran, Y. J., J. R. Martin & D. Zhang, eds (2022a), *Word* (Special Issue 'The grammar of nominal groups: Systemic functional linguistics perspectives'. *Word* 68.1 in press for 2022.

Doran, Y. J., J. R. Martin & D. Zhang, eds (2022b), *Word* (Special Issue 'The grammar of nominal groups: Systemic functional linguistics perspectives'. *Word* 68.2 in press for 2022.

Dreyfus, S., S. Humphrey, A. Mahboob and J. R. Martin (2016), *Genre Pedagogy in Higher Education: The SLATE Project*, Basingstoke: Palgrave Macmillan.

Firth, J. R. (1968), 'A Synopsis of Linguistic Theory', in F. R. Palmer (ed.), *Selected Papers of J.R. Firth, 1952–1959*, 168–205, London: Longmans.

Halliday, M. A. K. (1977), 'Text as Semantic Choice in Social Contexts', in T. A. van Dijk and J. Petöfi (eds), *Grammars and Descriptions: Studies in Text Theory and Text Analysis*, 176–225, Berlin: Walter de Gruyter.

Halliday, M. A. K. (1978), *Language as Social Semiotic: The Social Interpretation of Language and Meaning*, London: Edward Arnold.

Halliday, M. A. K. (1985), *An Introduction to Functional Grammar*, London: Arnold. (2nd edition 1994, 3rd edition revised by C.M.I.M. Matthiessen 2004, 4th edition revised by C.M.I.M. Matthiessen 2014).

Halliday, M. A. K. (1993), 'Towards a Language-based Theory of Learning', *Linguistics and Education*, 5 (2): 93–116.

Halliday, M. A. K. (2004), *The Language of Science* (Volume 5 in the Collected Works of M. A. K. Halliday, edited by J. J. Webster), London: Continuum.

Halliday, M. A. K. (2008a), 'Working with Meaning: Towards an Appliable Linguistics', in J. J. Webster (ed.), *Meaning in Context: Implementing Intelligent Applications of Language Studies*, 7–23, London: Continuum.

Halliday, M. A. K. (2008b), *Complementarities in Language*, Beijing: The Commercial Press.

Halliday, M. A. K. and W. S. Greaves (2008), *Intonation in the Grammar of English*, London: Equinox.

Halliday, M. A. K. and J. R. Martin, eds (1993), *Writing Science: Literacy and Discursive Power*, London: Taylor & Francis.

Hao, J. (2020), *Analysing Scientific Discourse from a Systemic Functional Linguistic Perspective: A Framework for Exploring Knowledge Building in Biology*, New York: Routledge.

Hasan, R. (2009), *Semantic Variation: Meaning in Society and in Sociolinguistics*, London: Equinox.

Hjlemslev, L. (1961), *Prolegomena to a Theory of Language*, Madison: The University of Wisconsin Press.

Hood, S. (2016), 'Systemic Functional Linguistics and EAP', in K. Hyland and P. Shaw (eds), *The Routledge Handbook of English for Academic Purposes*, 193–205, London: Routledge.

Hood, S. and P. Maggiora (2016), 'A Lecturer at Work: Language, The Body and Space in the Structuring of Disciplinary Knowledge in Law', in H. de Silva Joyce (ed.), *Language at Work in Social Contexts: Analysing Language Use in Work, Educational, Medical and Museum Contexts*, 108–28, Newcastle upon Tyne: Cambridge Scholars.

Irwin, D. and N. Liu (2019), 'Encoding, Decoding, Packing and Unpacking via Agnation: Reformulating General Knowledge into Disciplinary Concepts for Teaching English Academic Writing', *Journal of English for Academic Purposes*, 42: 1475–585. DOI: https://doi.org/10.1016/j.jeap.2019.100782.

Kartika-Ningsi, H. (2022), 'The Reading to Learn Bilingual Program: Taking Multilingualism into Genre-based Pedagogic Practicesm', in D. Caldwell, J. R. Martin, and J. Knox (eds), *Appliable Linguistics and Social Semiotics: Developing Theory from Practice*, npa, London: Bloomsbury (Bloomsbury Studies in Systemic Functional Linguistics).

Kim, M., J. Munday, P. Wang, and Z. Wang, eds (2021), *Systemic Functional Linguistics in Translation Studies*, London: Bloomsbury.

Knight, N. (2010), 'Wrinkling Complexity: Concepts of Identity and Affiliation in Humour', in M. Bednarek and J. R. Martin (eds), *New Discourse on Language: Functional Perspectives on Multimodality, Identity, and Affiliation*, 35–58, London: Continuum.

Kress, G. and T. van Leeuwen (2021), *Reading Images: The Grammar of Visual Design*, 3rd edn, London: Routledge.

Liardét, C. L. (2016), 'Grammatical Metaphor: Distinguishing Success', *Journal of English for Academic Purposes*, 22: 109–18.

Martin, J. R. (1992), *English Text: System and Structure*, Amsterdam: Benjamins.

Martin, J. R. (1998), 'Linguistics and the Consumer: The Practice of Theory', *Linguistics and Education*, 9 (4): 411–48.

Martin, J. R. (2006), 'Genre, Ideology and Intertextuality: A Systemic Functional Perspective', *Linguistics and the Human Sciences* (Special Issue on Genre edited by J. Bateman), 2 (2): 275–98.

Martin, J. R. (2008a), 'Incongruent and Proud: De/vilifying "Nominalisation"', *Discourse & Society*, 19 (6): 801–10.

Martin, J. R. (2008b), 'Innocence: Realisation, Instantiation and Individuation in a Botswanan Town', in N. Knight and A. Mahboob (eds), *Questioning Linguistics*, 32–76, Cambridge: Cambridge Scholars Publishing.

Martin, J. R. (2008c), 'Tenderness: Realisation and Instantiation in a Botswanan Town', 30–62, *Odense Working Papers in Language and Communication* (Special Issue of Papers from 34th International Systemic Functional Congress edited by Nina Nørgaard).

Martin, J. R. (2010a), 'Language, Register and Genre', in C. Coffin, T. Lillis, and K. O'Halloran (eds), *Applied Linguistics Methods: A Reader*, 12–32, London: Routledge.

Martin, J. R. (2010b), 'Semantic Variation: Modelling System, Text and Affiliation in Social Semiosis', in M. Bednarek and J. R. Martin (eds), *New Discourse on Language: Functional Perspectives on Multimodality, Identity and Affiliation*, 1–34, London: Continuum.

Martin, J. R. (2011), 'Bridging Troubled Waters: Interdisciplinarity and What Makes It Stick', in F. Christie and K. Maton (eds), *Disciplinarity: Functional Linguistic and Sociological Perspectives*, 35–61, London: Continuum.

Martin, J. R. (2012), 'Heart from Darkness: Apocalypse Ron', *Revista Canaria de Estudios Ingleses*, 65. November 2012 (Special issue on The Evaluative Uses of Language: the appraisal framework), 67–99.

Martin, J. R. (2014), 'Evolving Systemic Functional Linguistics: Beyond the Clause', *Functional Linguistics*, 1 (3).

Martin, J. R. (2016), 'Meaning Matters: A Short History of Systemic Functional Linguistics', *Word*, 61 (2): 35–58.

Martin, J. R. (2020), 'Genre and Activity: A Potential Site for Dialogue between Systemic Functional Linguistics (SFL) and Cultural Historical Activity Theory (CHAT)', *Mind Culture Activity*, 27 (3) (Special Issue on SFL and CHAT edited by M. Cole): 216–32.

Martin, J. R. (2021), 'Pedagogic Discourse: Marshalling Register Variation', *Revista Signos*, 54 (107) (Special Issue in Honour of Giovanni Parodi): 771–98.

Martin, J. R. and Y. J. Doran, eds (2015), *Grammatical Descriptions*, London: Routledge (Critical Concepts in Linguistics: Systemic Functional Linguistics, Vol. 2).

Martin, J. R. and B. Quiroz (2021), 'Functional Language Typology: SFL Perspectives', in M. Kim, J. Munday, P. Wang and Z. Wang (eds), *Systemic Functional Linguistics in Translation Studies*, 7–33, London: Bloomsbury.

Martin, J. R. and D. Rose (2007), *Working with Discourse: Meaning beyond the Clause*, London: Continuum.

Martin, J. R. and D. Rose (2008), *Genre Relations: Mapping Culture*, London: Continuum.

Martin, J. R. and P. R. R. White (2005), *The Language of Evaluation: Appraisal in English*, London: Palgrave.

Martin, J. R., Y. J. Doran, and G. Figueredo, eds (2020), *Systemic Functional Language Description: Making Meaning Matter*, London: Routledge.

Martin, J. R., K. Maton, and Y. J. Doran, eds (2020a), *Accessing Academic Discourse: Systemic Functional Linguistics and Legitimation Code Theory*, London: Routledge.

Martin, J. R., K. Maton, and Y. J. Doran (2020b), 'Academic Discourse: An Interdisciplinary Dialogue', in J. R. Martin, K. Maton and Y. J. Doran (eds), *Accessing Academic Discourse: Systemic Functional Linguistics and Legitimation Code Theory*, 1–31, London: Routledge.

Martin, J. R., B. Quiroz and G. Figueredo, eds (2021), *Interpersonal Grammar: Systemic Functional Linguistic Theory and Description*, Cambridge: Cambridge University Press.

Martin, J. R., K. Maton and E. Matruglio (2010), 'Historical Cosmologies: Epistemology and Axiology in Australian Secondary School History', *Revista Signos*, 43 (74): 433–63.

Martin, J. R. and M. Zappvigna (2016), 'Rites of Passion: Remorse, Apology and Forgiveness in Youth Justice Conferencing', *Linguistics and the Human Sciences,* 12 (2–3) (Special Issue on Legal Discourse edited by Wang Zhenhua): 101–21.

Maton, K. (2014), *Knowledge and Knowers: Towards a Realist Sociology of Education*, London: Routledge.

Maton, K., J. R. Martin and Y. J. Doran, eds (2021), *Teaching Science: Language, Knowledge and Pedagogy*, London: Routledge.

Matthiesseen, C. M. I. M. and M. A. K. Halliday (1999), *Construing Experience through Meaning: A Language-based Approach to Cognition*, London: Cassell.

Monbec, L. (2020), 'Systemic Functional Linguistics for the EGAP Module: Revisiting Common Core', *Journal of English for Academic Purposes*, 43.

Mwinlaaru, I. and W. Xuan (2016), 'A Survey of Studies in Systemic Functional Language Description and Typology', *Functional Linguistics*, 3 (8).

Ngo, T., S. Hood, J. R. Martin, C. Painter, B. Smith and M. Zappavigna (2022), *Modelling Paralanguage Using Systemic Functional Semiotics*, London: Bloomsbury (Bloomsbury Studies in Systemic Functional Linguistics).

O'Halloran, K., S. Tan and P. Wignell (2019), 'SFL and Multimodal Discourse Analysis', in G. Thompson, W. L. Bowcher, L. Fontaine and D. Schöntahl (eds), *The Cambridge Handbook of Systemic Functional Linguistics*, 433–61, Cambridge: Cambridge University Press.

Painter, C., J. R. Martin, and L. Unsworth (2013), *Reading Visual Narratives: Image Analysis of Children's Picture Books*, London: Equinox.

Poynton, C. (1985), *Language and Gender: Making the Difference*, Geelong: Deakin University Press.

Ramirez, A. (2022), 'Reading to Learn, Learning to Teach: Emergent Bilingual Latinx Parents Read in English to Their Young Emergent Bilingual Children at Home', in D. Caldwell, J. R. Martin, and J. Knox (eds), *Appliable Linguistics and Social Semiotics: Developing Theory from Practice*, xx–xx, London: Bloomsbury (Bloomsbury Studies in Systemic Functional Linguistics).

Rose, D. (2020), 'Building a Pedagogic Metalanguage I: Curriculum Genres', in J. R. Martin, K. Maton and Y. J. Doran (eds), *Accessing Academic Discourse: Systemic Functional Linguistics and Legitimation Code Theory*, 236–67, London: Routledge.

Rose, D. and J. R. Martin (2012), *Learning to Write, Reading to Learn: Genre, Knowledge and Pedagogy in the Sydney School*, London: Equinox.

Stenglin, M. (2022), 'Binding and Bonding: A Retrospective and Prospective Gaze', in D. Caldwell, J. R. Martin and J. Knox (eds), *Appliable Linguistics and Social Semiotics: Developing Theory from Practice*, npa, London: Bloomsbury (Bloomsbury Studies in Systemic Functional Linguistics).

Szenes, E. (2021), 'The Linguistic Construction of Business Decisions: A Systemic-functional Linguistic Perspective', *Language, Context and Text*, 3 (2): 335–66.

Szenes, E. (2022), 'The Language of Business Reasoning: Analysing Student Writing in Higher Education', in D. Caldwell, J. R. Martin, and J. Knox (eds), *Appliable Linguistics and Social Semiotics: Developing Theory from Practice*, npa, London: Bloomsbury (Bloomsbury Studies in Systemic Functional Linguistics).

Szenes, E. and N. Tilakaratna (2021), 'Deconstructing Critical Reflection in Social Work and Business: Negotiating Emotions and Opinions in Reflective Writing', *Journal of English for Academic Purposes*, 49.

Tann, K. (2010), 'Imagining Communities: A Multifunctional Approach to Identity Management in Texts', in M. Bednarek and J. R. Martin (eds), *New Discourse on Language: Functional Perspectives on Multimodality, Identity, and Affiliation*, 163–94, London: Continuum.

Tann, K. (2012), 'The Language of Identity Discourse: Introducing a Systemic Functional Framework for Iconography', *Linguistics and the Human Sciences*, 8 (3): 361–91.

Thompson, G., W. L. Bowcher, L. Fontaine and D. Schöntahl, eds (2019), *The Cambridge Handbook of Systemic Functional Linguistics*, Cambridge: Cambridge University Press.

Wignell, P. (2007), *On the Discourse of Social Science*, Darwin: Charles Darwin University Press.

Zappavigna, M. and J. R. Martin (2018a), *Discourse and Diversionary Justice: An Analysis of Youth Justice Conferencing*, London: Palgrave Macmillan.

Zappavigna, M. and J. R. Martin (2018b), 'Communing Affiliation: Social Tagging as a Resource for Aligning around Values in Social Media', *Discourse, Context and Media*, 22 (special issue, *Discourse of Social Tagging* edited by C Lee): 4–12.

Part Two

Perspectives

4

Legitimation Code Theory: Addressing fragmentation in EAP

Steve Kirk

Introduction

EAP is fragmented. Great variability in routes into the field, institutional positioning, professional affordances and thus local configurations of EAP creates a complex, fractured landscape. Perspectives can become polarized, e.g. with respect to theory 'vs' practice, creating unnecessary boundaries between different forms of knowledge. A framework is needed that enables a more integrated understanding of EAP practices and the field. This chapter introduces Legitimation Code Theory (LCT) as offering one such framework.

Exploration begins with an overview of LCT, outlining key characteristics and concepts that enable it to address fragmentation. This includes, in particular, a focus on knowledge practices and how this opens up refined ways of conceptualizing and practising EAP. Discussion then focuses on the concept of semantic gravity, or the relative context dependence of meaning-making, to exemplify how LCT can be enacted for richer understandings of EAP materials design, teaching and student practice. The chapter thus illustrates how LCT offers EAP a powerful shared language, both to discuss the field in all its diversity, and to analyse and shape practice itself. This could enable a more integrated understanding of EAP practices and a more cumulative means to build the field.

A shared language for EAP: Legitimation Code Theory

LCT is a sociological framework for researching, shaping and changing practice. It is 'a conceptual toolkit and analytic methodology, rather than a paradigm or "-ism"' (Maton et al., 2016: 7). The framework has continued to evolve since its origins in the early 2000s in extensive dialogue with empirical research and draws on a range of theoretical influences. Most explicitly, LCT extends and integrates the sociological approaches of Pierre Bourdieu (e.g. 1996, 2000) and, in particular, Basil Bernstein (e.g. 1977, 1990, 2000). This has enabled making a wider range of phenomena visible for analysis, understanding and as the basis for practical action.[1]

LCT is a rapidly growing community with rapidly growing influence and impact (legitimationcodetheory.com). Its capacity to address problems and shape practice across disciplines and diverse international settings points suggestively to its potential for EAP in similarly diverse environments. Problem contexts include Australia, South Africa, the UK, the United States, Mexico and China. Research ranges from exploring parental school choice (Aris, 2020) and inclusive education (Walton and Rusznyak, 2020), to political discourse (Siebörger and Adendorff, 2017), teaching chemistry (Blackie, 2014), jazz (Richardson, 2019) and ballet (Lambrinos, 2019). Recent edited collections address concerns of knowledge building and social justice in higher education (Winberg et al., 2020), in teaching science (Maton et al., 2021) and, of particular value to EAP practitioners, in accessing academic discourse (Martin et al., 2020). The latter two volumes also showcase the fruitful interdisciplinary collaboration between LCT and systemic functional linguistics.

Practitioners in higher education and in EAP more specifically are demonstrating how LCT can be used to enhance current understandings and practices, particularly through integrating perspectives on knowledge-building. This includes work in academic literacies, particularly in South Africa (e.g. Clarence and McKenna, 2017) and enactments of LCT in educational practice for those who teach in university settings (Clarence, 2021). In EAP, a growing number of teaching professionals are addressing problems that LCT helps to make visible, such as the obscuring of knowledge and its effects on people and practices (Maton, 2014a). Focuses include examining and enhancing practice in EAP course design and enactment (Kirk, 2018; Monbec, 2018), in academic reading (Cowley-Haselden, 2020) and in academic writing (Brooke et al., 2019; Ingold and O'Sullivan, 2017; Kirk, 2017; Muir and Solli, 2019; Szenes et al., 2015). This work offers a tantalizing glimpse of LCT's potential to enrich existing approaches and dissolve unhelpful dichotomies, such as theory/practice and language/content, by integrating the means to see different forms of knowledge

---

[1] See Maton (2005, 2018) for insights into relations between LCT concepts and Bourdieu's approach. See Maton (2014a) for extensive discussion of how LCT concepts relate to Bernstein's concepts.

in practice and how these are woven together, e.g. in an EAP lesson or successful student assignment.

Knowledge, knowers and the 'rules of the game'

Central to the framework, as the name suggests, is the notion of legitimation. LCT construes society as comprising a complex of relatively autonomous fields (e.g. engineering, business, education, etc.), within which actors cooperate and compete for status, resources and legitimacy (Maton, 2014a: 24). Actors' practices are construed as strategic stances aimed at maximizing their positions within a given 'field of struggles', a perspective inspired by Bourdieu. In EAP, for example, we might think of two programmes in different institutions that run according to different principles. In one course, the coordinator and materials writers see EAP as language and skills work. Tasks for students focus on sentence-level 'academic grammar' and short texts drawn from outside the university. In the other course, the focus is on much longer and more challenging discipline-specific texts; language work emerges from engagement with this complex content. These contrasting perspectives on academic discourse embody quite different 'messages' about what constitutes legitimate practice and participation in academic literacy, and how success should be measured. LCT construes these underpinning messages, embodied in actors' practices, as 'languages of legitimation' (Maton, 2014a: 23–42).

Of particular value to EAP here is the insight that claims to legitimacy do not rest only on social power but also on more or less epistemologically powerful claims (Maton, 2000, 2014a). Implicit messages transmitted through materials or pedagogies about the value of discipline-embedded academic writing development, for instance, emerge from research practices and an empirical base of evidence (e.g. Hyland, 2002, 2004; Nesi and Garder, 2012; Sloane and Porter, 2010). Beliefs, pedagogies, curriculums and entire EAP departments are shaped in some way by such knowledge claims, in ways that interact with the power and influence that certain people hold but which are analytically distinct.

Knowledge in this sense is *real* in LCT, while nevertheless remaining fallible and subject to updates and improvements over time (cf. Bhaskar, 1975; Popper, 1959). The power exerted by a course director to thread a given linguistic framework throughout an EAP curriculum is distinct from the power the linguistic theory itself offers to students in revealing valued aspects of academic discourse. Social power and knowledge are intertwined, but irreducible to one another. Seeing that knowledge possesses its own powers and tendencies helps us see also that it cannot be reduced to the minds that have produced it; knowledge is distinct from *knowing* (Maton, 2014a: 7–8). There are always knowledges and always knowers in LCT, therefore; social fields are *knowledge–knower* structures (Maton, 2014a: 96).

By making knowledge itself more visible as a shaping force, these analytic distinctions offer EAP a more nuanced and integrated means of understanding the field, its practices and its tensions. Community practices, teacher discourse, EAP curricula, pedagogic decisions in the classroom, students' disciplines, assigned texts and written assessments can all be more richly understood in terms of the forms of knowledge they embody and the deeper messages they transmit about who and what matter. LCT distinguishes between the *focus* of practices (their content) and the *basis* of those practices – their languages of legitimation – to make clear that we are looking beyond surface appearances to these underlying organizing principles. Revealing the 'rules of the game' in EAP enables making visible the valorized measures of success in different practices and is thus of potentially significant value. For students, it might involve seeing how knowledge practices in their discipline shape valued forms of writing or speaking. For practitioners, it might involve seeing the organizing principles that have shaped a locally designed EAP programme (Kirk, 2018), helping to inform more effective teaching during a sessional contract. Such practices are illustrated further below.

Equally, however, seeing the rules of the game enables them more easily to be called into question, resisted, reimagined and perhaps reshaped, particularly where practices are perceived to be inequitable or ineffective. While most sociological approaches study only relations *to* knowledge, such as relations of class, race and gender to curriculum or pedagogy, LCT builds on Bernstein (2000) to enable also analysing relations *within* this knowledge. The knowledge embodied in EAP curricula across contexts may take different forms, for instance (cf. Kirk, 2018), reflecting different relations to concepts and students, and different capacities for cumulative knowledge-building (Maton, 2009). It is not a homogenous or neutral medium and is therefore also inherently ideological (cf. Bernstein, 2000: 27). Practitioners can explore the structuring effects of such knowledge practices for teaching and learning with LCT, seeing the principles that dominate and subjecting these to question and critique through a shared lens.

These organizing principles, giving rise to different languages of legitimation (e.g. as embodied in an EAP textbook or in the practices of students and teachers), are conceptualized in LCT as different species of *legitimation codes*. Different sets of concepts, or 'dimensions', have been developed to explore each species. There are currently three active dimensions of LCT: Specialization, Semantics and Autonomy. Each offers concepts to explore different kinds of principles underpinning practices, such as who and what are valorized, how meanings are made, and how bounded practices are from others. By looking beyond surface features, these concepts enable LCT to describe and analyse not just 'what is' but also what could *have been* and what *could be* (see illustrations below). Making alternatives to current practices visible enables seeing how things might be otherwise – key for imagining change and acting for social justice. LCT can thus be seen as a 'sociology of possibility' (Maton, 2014a: 3), offering practitioners a generative toolkit for going beyond 'armchair theorising' to address real-world challenges and problems in practice.

The recontextualization of knowledge and the field(s) of EAP

The problem of dichotomous, fragmented thinking in EAP can arise because different forms of practice become conflated, for instance when teachers reject theory as 'superfluous' (Cowley-Haselden and Monbec, 2019: 43) or as too technical to inform practice. This rather polarized stance overlooks how knowledge production in research has its own goals, norms and values. Considerable *recontextualization* work (Bernstein, 1990) may be needed to turn, e.g. discourse analytic research into pedagogic materials. Recognizing that there are different 'rules of the game' in research, course design and pedagogic practices, and that moving from one to another involves the recontextualization of knowledge, may be crucial to forging more productive, integrative relations between theory and practice.

LCT offers this integrated view by construing the university as an 'arena of struggle' (Bernstein, 1990: 206) comprising interacting but analytically distinguishable fields of: *production*, where new research knowledge is created; *recontextualization*, where this knowledge is selectively reorganized into curricula; and *reproduction*, where this 'curricularized' knowledge is then 'pedagogized' in teaching, learning and assessment practices (Bernstein, 1990; Maton, 2014a: 47–53). Seeing an analogous arena in EAP opens up refined, sociologically oriented ways of thinking about struggles among practitioners and debates within and between fields (Kirk, 2018). The practices of EAP research, curriculum development and classroom pedagogy each possess their own logics, tendencies and criteria for success. LCT sees a dialectal relationship between these fields, recognizing that developments and innovations may flow in different directions. Teacher work with students may feed back into reshaping pedagogic materials, for instance, and insights from the classroom may be theorized and published without necessarily influencing the curriculum.

One usefully available example of the recontextualization of knowledge across fields in EAP can be seen in the work of John Swales. Empirical and theorized insights from *Genre Theory* (Swales, 1990) have been selectively recontextualized and integrated with annotated texts, tasks and notes to develop the student-facing *Academic Writing for Graduate Students* (e.g. Swales and Feak, 2012). Such work may represent an important part of innovation in EAP materials development and, if theory is to inform practice in meaningful ways, a key facet of the EAP practitioner knowledge base (cf. Bruce, 2021; Ding and Bruce, 2017: 65–83). The 'border-crossing' practices required need clearer articulation and exploration, however, particularly to understand what may be gained or lost through recontextualization; LCT provides tools to do so, for instance by analysing how the relative abstraction and complexity of content shift from one context to another, changing affordances for learning and teaching. This offers a means of dissolving dichotomies between theory and practice to examine more productively and more critically how one can shape and be shaped by the other.

The degree of insulation/interaction between fields in EAP may vary significantly across local contexts, fragmenting access to knowledge and opportunities for development. The disciplinary academic may cross field boundaries in their everyday practice: Insights from the lab (research) become slides for a lecture (curriculum), which are then discussed with students in a seminar (pedagogy). In the EAP context, however, there may often be an unproductive division of labour: the researcher writes a paper for an academic journal that offers insights for practice, but that never becomes EAP student-facing material. EAP materials writers may neither engage with (or in) research and may not be teachers either. And EAP practitioners may be given no time for scholarship and may remain only consumers rather than producers of research knowledge (cf. Ding, 2016). Addressing some of these challenges requires addressing issues at the heart of the material experience of EAP, such as contracted and actively facilitated time for practitioners to engage in materials design and research. Nevertheless, LCT can help clear a conceptual path to such conversations by providing lenses and language to tease apart important analytic distinctions, and enabling richer understandings of how knowledge, knowers and contexts interact and influence each other to shape local affordances for practice and practitioners.

Seeing the contours of knowledge

One key area where LCT can contribute to a richer and more joined-up perspective on EAP is in concepts and tools that enable seeing how knowledge takes different forms in different practices, for instance in how a curriculum is sequenced and structured, in the unfolding of effective teaching and in successful student writing across genres. EAP researchers and practitioners have developed detailed and nuanced understandings of academic discourse across disciplines (e.g. Hyland, 2004; Nesi and Gardner, 2012) but not of knowledge. LCT can enrich existing approaches in EAP by making disciplinary knowledge practices visible, revealing valued measures of success and affordances for replication, challenge or change.

A good example of an LCT concept proving highly fruitful in education is semantic gravity. This is because the concept can be enacted in accessibly visual ways, both for principled analysis *of* practice and for practical analysis *in* practice, e.g. with students in the EAP classroom. The next section provides a brief introduction to semantic gravity and demonstrates its potential for EAP via three illustrations. These examples show how semantic gravity can help reveal and shape meaning-making practices in, respectively, EAP curriculum, classroom teaching and research student presentations. Taken together, the enactments highlight the flexible ways in which LCT concepts can be enacted to enable less fragmented and more integrated understandings of valued educational practices.

Practising EAP differently with LCT: Semantic gravity

Semantic gravity (SG) refers to the context dependence of meaning-making (Maton, 2013, 2014a, b, 2020). Semantic gravity is conceptualized as a continuum of strengths, from stronger (+) or more context-dependent to weaker (–) or less context-dependent. For example, the everyday conversations of students about life on campus or case study examples given by a lecturer in a seminar can be conceptualized as stronger semantic gravity, because they are more closely dependent on contexts than principles for teaching in an EAP staff handbook or theoretical concepts that students meet in an assigned reading on their degree. Shifts in semantic gravity can be profiled dynamically over time, e.g. to examine classroom practices or, over 'text time', to analyse how more contextualized and more abstract forms of knowledge are woven together in a high-scoring student assignment. Shifts back and forth between stronger and weaker semantic gravity are as *semantic gravity waves* and enable repackaging particularized understandings for other contexts. These have been shown to be key for cumulative knowledge building in education (Clarence, 2016; Macnaught et al., 2013; Maton, 2014a, b, 2020).

Studies enacting semantic gravity in educational research and practice are numerous and diverse, ranging from revealing problematic student practices in physics assessments (Georgiou, 2016) to scaffolding writing in teacher education (Sigsgaard, 2021). In EAP-type contexts, semantic gravity has been enacted for the design of curriculum (Monbec, 2018), for understanding students' knowledge-building practices in seminars (Cowley-Haselden, 2019) and for teaching different forms of academic writing (Brooke, 2017; Kirk, 2017, forthcoming; Macnaught, 2021; Muir and Solli, 2019). These projects, emerging from and for educational practice in EAP, are quickly demonstrating the value of semantic gravity for integrating understandings of knowledge practices into curriculum design and academic literacy pedagogies, enriching EAP learning and teaching.

Semantic gravity in EAP research: Exploring the structuring of curriculum materials

The first illustration of LCT enacted to explore EAP practices comes from a research study that explored the principles shaping the conception, design and teaching of a university summer pre-sessional curriculum in the UK (Kirk, 2018). In the research, semantic gravity was enacted as a continuum from stronger, contextualized meaning-making practices (e.g. student opportunities for spoken and written practice) to weaker, decontextualized meaning-making practices (e.g. the curricular concepts of 'thesis statement' and 'nominalization'). This enactment emerged in dialogue with curriculum documentation, pedagogic materials and analysis of classroom teaching, realizing semantic gravity for the particular EAP context. The resultant 'translation device' establishes a bridge between LCT concepts and the specifics of research data or educational practice[2]

---

[2] See also the illustrations below and Figures 4.3 and 4.8 for related but distinct enactments.

and is a key feature of the LCT architecture across dimensions (cf. Maton and Chen, 2016).

Analysis of curriculum materials revealed a 'signature profile' in the way many lessons were designed. Task sequences usually started by introducing an aspect of academic writing, such as writing a literature review or developing an argument, in relatively generalized or abstract terms. An exemplar text would then follow, with exploratory questions for students, aimed at identifying key insights from the text for a more grounded understanding of the more abstract lesson introduction. A follow-up discussion task might then explore student 'findings' in terms of the conceptual theme, on the way to planning a subsequent written or spoken task. Figure 4.1 shows this signature profile as a schematic semantic gravity wave.

With some variations, this profile was seen repeated across task sequences over the course of a lesson in the programme's in-house study books, creating regular movements between opportunities for textual engagement, student practice and higher-order understandings of key concepts in the curriculum. Figure 4.2 shows a schematic representation of this common patterning. This structuring of curricular knowledge within and across lessons was argued to provide the potential for cumulative knowledge-building on the EAP pre-sessional

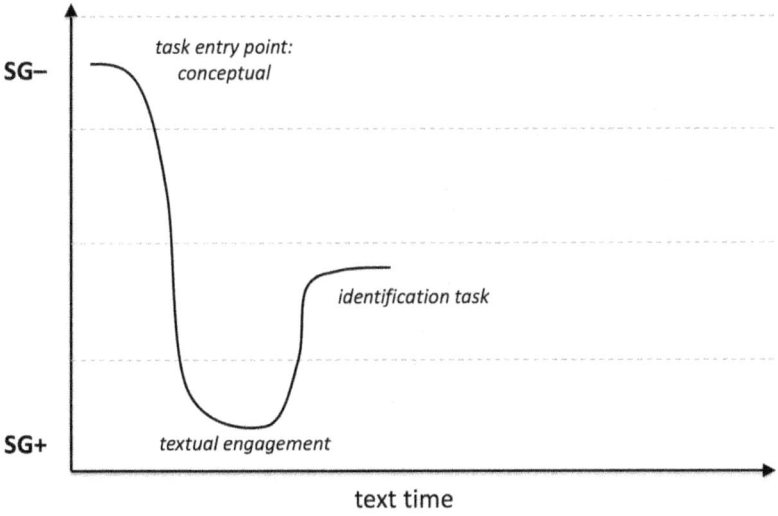

Figure 4.1 Signature semantic gravity wave in an EAP curriculum (adapted from Kirk, 2018: 248).

programme (Kirk, 2018). This is because recurrent shifts between unpacking decontextualized curriculum concepts and repackaging contextualized practices in terms of those curricular concepts, enacting semantic gravity waves, may facilitate transfer of learning from one lesson to another and thus constitute a key mechanism for cumulative knowledge-building (e.g. Macnaught et al., 2013). In contrast, curricular or teaching practices that unpack more conceptual content with examples or tasks but which do not then repack them would enact only downward shifts in semantic gravity, or 'down escalators' (Maton, 2013), segmenting learning into disparate chunks and potentially hindering knowledge-building. Semantic profiling can thus make explicit why the structuring of curriculum materials may be more/less effective for student learning, enabling the imagining of alternatives, and informing redesign practices that avoid segmented sequences of unconnected tasks and lessons, for the creation of more connected, integrated curricula.

In LCT, knowledge is real and has effects back on people and practices. The structuring of curricular knowledge thus has implications for the *forms of learning* that may be enabled or constrained – in this case, both experiential and conceptual. The organizing principles that realize EAP lessons-as-designed may well differ within and across programmes, reflecting differences in purpose or

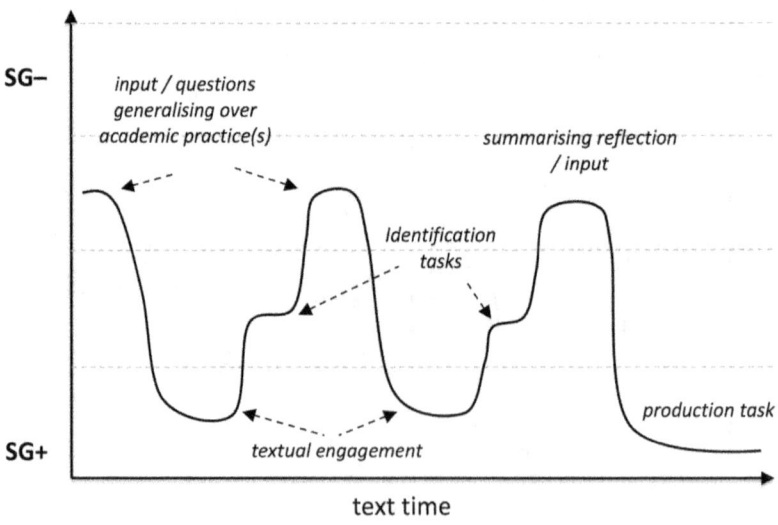

Figure 4.2 Schematic semantic gravity wave across task sequences in an EAP lesson (adapted from Kirk, 2018: 246).

conception of EAP. Making curricular meaning-making visible to course writers and teachers with semantic gravity thus offers the potential for more effective design, pedagogy, teacher development and agency. Once organizing principles are made explicit, practitioners can more easily scrutinize, re-enact or challenge existing practices, and see alternatives. Given the focus on knowledge practices that is enabled by LCT, critical considerations can include how far and in what ways the legitimation codes of students' target disciplines should shape the semantic profiles of design and pedagogic practices. This offers a means to cut through unnecessarily dichotomized distinctions between general- and specific-purposes EAP, towards more nuanced discussions of student knowledge-building and valuable forms of learning.

Visualizing pedagogic knowledge-building for EAP teacher development

Insights from this research can also inform teacher development, enabling more joined-up understandings of curriculum goals and pedagogies that avoid fragmenting learning in favour of more cumulative, integrated knowledge-building. Notions of 'signature profiles' and semantic gravity waving provide a visual means of exploring pedagogic choices and their effects, as teachers lift texts and tasks off the page (or slides) in their interactions with students. Extending the work above, therefore, semantic gravity has been enacted in developmental discussion of classroom teaching with EAP teachers. The brief illustrations below involve real-world examples from classroom observations and follow-up discussions with pre-sessional EAP staff.

In order to develop a principled *and* practical approach for talking with teachers about their pedagogic meaning-making practices, LCT terminology was 'translated' for practice (Kirk, 2017; Macnaught, 2021; Maton et al., 2016). Given the strong course focus on academic literacy development, 'stronger semantic gravity' became 'text-mediated student practice/experience'. Given also the importance of conceptual understandings of academic discourse, 'weaker semantic gravity' became 'EAP principles/concepts in the curriculum'. Between these two poles, a middle level of 'generalizations' was established to identify generic notions commonly referred to in the curriculum and by teachers, such as 'essay writing' and 'presentation skills'. This recontextualized and simplified the translation device developed for the research study, dividing the semantic gravity continuum into three heuristic 'levels'. This 'language of enactment' (Maton et al., 2016) draws inspiration from a translation device developed originally to teach reflective writing (Kirk, 2017, forthcoming) and is represented in Figure 4.3.

To demonstrate how semantic gravity can be enacted to empower teachers with more connected understandings of curriculum and pedagogy, the two examples that follow are taken from 'problematic' real-world instances of observed teaching[3] on the same EAP pre-sessional programme. This programme shifts from shared academic content and tasks to more differentiated, discipline-specific texts and assessments over three months. The observed classes both took place during the first month.

Teachers in these examples were recruited externally and so do not benefit from year-round in-house staff collaboration or development. The first relates to a class on research ethics. Students had attended a lecture and had also been assigned a reading relating to the theme. The lesson appeared in a sequence that culminated in students conducting their own mini-ethnography. The purpose of this session was to have students think about ethics for their own empirical projects. A set of exploratory questions were made available but Evelyn,[4] the experienced class teacher, otherwise had relative freedom to design the session as she wished.

In the observed class, Evelyn opened by leading a discussion of key concepts for the session. These included ethics, ethnocentrism, bias and criticality. Students then discussed the text they had been assigned before the class and answered the accompanying questions. Evelyn mediated these conversations, eliciting responses and adding her own input. She briefly displayed the assigned text on

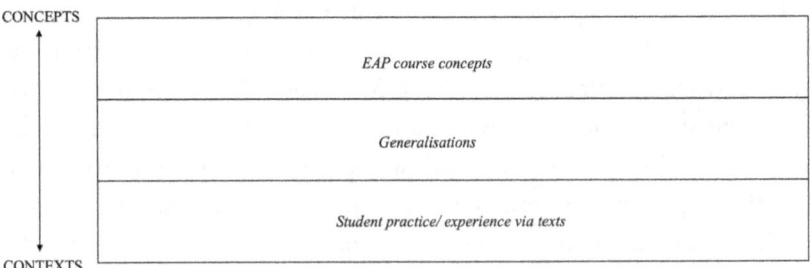

Figure 4.3 Translation device enacting semantic gravity for talking about teaching.

---

[3] Steve was the observer in these examples.
[4] A pseudonym. Both teachers discussed in this section have been anonymized.

the interactive whiteboard but otherwise most work in the class was conducted verbally. The resulting class was thus a very interesting but highly conceptual discussion of ethics. While discussing the merits of these interactions after the observation, the three-level diagram (Figure 4.3) was quickly introduced and the conceptual nature of the session then drawn as a high semantic gravity 'flatline' (cf Maton, 2014: 121; 142–3). Figure 4.4 reproduces this diagram.

Semantic flatlines may hinder cumulative knowledge-building (Maton, 2014: 142–3) by precluding students from connecting and integrating knowledge of different kinds. In this case, few opportunities were provided to unpack the abstract content, relating concepts to students' own contexts or examples in the text, and then to repack these examples in terms of the concepts to facilitate transfer. Possible alternative practices were thus discussed together, enabled by further semantic gravity wave diagrams. One key focus was the likely benefit to students' language and literacy development of integrating more text-mediated discussion of concepts. A second focus was the potential value of 'waving down' in teacher talk and tasks from abstract exploration of ethics, encouraging students to connect course concepts explicitly to their own ethnography project and future empirical work in their departments beyond the pre-sessional programme. Such practices would also enact 'signature' type profiles, as illustrated further above, waving between principles and opportunities for hands-on engagement, a key value and design feature on the EAP programme. These suggested enhancements, drawn together as different wave profiles with Evelyn and exemplified in Figure 4.5, enabled her to see overarching programme values and student needs more clearly, and offered a means of planning subsequent lessons with a more connected sense of how they fitted into the wider course.

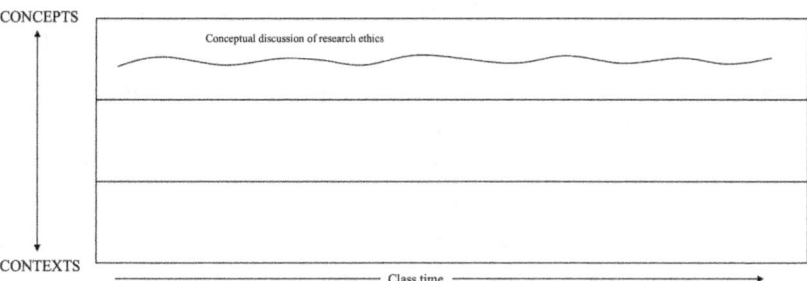

Figure 4.4 Conceptual class discussions represented for a teacher as a high semantic gravity flatline.

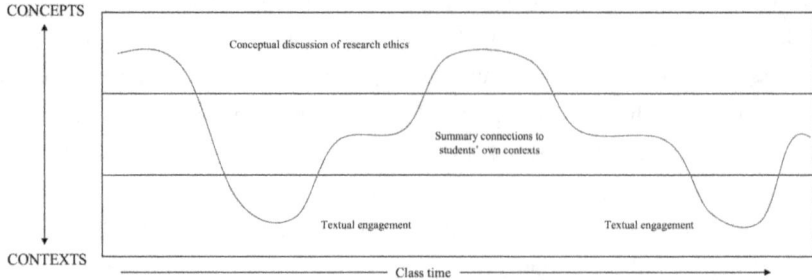

Figure 4.5 Enhancing EAP teaching practices by 'waving'.

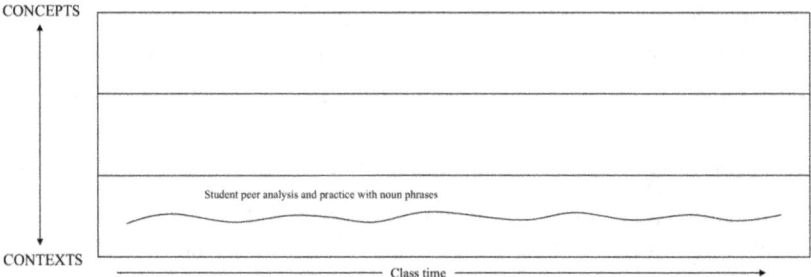

Figure 4.6 A low semantic gravity flatline in EAP lesson design and enactment.

The second example of teaching observations concerns a class on complex noun phrases. In this session students expand and contract noun phrases across a number of tasks, honing their understanding of meaning-making potential and sentence structure. The session title pointed to the usefulness of this work for reading academic texts. Tim, a teacher new to EAP and teaching on a summer pre-sessional for the first time, taught the lesson essentially as it appeared in the pages of the provided lesson materials. This represented a series of practice tasks that built progressively in complexity, but which did not embed explicit tasks exploring the usefulness of this work for students' unravelling of complex content in their disciplinary reading. Unlike many other lessons in the programme, therefore, the structuring principles underpinning the design resembled a low-level semantic gravity flatline. This was how the session was also enacted with students, moving segmentally from task to task in repeating cycles of practice and feedback on students' noun phrase construction. The design and teaching of the class are represented in Figure 4.6.

Post-lesson discussion focused initially on the creativity that Tim evidenced in lifting the lesson off the page. He had prepared cut-up versions of sentences for different student groups and had established a usefully interactive workshop-style session, with students collaborating to analyse and (re)arrange phrases. This had enabled some focused and useful experimentation with language. The recontextualized translation device (Figure 4.3) was then introduced and a low flatline drawn (Figure 4.6) to visualize the way the session had 'moved'. As with Evelyn, the effects of this flatlining for student learning were explored – in particular the likelihood that students had not connected the grammar games with their academic reading practices. This risked students isolating the learning as 'language practice', rather than taking away generative strategies that could be applied again and again in working with complex texts. Discussion of possible session enhancements therefore focused on the value of 'waving up to the *so-whats*' and to conceptual summaries from practice tasks, via explicit conversations with students that would help forge connections to wider aspects of their learning. The benefit of supplementing the materials was also explored, particularly having students work with longer texts already assigned for other purposes. This produced sketches of the kind reproduced in Figure 4.7.

Tracing semantic gravity waves with teachers in this way offers a practical means of exploring and integrating EAP course goals, curriculum knowledge and pedagogic practice. Related work with disciplinary academics, exploring the structuring of their lectures (Clarence, 2016, 2021), suggests LCT Semantics holds great potential for the practical analysis and development of teaching practices. Where time and logistics allow for pre-observation conversations and/or collaborative planning opportunities, such conversations can (also) take place before teaching, enabling earlier formative exploration of teacher choices. From the perspective of the observer, the second example above serves further to reveal possible shortcomings in materials design (something that was discussed with Tim) and the potential value of engineering task sequences that enact semantic gravity

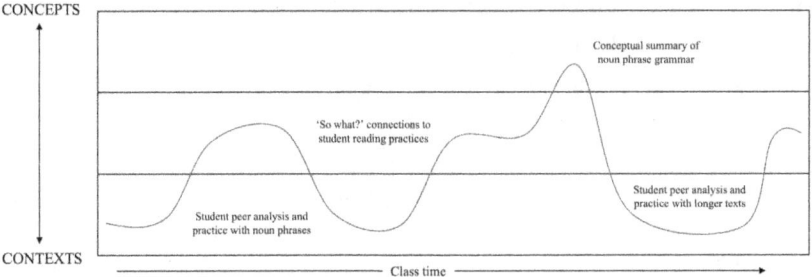

Figure 4.7 Semantic gravity waving to connect practice tasks with wider course learning.

waves, such that valued practices are embedded and modelled more explicitly. The approach can thus also be used in curriculum planning, in staff inductions and CPD sessions to revisit materials and recontextualization practices, to imagine and map possible alternatives, and to consider the forms of learning that such alternatives might afford, enabling a more critically integrated exploration of EAP practices.

Integrating knowledge work into 'skills' work

The final illustration, drawn from extensive work enacting semantic gravity across disciplines and academic levels over a number of years, focuses on doctoral students in education preparing to speak at a peer conference. The example shows how semantic gravity can be enacted to move beyond notions of 'presentation skills' as a generic and separate area of development, such that students integrate understandings of effective speaking with the knowledge-building practices of their research. Students must present their fledgling work, often at varying stages of development, to fellow research students who may well not be experts in the same sub-field or theoretical perspectives. Many of these students may be nervous about presenting their ideas in public and an intervention was designed to build confidence and provide a simple toolkit to help student thinking and planning of their talks.

Semantic gravity was chosen to inform this work given students' need to weave together different forms of knowledge, such as examples from their data, general insights for a non-specialist audience and theoretical frameworks. This led to developing a slightly different translation device from the curricular research and staff observation contexts discussed above. As noted earlier, LCT concepts like semantic gravity are defined in non-essentialist terms, enabling them to take on particularized forms in dialogue with a given problem context (cf. Maton and Chen, 2016). This illustrates the creative flexibility offered by LCT concepts for research and educational practice. The enactment of the semantic gravity continuum for planning conference talks[5] is shown in Figure 4.8, as it appeared on the session worksheet.

The session begins with discussion of how students feel about presenting and the value (or not) of 'being yourself' when speaking in public. Students

---

[5] It is worth noting that similar enactments can also be used to analyse and plan writing with students (e.g. Kirk, forthcoming; Muir and Solli, 2019; Sigsgaard, 2021). In the case of doctoral writing, this might include exploring how data, theory and generalized conclusions are woven together in a discussion chapter. For new perspectives enacting LCT to explore doctoral writing, see e.g. Wilmott (2020).

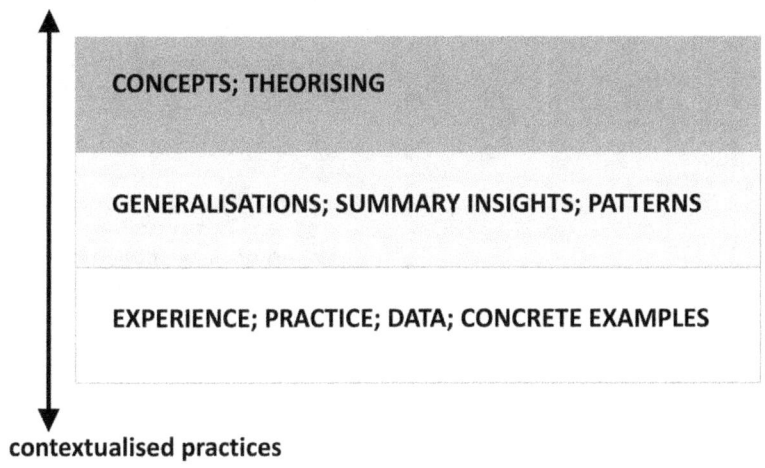

Figure 4.8 Translation device enacting semantic gravity for planning conference talks.

then consider their imagined audience, their needs and expectations, and how this might inform selection of content, level of detail and key 'takeaways' for participants. Text on the provided worksheet then introduces semantic gravity concepts, recontextualized in ways analogous to discussions earlier in this section:

> *What is the background of your audience? Are they practitioners? Researchers? Researchers interested in practice? Practitioners wanting to engage with theory? How might this affect the design choices you make in your talk?*

> *A useful way to help think about this is in terms of movements between more/less concrete and more/less conceptual content:*

An illustrative semantic gravity wave is then introduced to show how one section of an imagined talk might be profiled over time. In this illustration, the speaker begins with a grounded story from data or practice. They then reinterpret this experience through a theoretical lens, before suggesting how this shifts their perspective on the experience, enabling new understandings. Such a sequence might serve, for instance, to introduce the speaker's motivation for their chosen research focus. This notional semantic gravity wave is reproduced here as Figure 4.9.

While such a sequence may be unsurprising for some students, the visual means of mapping possible structures offers an accessible and explicit tool

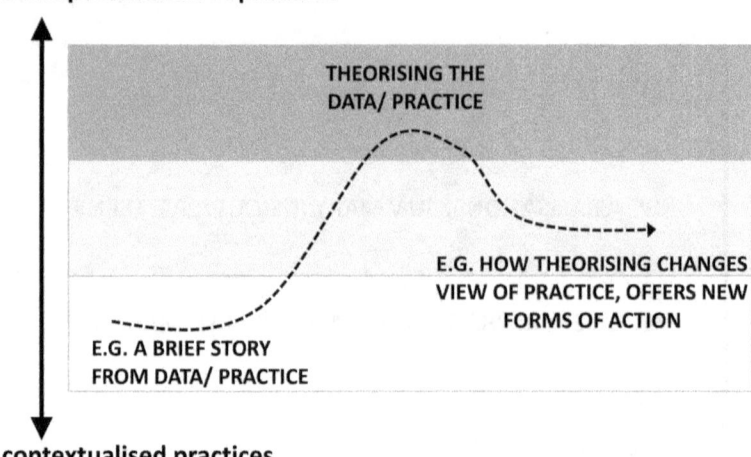

Figure 4.9 Semantic gravity wave profiling one section of a notional conference talk.

for interrogating different approaches and exploring alternatives. Students are invited to consider their own research, thoughts for their presentation focus and how a possible 'storyline' might be sketched as a wave profile. To facilitate this, a later worksheet task extends the shared metalanguage to enable students to discuss different areas of their talk:

> Think about the macro-structure of your talk. Using the above diagrams and the notion of 'waves' between different forms of content, consider the following:

a) What do you think the **entry point** should be for your talk? High, with a concept / theory? Low, with a case study illustration, story or example? In the middle, with some general observations or summary insights?

b) How high or low does your talk then need to wave? When might you need to **wave up** into concepts and/or theoretical frameworks? When might you need to **wave down** into concrete illustrations and examples?
   Remember to bear the audience experience in mind: What do they *need* to hear? What might they *want* to hear?

c) Finally, what do you think the **exit point** is for your talk?
   A talk will often end 'in the middle', with summary insights and messages for practice / research / policy / etc. You may feel it needs to end elsewhere, however ...

There are, of course, many possibilities for a session of this kind. In a mixed disciplinary group, students might work with researchers from other disciplines, comparing disciplinary audience expectations and possible talk profiles. Students might watch extracts of conference talks, trace the semantic gravity profile enacted and discuss the effects of this structuring on understanding and engagement. Participants might also explore how their talks might be differently structured for a non-academic audience. While generic considerations of eye contact, clear signposting and volume of text on slides remain important, semantic gravity profiling enables integrating more substantive work that puts students' research also at the heart of successful academic speaking.

Given that LCT is a sociological rather than linguistic theory, focus on language work can be woven flexibly into sessions of this kind to foster more integrated learning. Systemic functional linguistics is proving powerful in combination with LCT to explore academic discourse (Martin et al., 2020) but EAP practitioners might integrate other approaches. In both spoken and written work, students can be encouraged to notice, e.g., language choices that signal the strengthening and weakening of semantic gravity in different phases of a talk or text. To take simple examples, these might include 'waving down constructions', such as *for instance …* and *in one case study …*, and 'waving up constructions', such as *in general, therefore …* and *one possible interpretation of this finding is …* In conjunction with semantic gravity profiling, such work can help students connect language learning with disciplinary learning, scaffolding understanding of speaker/writer intentions and of how knowledge unfolds over the course of a talk or text, and providing possible models for their own practice.

Towards more integrated understandings and practices in EAP

LCT concepts like semantic gravity offer both principled and practical means of overcoming fragmented thinking and practices in EAP, enabling more integrative and empowering ways of thinking, designing, developing and teaching. The wider framework offers a rich palette of concepts and associated tools to empower EAP practitioners to see beyond either/or modes of thinking towards *both–and* approaches. Semantic gravity is only one such concept, enabling a richer and more nuanced view of EAP that integrates understandings of knowledge-building to enhance diverse practices, from curriculum-making to teacher decisions and student speaking.

LCT concepts such as semantic gravity also enable seeing *why* knowledge in different contexts may shape both students and practitioners differently, by revealing how different approaches to language work, textual engagement, materials design and classroom practice embody differently structured knowledge practices. Engagement over time in EAP provision realized as generic skills training versus a course that integrates substantive discussion of disciplinary readings, for example, may shape participant dispositions in ways that are significant to affordances for success and agency. Such insights raise new kinds of questions for EAP: What kinds of knowledge are being made available to students into this textbook? How is this course shaping who students become, who practitioners become? What *form* of learning is enabled by this teaching practice? And how far does engaging with *this text*, in *this way*, develop dispositions that are valued in students' departments?

Returning to the bigger picture of the EAP profession, such perspectives further enable seeing why it matters to integrate sociological perspectives into explorations of EAP (see other chapters in this volume) and to understand the sociohistoric, economic and political forces that have shaped the material conditions for EAP on the ground (Ding and Bruce, 2017; Hadley, 2015). The legitimation codes underpinning EAP units, curricula and as embodied in teacher practices will be differently shaped by, for instance, the variable qualifications with which practitioners enter the profession, variable access to scholarship and development given relative scarcity of full-time contracts, and variable institutional views of EAP, including in quick-fix, marketized terms of recruiting international students (Turner, 2004). Semantic gravity and other LCT concepts can reveal how these codes may sometimes engender fragmented, ineffective practices, e.g. in separating 'skills' work from knowledge work or in teaching that flatlines, precluding higher-order understandings for cumulative learning and transfer. LCT can thus help connect the 'macro' and the 'micro' in EAP, enabling valuable insights for considerations of practitioner agency and for understandings of more/less enabling and empowering forms of practice.

Conclusion

LCT opens up EAP to examination and development in terms of its knowledge practices, enabling exploration of what is legitimated in curricula and pedagogies, how this shapes who is deemed a legitimate 'EAP knower', and how EAP itself is conceived, realized and reshaped within particular institutional contexts. The framework can help integrate understandings of EAP knowledge practices, actors and contexts, and their effects on each other, to facilitate more cumulative knowledge-building in the profession. LCT's primary orientation is towards problem-solving and thus to developing tools and approaches that can be creatively and generatively *enacted* for better, more accessible and more equitable education. It offers EAP, therefore, a principled *and* practical addition to the practitioner knowledge base. This chapter has provided a glimpse of the possibilities.

The potential of LCT for EAP is only just beginning to be exploited. More intrepid explorers are needed. One of the best ways into these possibilities is through the LCT community. LCT offers a powerful shared language for EAP professionals to explore their craft, not just with each other, but with like-minded colleagues across the disciplines, from music researchers to science educators. Contact the LCT Centre for Knowledge Building. Consider joining a regional group. Explore the website (legitimationcodetheory.com) and message people directly. LCT has both knowers and knowledge at its heart; the people are as valuable as the papers for learning more. If you haven't already, jump in and join a conversation.

Acknowledgement

I would like to thank Prof. Karl Maton for generous time and advice over Zoom and email during early preparation and drafting of this chapter.

References

Aris, S. M. (2020), 'Understanding School Choice: What Parents Prioritise in High Schools', Doctoral dissertation, University of Sydney.

Bernstein, B. (1977), *Class, Codes and Control, Volume III: Towards a Theory of Educational Transmissions*, 2nd edn, London: Routledge & Kegan Paul.

Bernstein, B. (1990), *Class, Codes and Control, Volume IV: The Structuring of Pedagogic Discourse*, London: Routledge.

Bernstein, B. (2000), *Pedagogy, Symbolic Control and Identity: Theory, Research, Critique*, revised edn, Oxford: Rowman & Littlefield.

Bhaskar, R. (1975), *A Realist Theory of Science*, London: Verso.

Blackie, M. A. (2014), 'Creating Semantic Waves: Using Legitimation Code Theory as a Tool to Aid the Teaching of Chemistry', *Chemistry Education Research and Practice*, 15 (4): 462–9.

Bourdieu, P. (1996), *The Rules of Art: Genesis and Structure of the Literary Field*, Stanford: Stanford University Press.

Bourdieu, P. (2000), *Pascalian Meditations*, Cambridge: Polity.

Brooke, M. (2017), 'Using "Semantic Waves" to Guide Students through the Research Process: From Adopting a Stance to Sound Cohesive Academic Writing', *Asian Journal of the Scholarship of Teaching and Learning*, 7 (1): 37–66.

Brooke, M., L. Monbec and N. Tilakaratna (2019), 'The Analytical Lens: Developing Undergraduate Students' Critical Dispositions in Undergraduate EAP Writing Courses', *Teaching in Higher Education*, 24 (3): 428–43.

Bruce, I. (2021), 'Towards an EAP without Borders: Developing Knowledge, Practitioners, and Communities', *International Journal of English for Academic Purposes: Research and Practice*, (Spring 2021): 23–36. https://www.liverpooluniversitypress.co.uk/journals/article/61071.

Clarence, S. (2016), 'Exploring the Nature of Disciplinary Teaching and Learning Using Legitimation Code Theory Semantics', *Teaching in Higher Education*, 21 (2): 123–37.

Clarence, S. (2021), *Turning Access into Success: Improving University Education with Legitimation Code Theory*, London: Routledge.

Clarence, S. and S. McKenna (2017), 'Developing Academic Literacies through Understanding the Nature of Disciplinary Knowledge', *London Review of Education*, 15 (1): 38–49.

Cowley-Haselden, S. and L. Monbec (2019), 'Emancipating Ourselves from Mental Slavery: Affording Knowledge in Our Practice', in M. Gillway (ed.), *Addressing the State of the Union: Working Together = Learning Together*, proceedings of the 2017 BALEAP conference, 39–46, Reading: Garnet Education.

Cowley-Haselden, S. (2020), 'Building Knowledge to Ease Troublesomeness: Affording Theory Knowledgeability through Academic Reading Circles', *Journal of University Teaching & Learning Practice*, 17 (2): 8.

Ding, A. (2016), 'Challenging Scholarship: A Thought Piece', *The Language Scholar*, 6–18. Available online: https://languagescholar.leeds.ac.uk/wp-content/uploads/sites/3/2016/12/Language-Scholar-Winter-2016-Issue-0.pdf#page=5 (accessed 17 May 2021).

Ding, A. and I. Bruce (2017), *The English for Academic Purposes Practitioner: Operating on the Edge of Academia*, London: Palgrave Macmillan.

Georgiou, H. (2016), 'Putting Physics Knowledge in the Hot Seat: The Semantics of Student Understandings of Thermodynamics', in K. Maton, S. Hood and S. Shay (eds), *Knowledge-building: Educational Studies in Legitimation Code Theory*, 176–92, London: Routledge.

Hadley, G. (2015), *English for Academic Purposes in Neoliberal Universities: A Critical Grounded Theory*, Heidelberg, Germany: Springer.

Hyland, K. (2002), 'Specificity Revisited: How Far Should We Go Now?' *English for Specific Purposes*, 21 (4): 385–95.

Hyland, K. (2004), *Disciplinary Discourses: Social Interactions in Academic Writing*, Ann Arbor, MI: University of Michigan Press.

Ingold, R. and D. O'Sullivan (2017), 'Riding the Waves to Academic Success', *Modern English Teacher*, 26 (2): 39–43.

Kirk, S. (2017), 'Waves of Reflection: Seeing Knowledges in Academic Writing', in J. Kemp (ed.), *EAP in a Rapidly Changing Landscape: Issues, Challenges and Solutions*, proceedings of the 2015 BALEAP conference, 109-18, Reading: Garnet Publishing.

Kirk, S. (2018), 'Enacting the Curriculum in English for Academic Purposes: A Legitimation Code Theory Analysis', Doctoral dissertation, Durham University. Available online: http://etheses.dur.ac.uk/12942/

Kirk, S. (forthcoming), 'Enacting Reflective Practice in Sport and Exercise Sciences: Pedagogic and Integrative Perspectives', in N. Tilakaratna and E. Szenes (eds), *Demystifying Critical Reflection: Improving Pedagogy and Practice with Legitimation Code Theory*, London: Routledge.

Lambrinos, E. (2019), 'Building Ballet: Developing Dance and Dancers in Ballet', Doctoral dissertation, University of Sydney.

Macnaught, L. (2021), 'Demystifying Reflective Writing in Teacher Education with Semantic Gravity', in C. Winberg, S. McKenna and K. Wilmot (eds), *Building Knowledge in Higher Education: Enhancing Teaching and Learning with Legitimation Code Theory*, 19-36, London: Routledge.

Macnaught, L., K. Maton, J. R. Martin and E. Matruglio (2013), 'Jointly Constructing Semantic Waves: Implications for Teacher Training', *Linguistics and Education*, 24 (1): 50–63.

Martin, J. R., K. Maton and Y. J. Doran, eds (2020), *Accessing Academic Discourse: Systemic Functional Linguistics and Legitimation Code Theory*, London: Routledge.

Maton, K. (2000), 'Languages of Legitimation: The Structuring Significance for Intellectual Fields of Strategic Knowledge Claims', *British Journal of Sociology of Education*, 21 (2): 147–67.

Maton, K. (2005), 'A Question of Autonomy: Bourdieu's Field Approach and Policy in Higher Education', *Journal of Education Policy*, 20 (6): 687–704.

Maton, K. (2009), 'Cumulative and Segmented Learning: Exploring the Role of Curriculum Structures in Knowledge-Building', *British Journal of Sociology of Education*, 30 (1): 43–57.

Maton, K. (2013), 'Making Semantic Waves: A Key to Cumulative Knowledge Building', *Linguistics and Education*, 24 (1): 8–22.

Maton, K. (2014a), *Knowledge and Knowers: Towards a Realist Sociology of Education*, London: Routledge.

Maton, K. (2014b), 'A TALL Order? Legitimation Code Theory for Academic Language and Learning', *Journal of Academic Language and Learning*, 8 (3): A34–A48.

Maton, K. (2018), 'Thinking Like Bourdieu: Completing the Mental Revolution with Legitimation Code Theory', in J. Albright, D. Hartman and J. Widin (eds), *Bourdieu's Field Theory and the Social Sciences*, 249–68, London: Palgrave Macmillan.

Maton, K. (2020), 'Semantic Waves: Context, Complexity and Academic Discourse', in J. R. Martin, K. Maton and Y. J. Doran (eds), *Accessing Academic Discourse: Systemic Functional Linguistics and Legitimation Code Theory*, 59–85, London: Routledge.

Maton, K., L. Carvalho and A. Dong (2016), 'LCT in Praxis: Creating an e-Learning Environment for Informal Learning of Principled Knowledge', in K. Maton, S. Hood and S. Shay (eds), *Knowledge-building: Educational Studies in Legitimation Code Theory*, 72–92, London: Routledge.

Maton, K. and R. T.-H. Chen (2016), 'LCT in Qualitative Research: Creating a Translation Device for Studying Constructivist Pedagogy', in K. Maton, S. Hood and S. Shay (eds), *Knowledge-building: Educational Studies in Legitimation Code Theory*, 27–48, London: Routledge.

Maton, K., S. Hood and S. Shay, eds (2016), *Knowledge-building: Educational Studies in Legitimation Code Theory*, London: Routledge.

Maton, K., J. R. Martin and Y. J. Doran, eds (2021), *Teaching Science: Knowledge, Language, Pedagogy*, London: Routledge.

Monbec, L. (2018), 'Designing an EAP Curriculum for Transfer: A Focus on Knowledge', *Journal of Academic Language and Learning*, 12 (2): A88–A101.

Muir, T. and K. Solli (2019), 'The Real and the Unreal: English for Research Purposes in Norway', in J. Corcoran, K. Englander and L.-M. Mureşan (eds), *Pedagogies and Policies for Publishing Research in English: Local Initiatives Supporting International Scholars*, 91–105, New York: Routledge.

Nesi, H. and S. Gardner (2012), *Genres across the Disciplines: Student Writing in Higher Education*, Cambridge: Cambridge University Press.

Popper, K. (1959), *The Logic of Scientific Discovery*, London: Hutchinson.

Richardson, S. A. (2019), 'Teaching Jazz: A Study of Beliefs and Pedagogy Using Legitimation Code Theory', Doctoral dissertation, University of Sydney.

Siebörger, I. and R. Adendorff (2017), 'We're Talking about Semantics Here: Axiological Condensation in the South African Parliament', *Functions of Language*, 24 (2): 196–233.

Sigsgaard, A. V. (2021), 'Making Waves in Teacher Education: Scaffolding Students' Disciplinary Understandings by "Doing" Analysis', in C. Winberg, S. McKenna and K. Wilmot (eds), *Building Knowledge in Higher Education: Enhancing Teaching and Learning with Legitimation Code Theory*, 37–54, London: Routledge.

Sloane, D. and E. Porter (2010), 'Changing International Student and Business Staff Perceptions of in-Sessional EAP: Using the CEM Model', *Journal of English for Academic Purposes*, 9 (3): 198–210.

Swales, J. M. (1990), *Genre Analysis: English in Academic and Research Settings*, Cambridge: Cambridge University Press.

Swales, J. M. and C. B. Feak (2012), *Academic Writing for Graduate Students: Essential Tasks and Skills*, vol. 1, 3rd edn, Ann Arbor, MI: University of Michigan Press.

Szenes, E., N. Tilakaratna, and K. Maton (2015), 'The Knowledge Practices of Critical Thinking', in M. Davies and R. Barnett (eds), *The Palgrave Handbook of Critical Thinking in Higher Education*, 573–91, London: Palgrave Macmillan.

Turner, J. (2004), 'Language as Academic Purpose', *Journal of English for Academic Purposes*, 3: 95–109.

Walton, E. and L. Rusznyak (2020), 'Cumulative Knowledge-building for Inclusive Education in Initial Teacher Education', *European Journal of Teacher Education*, 43 (1): 18–37.

Wilmot, K. (2020), 'Building Knowledge with Theory: Unpacking Complexity in Doctoral Writing', *Critical Studies in Teaching and Learning*, 8 (2): 18–38.

Winberg, C., S. McKenna and K. Wilmot, eds (2020), *Building Knowledge in Higher Education: Enhancing Teaching and Learning with Legitimation Code Theory*, London: Routledge.

5

Social realism and genre theory: Knowledge-building in EAP

Ian Bruce

Introduction

English for Academic Purposes (EAP) is a relatively new and rapidly developing field of English language teaching, a field in which practitioners and researchers are involved in an ongoing process of knowledge-building and knowledge-refining. The knowledge base of EAP draws upon a number of areas of linguistic and educational enquiry, including genre studies, corpus linguistics, systemic functional linguistics, academic literacies and critical pedagogy. Insights from these and from other areas of research and theory inform the curriculum and pedagogic practice of EAP practitioners. However, driven by EAP's strong focus on meeting student needs and problem-solving, the knowledge base of the field, pragmatically drawing on these diverse research streams, has not been related strongly to any particular overarching or unifying sociological theory of knowledge or knowledge-building, which is the issue that I will explore in this chapter.

In approaching this issue of a theory of knowledge-building for EAP, I am focusing specifically on the research stream of *genre studies*, a key contributor to the EAP knowledge base. In this chapter, I propose to locate EAP genre-based research and genre-based pedagogy under the sociological theory of knowledge known as *social realism* (Moore, 2013; Young, 2008, 2010). 'Social realism' (SR) distinguishes between knowledge and experience, theoretical and everyday knowledge, and it acknowledges that theoretical knowledge exists in particular domains or disciplines. In the chapter I argue that locating genre theory and research within the key theoretical parameters of social realism provides a basis for conceptual and methodological judgements when planning, executing and applying the findings of genre studies in the field of EAP, and specifically, it provides a way of addressing some of the key issues relating to construct validity that have persisted within this area of research for some time. The chapter is divided into four sections.

- The first section introduces the field of EAP, its functional roles and its strong focus on writing instruction that uses genre-based pedagogy as a central tool for *recontextualizing* and *reproducing* knowledge (Bernstein, 2000).
- The second section presents a brief overview of two theoretical and research approaches towards genre studies that aim to inform writing pedagogy, but raises the issue of the current lack of construct validity in defining and researching genres by considering what each approach actually operationalizes.
- The third section then discusses the research activity of EAP genre studies, proposing that this area of research activity be framed by the theory of social realism as a basis for knowledge-building and consolidating practitioner knowledge in this area. In this section, I discuss a particular theory of genre that I have proposed, the social genre/cognitive genre model (Bruce, 2008a), acknowledging both the ontological reality of genres (as categories of texts) and the socially constructed and intersubjective nature of the epistemological judgements involved when analysing and characterizing the nature of particular genres and the knowledge types that they employ.
- The fourth and final section concludes by providing discussion of the implications for the activity of academic writing pedagogy when genre theory and research is framed by social realism, and by specifically addressing the issue of relating the types of abstract and procedural knowledge to previously acquired frames and writing experiences.

The field of EAP: Recontextualizing and reproducing knowledge through genre-based pedagogy

In the first section of this chapter, I reflect on the field of EAP, its functional roles and its strong focus on writing instruction with a focus on academic genres, which provide the communicative vehicle for recontextualizing and reproducing knowledge (Bernstein, 1990) or what Maton (2014) refers to as 'curriculizing' knowledge.

Flowerdew and Peacock (2001: 8) define EAP as 'the teaching of English with the specific aim of helping learners to study, conduct research or teach in that language'. In this definition, EAP is described in terms of the end goals of its students. However, when considering the *processes* of EAP teaching and learning as part of a definition of the field (Ding and Bruce, 2017), my co-author and I proposed that EAP is characterized by:

- a concern with students' literacy development rather than overall language proficiency development;
- a focus on developing discourse competence;
- consideration of the academic rather than more general social uses of language; and
- a commitment to the academy rather than to wider society.

Given these characteristics, EAP courses tend to have a major focus on the requirements of academic writing for the reason that mastery of this language skill is central to knowledge acquisition and assessment in university courses. As a basis for the development of academic literacy (and specifically academic writing) skills, I propose that the overall goal of EAP courses is students' development of *discourse competence*, which I define as the abilities to process and create extended academic texts in order to communicate and participate in the previously mentioned activities of study, teaching and research. The approach to the development of discourse competence in EAP courses may be *discipline-specific*, with a focus on the texts and related discourse knowledge of a particular discipline, such as an EAP course for students preparing to study engineering. On the other hand, its development may require a broader, *discipline-contrasting* approach in contexts where practitioners are teaching classes for students studying or preparing to study in a range of disciplines. This approach will involve a focus on knowledge development by comparing the different ways in which subject disciplines realize common academic assignment genres.

Teaching and learning the writing of academic genres is, therefore, a central activity in EAP courses. I use the term 'genre' here to refer to a conventionalized category of texts that fulfils a commonly recognized purpose (or purposes) for knowledge communication within a particular context. EAP courses focus on those genres that regularly occur in academic contexts, such as essays, literature reviews, lab reports, dissertations and academic presentations. EAP practitioners are often tasked with teaching students how to master the writing of these genres and, to that end, often use what is termed *genre-based pedagogy* or *genre-based instruction*. This is a top-down approach that begins with an example text (or sample of texts) of a particular genre category, and involves identification and analysis of key features of the target genre, knowledge that then becomes the basis for supported and later more individual construction of new examples of the same genre (see, for example, Burns and Joyce, 1991; Callaghan and Rothery, 1988). Because an analytical and productive understanding of academic genres is central to discourse competence development, much EAP research has aimed to uncover the types of declarative and procedural knowledge required to support this type of pedagogy and knowledge development (e.g. Nesi and Gardner, 2012).

In terms of their social operations, I propose that academic genres are used to communicate what Bernstein (2000: 160) refers to as *vertical discourses*, referring to the structuring of specialist knowledge within disciplines: 'vertical discourse consists of specialized symbolic structures of specific knowledge'. Academic genres are conventionalized categories of texts used to recontextualize and communicate this specialized knowledge within disciplines. That is, they are communicative or rhetorical vehicles that provide the textual and discursive means to facilitate the communication of such knowledge structures. Essentially, in this chapter I am proposing that:

- genre theory is a way of *curriculizing* the communicative forms and requirements that relate to specialist academic knowledge and
- genre-based instruction is a way of *pedagogizing* that knowledge communication (Lilliedahl, 2015: 42).

In relation to the development of discourse competence, it seems that a genre-based approach to the teaching of academic writing in EAP courses has three major strengths enabling a focus on: units of language above sentence level; the organizational or procedural elements of extended written text, and it makes it possible to retain linguistic components as functioning features of a larger unit of discourse, thereby avoiding atomistic approaches to language teaching. As Paltridge (2001: 6) observes:

> [a] genre-based approach to language program development aims to incorporate discourse and contextual aspects of language use that are often under attended to in programs based only on the lower-level organizational units of language, such as structures, functions, or vocabulary.

Genre-based pedagogy in EAP draws upon a considerable amount of research that has examined the written genres that occur in academic contexts, such as research articles and dissertations, and spoken events, such as academic presentations and lectures. In particular, two streams of genre research have contributed to EAP: these are the English for Specific Purposes (ESP) approach to genre, based on Swales's work (1990, 1998, 2004) and the approach to genre influenced by Systemic Functional Linguistics (SFL) (Martin, 1984; Martin and Rose, 2008). In the following section, I briefly review these two approaches, considering what they operationalize and their theoretical provenances.

The genre problem

Genre theory and research as it informs EAP is complex, including different theoretical approaches and competing terminologies that refer to similar or overlapping constructs. Genre, in effect, is a theoretical concept referring to conventionalized categories of written text or spoken language event. The synthesis of knowledge elements that combine to create these texts or language events forms the underlying constructs. In research, the construct validity of a classificatory concept (such as genre) relates to its effectiveness in being able to identify and mirror (or operationalize) all of the elements of the entity that it claims to represent. Concerning construct validity, Cohen et al. (2018: 256) state 'in this sort of validity, agreement is sought on the operationalized forms of the construct ... Is the researcher's understanding similar to what is generally accepted to be the construct?' This suggests that construct validity involves general agreement by those working in a particular research field about the characteristics of the underlying constructs that relate to a particular variable, in this case 'genre'. However, the field of genre studies, on which EAP draws, currently contains several competing theories, and has some way to go before there is general agreement about the constructs that relate to genre as a classificatory concept. In a previous work (Bruce, 2020: 33), I discussed this issue in relation to the areas of discursive and textual knowledge that theories of genre aim to operationalize. Specifically, I considered theories of genre in terms of their capacities to operationalize knowledge when characterizing particular genres in four areas: the type of language use (such as written or spoken language); organization of the conceptual content that they communicate, both empirical and abstract (including knowledge that is referred to both explicitly and implicitly); organizational (procedural) knowledge; and the systems of the language. In this section, I will briefly revisit the key elements of the two theories of genre used most frequently to inform EAP, the ESP approach and the approach influenced by SFL. I will consider each of the two genre approaches in terms of the types of knowledge that each operationalizes in the four areas of: language use (context), conceptual content, organizational knowledge and linguistic knowledge.

Genre theorists influenced by SFL, when characterizing genres, draw upon the SFL concept of *register* to analyse the operation of language in a particular social situation. Register has three socio-semantic dimensions: field (what is happening), tenor (those involved) and mode (the role of language) (Martin, 1992: 494). In register analysis, different aspects of the lexicogrammar of a language are linked to the meaning-making of these three socio-semantic dimensions. While some SFL theorists see the connections between the register variables and linguistic knowledge as deterministic, others see them as somewhat more probabilistic. The approach to genre influenced by SFL sees genres as 'recurring configurations of field, tenor, mode meanings that occur in a culture' (Hood, 2016: 194). Some SFL-influenced genre analyses identify organizational patterns in texts. For example, Martin and Rose (2008: 143) characterize school science genres in terms of more abstract 'stages and phases', and Hasan (1989: 64–5) describes the essential functional stages of shopping encounters in terms of the actual actions involved. Other SFL-influenced genre studies focus more on the characteristic linguistic elements that relate to register found in a particular genre, such as Humphery and Hao's (2011) analysis of university biology texts.

In a seminal definition of the ESP approach, Swales (1990: 58) states that genres are 'a class of communicative events, the members of which share the same communicative purpose'. Earlier ESP genre studies were primarily textual. While genres were identified in terms of their communicative purposes, their internal organization were analyzed in terms of 'rhetorical moves and steps'. Swales (2004: 228–9) defines a move as a 'discoursal or rhetorical unit that performs a coherent communicative function in a written or spoken discourse'. Dudley-Evans (1994: 226) suggests that 'decisions about the classifications of the moves are made on the basis of linguistic evidence, comprehension of the text and understandings of the expectations that both the general academic community and the particular discourse community have of the text'. After the earlier textual studies, ESP genre theorists advocated combining textual analysis with ethnography when researching academic genres (Bhatia, 2004) as a way of acknowledging the importance of context in genre research. Similarly, Swales (1998) advocates an approach that he called *textography*, which involves combining textual analysis with ethnographic interviews.

Accounting for the types of language use (contextual) that shape genres as conventionalized language events or categories of text was not a strong feature of earlier ESP analyses of genre, with the exception of Bhatia's (1993) research on the genre of the legal case. In the approach to genre influenced by SFL, contextual elements are limited to identification of the register elements of field, tenor and mode, which become a basis for identifying linguistic elements that may characterize a genre. Later, however, key ESP genre theorists (Bhatia, 2004; Swales, 1998) argued for a greater emphasis on context by combining ethnographic and textual analyses. For example, the approach to genre that Swales (1998) terms *textography* involves both ethnographic interviews with writers and textual analyses, and has been taken up by some ESP genre researchers (e.g. Paltridge, 2004; Paltridge et al., 2012). It is fair to say that both the SFL-influenced and ESP approaches acknowledge the importance of contextual knowledge to the characterization of genres, but there is some variation in the degree and quality of contextual information found in genre studies that inform EAP.

In accounting for the structuring of the conceptual content of genres, both empirical or abstract, neither of the two genre approaches draws on theory and research from cognitive science related to category theory, such as prototypes (Rosch, 1978) or schema theory (e.g. Lakoff, 1987; Oller, 1995; Sanford and Garrod, 1981). Neither acknowledges that human categorization and the cognitive structuring of different types of domain knowledge may exert an influence on the representation of such knowledge within a text. SFL generally, and genre theorists influenced by SFL set up a probabilistic or deterministic link between the variables of register and lexicogrammatical features, but have 'a lack of interest in cognition' (Van Dijk, 2008: 29). Also, while the ESP approach to genre allows that a genre itself (as a category) can include more or less prototypical examples of the category (Swales, 1990), there is no focus on how the human cognitive structuring of the types of knowledge actually communicated by a genre may influence its actual representation within a text.

In accounting for both textual organization and linguistic elements, genre studies that inform EAP vary somewhat in approach. ESP studies account for the internal textual organization of genres in terms of rhetorical moves and steps, which relate to what Carrell (1987) and Oller (1995) refer to as *content schemata*, but they include no focus on more general, text-organizing patterns, such as *general particular* or *problem solution* (Hoey, 1983) – what Carrell (1987) refers to as *formal schemata*. While some SFL-influenced genre studies may include the element of the textual staging (e.g. *schematic structures,* Eggins, 1994) or more abstract procedural *stages and phases* (Martin and Rose, 2008; Rose, 2011), other

SFL genre studies focus more exclusively on register variables and their typical realization by lexicogrammatical elements, such as in Humphrey and Hao's (2011) characterization of biology texts. Similarly, ESP genre studies sometimes relate linguistic elements to the particular 'moves' or 'steps' of a genre, such as Swales's proposal for the use of linguistic devices that signal a negative viewpoint at the beginning of Move 2 of research article introductions.

Thus, in relation to the key research requirement of construct validity, genre studies (including those that inform EAP) have some way to go before: (a) there can be said to be agreement on offering a comprehensive operationalization of the various types of knowledge that could potentially characterize particular genres and (b) there is general agreement among theorists and researchers on the constructs that relate to genre as a classificatory concept. To date, approaches to theorizing and operationalizing genre knowledge have essentially been pragmatic enterprises with educational ends, usually some aspect of language teaching and discourse competence development. Exemplifying the pragmatism and multiple theories and research that informed his proposal for genre, Swales (1990: 14) acknowledges the influences of: variety studies, skill and strategy studies, situational approaches, notional-functional approaches, discourse analysis, sociolinguistics, writing context studies and cultural anthropology. In the case of SFL-influenced approaches to genre, the use of genres in school pedagogy as a means for literacy development is based on Bernstein's (1990) recontextualizing principle (see, for example, Christie and Martin, 2005). Genres are seen as recurring language events within a culture that may be reflective of dominant ideologies and symbolic control and may be made accessible to learners from different socio-economic backgrounds by means of a research-informed, interventionist pedagogy. While not disagreeing with this position relating to the importance of a pedagogic focus on genres and that of student need to develop genre knowledge, it is the nature of genre knowledge itself that is at issue here, and it is this issue that is addressed in the following section.

Social realism and genre knowledge

To establish construct validity in genre studies, three issues need to be addressed. The first is the need for an ontology of genres – an articulation of the nature of genre knowledge as a basis for investigating, discussing, teaching and learning this type of knowledge. The second issue is epistemological – the need for agreement on the operationalization of genre for the purposes of research and, in particular, research that informs EAP pedagogy. The third issue is the need to develop a consensus on the first two issues among genre theorists and researchers, and especially among those whose studies inform the field of EAP. In this section, I will address these three issues in two ways: firstly, by locating genre studies within a broader theory of knowledge – that of social realism; and secondly, by revisiting a particular model of genre knowledge.

To provide a theoretical framework for genre studies that addresses both the ontological and epistemological problems of the field (including the diversity of approaches to researching genres), I propose that genre studies be located within the overarching theory of knowledge known as *social realism*. Social realism is a sociological theory of knowledge and knowledge-building in education, which emerges from a number of sources, but principally from the philosophical theory of *critical realism* based on the ideas of Bhaskar (1975). Social realism has three main principles: *ontological realism*, *epistemological relativism* and *judgemental rationality* (Archer et al., 1998). These three principles are introduced here briefly and related to genre knowledge.

Ontology is the theory of, or our understanding of existence or being – the world as it actually exists. A realist approach to ontology suggests that 'knowledge is about something other than itself: there exists a reality beyond our symbolic realm' (Maton and Moore, 2010: 4). Therefore, following the approach of ontological realism, I propose a genre to be a conventionalized category of texts (spoken or written) regularly used to achieve a set of socially recognized purposes within a particular social or disciplinary setting. Following this approach, a genre has an independent, objective existence beyond the mind that creates or processes texts of this category. Accordingly, genres have characteristics that may be identified in terms of a range of different (but integrated) knowledge types. For example, a particular genre or category of texts may be described in terms of procedural knowledge, such as how the content of the text is conventionally organized (in terms of moves or schematic structures), or its more general textual organization, such as general particular, problem solution discourse patterns (Hoey, 1983). A certain genre may also display regular and frequent use of certain stance-creating devices, such as described in terms of Hyland's (2005) metadiscourse model, or it may contain systematic use of certain cohesive devices described in linguistic terms or particular coherence relations described in semantico-pragmatic terms.

Epistemology relates to what constitutes knowledge and how it is proven and validated in a particular domain or subject area. Epistemology, therefore, is closely related to the research methods – the methods of enquiry – of that subject. Cohen, Manion and Morrison state that epistemology refers to 'ways of researching and enquiring into the nature of reality and the nature of things' (2018: 3). In the second half of the twentieth century, those studying both the philosophy and sociology of science emphasized the *situatedness* of both the creation and communication of knowledge, 'situatedness' referring to the influences of historical, cultural, social and institutional contexts on the methods of scientific research (e.g. Gilbert and Mulkay, 1984; Knorr Cetina, 1999; Latour and Woolgar, 1986). A relativist approach to epistemology, therefore, acknowledges that 'we can only "know" the world in terms of socially produced knowledge which changes over time and across socio-cultural contexts' (Maton and Moore, 2010: 4). This approach, therefore, suggests that ways in which we investigate and characterize a particular phenomenon (such as a genre) may vary according to the contextual influences on, and theoretical views and methodological preferences of researchers, which may differ in terms of the time and place, when and where the research occurs. Thus, in the case of building *knowledge about* an academic genre, such as an MA thesis, which, although it may have an independent objective ontological existence as a conventionalized discursive and textual form, can be investigated and characterized in different ways by those following different theories and different research traditions. Different research traditions may produce different insights about the target genre, but, importantly, those insights, of themselves, do not constitute or materially alter the genre itself or its actual characteristics.

In resolving the different types of insight about an entity, such as a genre, the third aspect of social realism, *judgemental rationality*, suggests that, although knowledge creation is situated and socially influenced, there are still 'rational, intersubjective bases for determining the relative merits of competing knowledge claims' (Maton and Moore, 2010: 4). Similarly, about judgemental rationality, Moore (2010: 152) states:

> Judgements are less than absolutes in that they acknowledge their fallibility. They are more than preference in that they submit themselves to historically evolved rules of collective evaluation.

Judgemental rationality suggests that when assessing knowledge claims, you apply a criterion, which, as Bhaskar states, 'refers to the real world – the ontological realism that allows you to differentiate between conflicting beliefs about the world' (Scott and Bhaskar, 2015: 20). Thus, although you may claim that a genre that involves argumentation is characterized by a particular move structure or by clusters of causal, coherence relations, a corpus study of a sample of texts from the genre may provide empirical, linguistic evidence to support or refute such claims.

Emphasizing the social dimension of genre knowledge and its conventionalized nature, I propose that genres (as categories of texts) constitute what Durkheim (1976: 15–16) calls *collective representations*, which are concepts that 'help to order and make sense of the world, but they also express, symbolize, and interpret social relationships' (Oxford Reference, n.d.). In developing Durkheim's idea of 'collective representations', Schmaus (1994: 263) proposes that 'to the extent that science aims at the *growth* of knowledge, it is characterized by both *cognitive norms* and *cognitive values*. Cognitive values specify the *aims* of science, while cognitive norms specify the *norms* to achieve those goals'. In addressing the concept of genres as categories of conventionalized texts used to communicate knowledge in certain academic disciplinary contexts, I propose that the cognitive values that Schmaus identifies includes the socially recognized communicative purposes of the discipline within which a genre occurs, while the cognitive norms refer to the genre-internal structures that govern the internal organization and selection of textual resources integrated within a particular text that belongs to a genre category.

The second issue raised in this section is the need for a comprehensive operationalization of genre knowledge to inform EAP. In the previous section, I reviewed the two existing approaches to genre that inform EAP in relation to: language use (context), conceptual content, organizational knowledge, and linguistic knowledge. Both (approaches) address some of these areas with a considerable degree of complexity, but it seems that there is still potential for further work on the issue of operationalizing genre knowledge as a framework for research, one that includes both the cognitive values and cognitive norms that Schmaus (1994) proposes. In accounting for the different dimensions of genre knowledge and as an attempt at addressing the operational issue, I have previously proposed the model of *social genre* and *cognitive genre* (Bruce, 2008a, 2013, 2018, 2020), which aims to take these broader, over-arching concepts (of genres as 'collective representations' involving both 'cognitive values' and 'cognitive norms') and flesh them out in terms of a range of different knowledge elements.

As mentioned previously, genre, in effect, is a theoretical concept referring to conventionalized categories of written text or spoken language event. Because creating and processing genres to communicate knowledge centrally involves human categorization, I suggest that any theory of genre needs to be underpinned by principles from category theory in cognitive science. Three key principles that can be applied to genre categories are:

- the role of purpose or intentionality in category formation (Barsalou, 1983; Murphy and Medin, 1985);
- the use of top-down knowledge hierarchies in the internal organizational structure of complex categories (Miller, 1984; Rumelhart and Ortony, 1977); and
- the role of prototypes in category formation (Rosch, 1978).

In relating these principles from categorization theory to genre analysis, I have previously proposed the *social genre/cognitive genre model* (Bruce, 2008a, 2013, 2018, 2020), which I have used in studies of a variety of genres. The first principle – that categories (genres being complex textual categories) are formed in response to different types of intention or purpose – is reflected in the different types of purpose that instantiate the social genre and cognitive genre elements of the model.

> Social genre – refers to socially recognized constructs according to which whole texts are classified in terms of their *overall social purpose* …. Purpose here is taken to mean the intention to communicate consciously a body of knowledge related to a certain context to a certain target audience.
>
> Cognitive genre – refers to the overall cognitive orientation and internal organization of a segment of writing that realizes a single, *more general rhetorical purpose* [such as] to recount a sequence of events, to explain a process, to present an argument.
>
> (Bruce, 2008b: 39)

Social genres are conventionally recognized categories of whole texts that occur in particular contexts for certain audiences, and sometimes involve formulaic patterns in the selection and staging of content. Cognitive genres are often segments of texts within larger social genres. The term 'cognitive' is used because they involve the use of abstract, procedural knowledge. Each is instantiated (triggered) by a particular *general* rhetorical purpose (e.g. argue, explain) that influences the micro-level organization of the text, relationships between propositions and linguistic choices relating to cohesion and coherence. Although a specific example of a particular social genre may exhibit features of a single cognitive genre (e.g. an instruction manual will use Explanation, probably recursively), it is more common for examples of social genres to

Table 5.1 The social genre/cognitive genre model.

Social genre elements

- Context (Widdowson, 2004)
- Epistemology (Lea and Street, 1998)
- Stance (Hyland, 2005)
- Content schemata (Hasan, 1989; Swales, 1990)

Cognitive genre elements

- Gestalt patterns of ideas (Johnson, 1987)
- General textual patterns (Hoey, 1983, 2001)
- Relations between propositions (Crombie, 1985)

Source: I. Bruce (2015, Table 1: 47).

exhibit features of more than one cognitive genre. For example, a personal letter (a social genre) may draw upon different cognitive genres in relation to the different communicative purposes that may characterize the sections of the overall message as it unfolds (e.g. recounting a series of events, providing an explanation, presenting an argument).

The second principle from categorization theory is that complex categories have a top-down, internal organizational structure (Miller, 1984; Rumelhart and Ortony, 1977). Because of the complexity of discourse creation, the model proposes that writers make choices from a range of discursive elements that relate to the achievement of different types of social and general rhetorical purpose. Table 5.1 outlines the different elements of the proposed model (that *may* influence textual choices) and the subsequent bullet points briefly unpack each of these elements (summarized from Bruce, 2013).

- *Context:* Widdowson (2004: 54) characterizes context in terms of schematic knowledge that involves both 'intralinguistic and extralinguistic factors'. I suggest that, in relation to academic genres, 'extralinguistic factors' involve the specialist, technical knowledge of the field to which the text belongs, and 'intralinguistic factors' include the socially driven forms of communication used in the particular field.
- *Epistemology* is how experts working in a particular field perceive and use knowledge. To understand how subject experts view knowledge, a necessary

co-condition is to understand how they create and validate (or prove) knowledge – the knowledge-creating paradigms used strongly influence its knowledge-communicating forms, such as its written and spoken genres.
- *Stance* (and engagement) involves the use of the set of ten language devices which Hyland (2005: 49) groups together under the term of *metadiscourse*, devices such as *hedges, boosters* and *transitions*. Hyland claims that these are used to make the propositional content of a text 'coherent, intelligible and persuasive to a particular audience' (p. 39).
- *Content Schemata*: These are regularly occurring, conventionalized patterns that *may* be used in organizing the content of a social genre, each stage of which fulfils a particular communicative or rhetorical purpose. The approach to genre influenced by SFL describes such patterns as *schematic structures* (Eggins, 1994) or *functional stages* (Hasan, 1989), and the English for Specific Purposes approach describes them as *moves and steps* (Swales, 1990). The rhetorical purpose that gives rise to a particular 'stage' or 'move' may relate quite closely to the disciplinary content of the text, such as in Bhatia's (1993) analysis of legal cases (e.g. *establishing the facts of the case, arguing the case*) or may be described in less content-specific terms, such as in Connor and Maurenan's (1999) analysis of grant proposals (e.g. *territory, gap, goal, means*). However, the type of context- and content-related rhetorical purpose that motivates these stages (or 'moves') differs from the more general types of rhetorical purpose (e.g. *argue, explain*) that instantiate the cognitive genre elements of the model; these are described under the next point.
- *Cognitive genres* refer to segments of writing that aim to achieve one particular, general rhetorical purpose, such as to argue, explain or recount. Such segments of writing are sometimes called *text types* and described in terms of linguistic features (see, for example, Biber, 1989; Quinn, 1993). However, in this model, they are conceptualized in terms of a top-down, internal organizational structure that involves:
    - gestalts called *image schemata* (Johnson, 1987) that reflect the higher-level organization of ideas (e.g. WHOLE PART, UP DOWN, LINK);
    - *discourse patterns* (Hoey, 1983, 2001) that relate to the organization of the actual written text (e.g. *Problem Solution*); and
    - *interpropositional relations* (Crombie, 1985) that account for lower-level, more specific, binary coherence relations, e.g. Reason Result, Condition Consequence, Means Purpose, Concession Contraexpectation.

The social genre/cognitive genre model is an attempt to address the complexity of genre knowledge and to respond to issues relating to the comprehensiveness and adequacy of existing genre theories used within the field of EAP – the construct validity problem. The model is not claimed to be the final word on genre knowledge, but in presenting it here, the aim is to address the operationalization issue by providing a comprehensive framework (*of potential genre knowledge elements*) as a basis for implementing the social realist principle of judgemental rationality and intersubjective judgements when investigating and characterizing a particular genre.

Social realism: Genre knowledge and genre-based pedagogy

In relating the theory of social realism to genre studies and genre-based pedagogy in EAP, my aim here is not to upend or radically overhaul this area of pedagogic knowledge and practice, but rather to take what has been a relatively successful but pragmatic and outcomes-focused area of instructional activity and research inquiry, and to address some fundamental theoretical issues relating to knowledge and knowledge-building. EAP students entering undergraduate or postgraduate study need access to, and to develop facility in the use of the textual and discursive forms used to communicate within particular academic fields. Effectively, they need to master the genres that are the vehicles of communication of the specialist knowledge of particular disciplines. In order to be able to provide the type of instruction necessary to prepare students to meet the requirements of academic writing, EAP courses of instruction need to access knowledge about genres as complex communicative forms. They then need to implement a genre-based pedagogy that provides systematic approaches to helping students develop knowledge of, and the ability to use these complex textual and discursive forms.

To meet these requirements, a suitable genre-based pedagogy, therefore, needs to be constructed around two elements: first a clear (and comprehensive) articulation of the genre knowledge to be presented; and secondly, cycles of teaching and learning that provide a relevant pedagogical progression that unpacks genre knowledge and supports its acquisition and use by students. Much of this chapter has been devoted to the first element relating to framing and investigating genre knowledge. In this, I have argued for a social realist approach, and also for broader knowledge frameworks (such as the proposed social genre/cognitive genre model) to address the genre knowledge/construct validity issue. However, in this section I move to a brief discussion of the second element, that of genre-based pedagogy (genre-based instruction), and include suggestions about how this may be implemented. I also address some of the arguments that have previously been raised about applying social realism to curriculum and pedagogy.

In this discussion, I invoke two sets of *image schema* concepts of Johnson (1987) as a way of characterizing and contrasting the operational progressions of two pedagogical approaches: one that is linear and one that is hierarchical. An image schema is an embodied, pre-linguistic structural concept (usually spacio-temporal), learned in early life, and used metaphorically to make sense of, and give coherence to human experiences in different domains. Image schemata can relate to processing static or dynamic information. Specifically, I propose that at an organizational level, pedagogies may follow a linear progression, which may be described in terms of the image schema concept that Johnson (1987) terms SOURCE PATH GOAL (SPG). This type of pedagogy follows a cumulative, linear approach, where knowledge is progressively introduced and developed, eventually leading to a desired learning outcome or goal. An SPG pedagogy is not necessarily simplistic and may involve a considerable degree of complexity, such as the cumulative knowledge-building through a series of *semantic waves*, such as proposed by Maton (2014). The progression of this type of SPG pedagogy is digressive through different knowledge types, but its essential directionality is linear. While acknowledging the ubiquity, and not decrying the usefulness of an SPG approach to knowledge-building in many contexts, I suggest that pedagogy may also follow a non-linear, hierarchical progression, which can be characterized in terms of a combination of the two image schemata that Johnson (1987) terms WHOLE PART and UP DOWN. Categorization theory tells us the internal organization of complex categories (that integrate different types of knowledge, such as genres) is hierarchical. Pedagogy that aims to teach awareness and mastery of this type of category knowledge needs to be able to articulate and unpack this hierarchy (the PART), but also to preserve its integrative character (the WHOLE), something that is difficult to achieve if a linear pedagogy is adopted.

Essentially, I propose that genre-based pedagogy (genre-based instruction) as it has developed follows a WHOLE PART/UP DOWN schematic progression, which is commensurable with understanding, and learning to create the complex textual forms used to communicate the specialist knowledge of academic subjects. This pedagogical approach, therefore, begins with genres as operational wholes. It then involves a top-down analysis and practice of the parts (of the whole) before student writers then undertake supported and then more autonomous reconstructions of the whole, creating their own examples of texts of the genre category.

As mentioned earlier in this chapter, this approach is not new and has its provenance in Australian literacy education in schools (Burns and Joyce, 1991; Callaghan and Rothery, 1988). In relation to academic genres, I have proposed that genre-based pedagogy involves two principal phases – *analysis* and *synthesis* (Bruce, 2020: 156–8). In the analysis phase, using a sample text or group of similar texts (exemplifying a particular genre), students engage with tasks that identify and deconstruct the contextual, organizational and linguistic features of the text in order to identify and acquire the types of procedural and declarative knowledge necessary for creating their own examples of the same genre. In the synthesis phase, students undertake joint, supported constructions of new examples of the target genre before moving on to create further exemplar texts, more autonomously. The important element of this pedagogical approach is to preserve the integrity of the genre as an operational whole and avoid falling into atomistic, synthetic approaches to teaching genre knowledge.

Criticisms of the social realist approach to knowledge and knowledge-building have centred on what they see as a rigid, binary division of knowledge between specialized, theoretical knowledge (Durkheim's 'sacred' category) and real-world everyday knowledge (e.g. Zipin et al., 2015). In response, I suggest that this opposition is based on an excessively hermetic view of the two categories of knowledge, and fails to account for the multi-layered, overlapping knowledge elements that integrate within genres as complex discursive and textual categories that aim to fulfil specific types of communicative and rhetorical purpose. Here I argue that the categorization and organization of 'sacred' (specialist) knowledge – the procedural knowledge central to genre construction – still involve fundamental human approaches to knowledge structuring that Johnson (1987) would argue actually relate to real-world concepts, such as temporal, spatial and causal concepts. Effectively unpacking these structures and the types of language involved, therefore, depends on the types of framing and analysis undertaken as part of the pedagogical process. Here, rather than a binary cycling between 'sacred' and 'secular' (in the movement towards a pedagogic goal – such as in the semantic wave approach), a genre-based pedagogy involves a progressive, top-down unpacking of *multiple* layers of knowledge that are closely integrated with each other. These knowledge layers may include context, subject content, conventionalized organizational patterns, abstract procedural knowledge, referential systems, metadiscourse devices, coherence relations and cohesive devices (that may include reference). An appropriate pedagogy, therefore, needs to account for both the *complexity* and *integrative nature* of the knowledge types that combine within any genre.

Conclusion

At the beginning of the third section of this chapter, I proposed that, to address the construct validity problem in genre studies, there needed to be three things: a clear ontology of genre knowledge, an established epistemology of genres – the types of knowledge that constitute the underlying constructs of the concept of genre and how they may be investigated – and, thirdly, agreement on the first two issues. Given the complexity of the phenomena of genres and the diverse ways in which they have previously been operationalized, I propose that social realism provides a useful basis for knowledge-building and knowledge-communicating that involves genres in the field of EAP. Following the social realist approach, I propose that academic genres, as conventionalized categories of texts, have identifiable, real-world properties, a real ontological existence that is amenable to analysis. In relation to their epistemology, I suggest that they are complex discursive and textual categories and, as such, integrate a range of different types of knowledge. Given this complexity, researching genres may involve different approaches in different contexts, which offer different insights about their constituency and functional uses. However, judgemental rationality – intersubjective disclosure, interaction and transparency around the methodology of genre research – can collectively contribute to a more complete understanding of the nature of these complex entities. Potentially, judgemental rationality is the key element to solving the construct validity problem in genre studies, where 'agreement is sought on the operationalized forms of the construct' (Cohen et al., 2018: 256).

Given the complexity of genre analysis and categorization and the multiple theoretical approaches employed, judgemental rationality would involve an approach that is based on principles of salience and transparency when identifying genre-defining elements. When tackling a particular genre, such an approach would require an analysis that draws selectively on a broad, consensus framework of genre-constructing knowledge elements from the different theories, such as socially constructed elements, more abstract cognitive elements and linguistic elements. In effect, judgemental rationality is where the social element in genre research emerges and becomes most visible, and potentially political. However, it also provides the means for moving genre theory beyond ideas which, for some, have become non-negotiable doxa that result in foreclosing on a more reasoned, cross-theoretical approach to genre analysis.

References

Archer, M. S., R. Bhaskar, A. Collier, T. Lawson and A. Norrie, eds (1998), *Critical Realism: Essential Readings*, London: Routledge.
Barsalou, L. W. (1983), 'Ad hoc Categories', *Memory & Cognition*, 11 (3): 211–27.
Bernstein, B. B. (1990), *Class, Codes and Control*, vol. 4, *The Structuring of Pedagogic Discourse*, London: Routledge.
Bernstein, B. (2000), *Pedagogy, Symbolic Control, and Identity*, Lanham, MD: Rowman & Littlefield Publishers.
Bhaskar, R. (1975), *A Realist Theory of Science*, Leeds: Leeds Books.
Bhatia, V. K. (1993), *Analysing Genre: Language Use in Professional Settings*, Harlow, England: Longman.
Bhatia, V. K. (2004), *Worlds of Written Discourse*, London: Continuum.
Biber, D. (1989), 'A Typology of English Texts', *Linguistics*, 27 (1): 3–44.
Bruce, I. (2008a), *Academic Writing and Genre: A Systematic Analysis*, London: Continuum.
Bruce, I. (2008b), 'Cognitive Genre Structures in Methods Sections of Research Articles: A Corpus Study', *Journal of English for Academic Purposes*, 7 (1): 38–54.
Bruce, I. (2013), 'A Role for Genre-based Pedagogy in Academic Writing Instruction?': An EAP Perspective, *TEXT: Special Issue: Scores from Another Ground: Writing in New Zealand*, (21): 1–15. Available online: https://hdl.handle.net/10289/8510.
Bruce, I. (2015), 'Resisting Neoliberalism through Political and Social Critique: The Guardian Column of Polly Toynbee', *Discourse, Context & Media*, 10: 45–52.
Bruce, I. (2018), 'The Textual Expression of Critical Thinking in PhD Discussions in Applied Linguistics', *ESP Today: Journal of English for Specific Purposes at Tertiary Level*, 6 (1): 2–24.
Bruce, I. (2020), *Expressing Critical Thinking through Disciplinary Texts: Insights from Five Genre Studies*, London: Bloomsbury Academic.
Burns, A. and H. Joyce (1991), 'The Teaching-learning Cycle', in J. Hammond, S. Solomon and S. Hood (eds), *English for Social Purposes: A Handbook for Teachers of Adult Literacy*, Sydney: National Centre for English Language Teaching and Research.
Callaghan, M. and J. Rothery (1988), *Teaching Factual Writing: A Genre-Based Approach: The Report of the DSP Literacy Project, Metropolitan East Region*. Metropolitan East Disadvantaged Schools Program.
Carrell, P. L. (1987), 'Content and Formal Schemata in ESL Reading', *TESOL Quarterly*, 21 (3): 461–81.

Christie, F. and J. R. Martin (2005), *Genre and Institutions: Social Processes in the Workplace and School*, London: Continuum.

Cohen, L., L. Manion and K. Morrison (2018), *Research Methods in Education*, Abingdon: Routledge.

Connor, U. and A. Mauranen (1999), 'Linguistic Analysis of Grant Proposals: European Union Research Grants', *English for Specific Purposes*, 18 (1): 47–62.

Crombie, W. (1985), *Process and Relation in Discourse and Language Learning*, Oxford, England: Oxford University Press.

Ding, A. and I. Bruce (2017), *The English for Academic Purposes Practitioner*, Cham, Switzerland: Springer.

Dudley-Evans, T. (1994), 'Genre Analysis: An Approach to Text Analysis for ESP', in M. Coulthard (ed.), *Advances in Written Text Analysis*, 233–42, London: Routledge.

Durkheim, É. (1976), *The Elementary Forms of the Religious Life*, London: Allen and Unwin.

Eggins, S. (1994), *An Introduction to Systemic Functional Linguistics*, London: Continuum International Publishing Group, Limited.

Flowerdew, J. A. and M. Peacock (2001), *Research Perspectives on English for Academic Purposes*, Cambridge: Cambridge University Press.

Gilbert, G. N. and N. Mulkay (1984), *Opening Pandora's Box: A Sociological Analysis of Scientists' Discourse*, Cambridge: Cambridge University Press.

Hasan, R. (1989), 'The Identity of a Text', in M. A. K. Halliday and R. Hasan (eds), *Language, Text and Context*, 97–118, Oxford: Oxford University Press.

Hoey, M. (1983), *On the Surface of Discourse*, London: Allen and Unwin.

Hoey, M. (2001), *Textual Interaction: An Introduction to Written Discourse Analysis*, London: Routledge.

Hood, S. (2016), 'Systemic Functional Linguistics and EAP', in K. Hyland and P. Shaw (eds), *The Routledge Handbook of English for Academic Purposes*, 217–29, Abingdon: Routledge.

Humphrey, S. and J. Hao (2011), 'Deconstructing Written Genres in Undergraduate Biology', *Linguistics & the Human Sciences*, 7 (1–3): 29–53.

Hyland, K. (2005), *Metadiscourse: Exploring Interaction in Writing*, London: Bloomsbury Academic.

Johnson, M. (1987), *The Body in the Mind: The Bodily Basis of Meaning, Imagination, and Reason*, Chicago: University of Chicago Press.

Knorr Cetina, K. (1999), *Epistemic Cultures: How the Sciences Make Knowledge*, Cambridge, MA: Harvard University Press.

Lakoff, G. (1987), *Women, Fire, and Dangerous Things*, Chicago: Chicago University Press.

Latour, B. and S. Woolgar (1986), *Laboratory Life: The Construction of Scientific Faces*, Princeton, NJ: Princeton University Press.

Lea, M. R. and B. V. Street (1998), 'Student Writing in Higher Education: An Academic Literacies Approach', *Studies in Higher Education*, 23 (2): 157–72.

Lilliedahl, J. (2015), 'The Recontextualisation of Knowledge: Towards a Social Realist Approach to Curriculum and Didactics', *Nordic Journal of Studies in Educational Policy*, 1: 40–7.

Martin, J. (1984), 'Language, Register and Genre', in F. Christie (ed.), *Language Studies: Children Writing. Reader*, 21–30, Victoria: Deakin University Press.

Martin, J. R. (1992), *English Text: System and Structure*, Philadelphia: John Benjamins Publishing.

Martin, J. R. and D. Rose (2008), *Genre Relations: Mapping Culture*, London: Equinox.

Maton, K. (2014), *Knowledge and Knowers: Towards a Realist Sociology of Education*, London: Routledge.

Maton, K. and R. Moore (2010), *Social Realism, Knowledge and the Sociology of Education: Coalitions of the Mind*, London: Continuum.

Miller, C. R. (1984), 'Genre as Social Action', *Quarterly Journal of Speech*, 70 (2): 151–67.

Moore, R. (2010), 'Knowledge Structures and the Canon: A Preference for Judgements', in K. Maton and R. Moore (eds), *Social Realism, Knowledge and the Sociology of Education: Coalitions of the Mind*, 131–52, London: Continuum.

Moore, R. (2013), 'Social Realism and the Problem of the Problem of Knowledge in the Sociology of Education', *British Journal of Sociology of Education*, 34 (3): 333–53.

Murphy, G. L. and D. L. Medin (1985), 'The Role of Theories in Conceptual Coherence', *Psychological Review*, 92 (3): 289–316.

Nesi, H. and S. Gardner (2012), *Genres across the Disciplines: Student Writing in Higher Education*, Cambridge, UK: Cambridge University Press.

Oller, J. W., Jr (1995), 'Adding Abstract to Formal and Content Schemata: Results of Recent Work in Peircean Semiotics', *Applied linguistics*, 16 (3): 273–306.

Oxford Reference (n.d.), 'Collective Representations'. Available online: https://www.oxfordreference.com/view/10.1093/oi/authority.20110803095624310.

Paltridge, B. (2001), *Genre and the Language Learning Classroom*, Ann Arbor: University of Michigan Press.

Paltridge, B. (2004), 'The Exegesis as a Genre: An Ethnographic Examination', in L. J. Ravelli and R. A. Ellis (eds), *Analysing Academic Writing: Contextualized Frameworks*, 84–103, London: Continuum.

Paltridge, B., S. Starfield, L. Ravelli and S. Nicholson (2012), 'Doctoral Writing in the Visual and Performing Arts: Two Ends of a Continuum', *Studies in Higher Education*, 37 (8): 989–1003.

Quinn, J. (1993), 'A Taxonomy of Text Types for Use in Curriculum Design', *EA Journal*, 11 (2): 33–46.

Rosch, E. H. (1978), 'Principles of Categorization', in E. H. Rosch and B. B. Lloyd (eds), *Cognition and Categorization*, 27–47, Hillsdale, NJ: Erlbaum.

Rose, D. (2011), 'Beyond Literacy: Building an Integrated Pedagogic Genre', *The Australian Journal of Language and Literacy*, 34 (1): 81–97.

Rumelhart, D. E. and A. Ortony (1977), 'The Representation of Knowledge in Memory', in R. C. Anderson, R. J. Spiro and W. E. Montague (eds), *Schooling and the Acquisition of Knowledge*, 99–135, Hillsdale, NJ: Erlbaum.

Sanford, A. and S. C. Garrod (1981), *Understanding Written Language*, Chichester: John Wiley.

Scott, D. and R. Bhaskar (2015), *Roy Bhaskar: A Theory of Education*, Cham, Switzerland: Springer International Publishing.

Schmaus, W. (1994), *Durkheim's Philosophy of Science and the Sociology of Knowledge: Creating an Intellectual Niche*, Chicago: University of Chicago Press.

Swales, J. M. (1990), *Genre Analysis: English in Academic and Research Settings*, Cambridge, UK: Cambridge University Press.

Swales, J. M. (1998), *Other Floors, Other Voices: A Textography of a Small University Building*, Mahwah, NJ: Lawrence Erlbaum.

Swales, J. M. (2004), *Research Genres: Explorations and Applications*, Cambridge: UK Cambridge University Press.

Van Dijk, T. A. (2008), *Discourse and Power*, Basingstoke: Palgrave Macmillan.

Widdowson, H. G. (2004), *Text, Context, Pretext: Critical Issues in Discourse Analysis*, Malden, MA: Blackwell.

Young, M. (2008), 'From Constructivism to Realism in the Sociology of the Curriculum', *Review of Research in Education*, 32 (1): 1–28.

Young, M. (2010), 'Why Educators Must Differentiate Knowledge from Experience', *Journal of the Pacific Circle Consortium for Education*, 22 (1): 9–20.

Zipin, L., A. Fataar and M. Brennan (2015), 'Can Social Realism Do Social Justice? Debating the Warrants for Curriculum Knowledge Selection', *Education as Change*, 19 (2): 9–36.

6

Critical realism: What can it do for EAP?

Julia Molinari

Introduction

This chapter adopts a critical realist lens to analyse the ways in which change can be understood and at what level it can be located across three interconnected domains of EAP socio-academic reality: the micro-level of everyday practices and experiences; the meso-level of actual and potential contexts; and the macro-level of deep structures and mechanisms. Following a historical overview to set the scene for why and how EAP lends itself to critical realist scrutiny, I explain what critical realist theory is and how it can be methodologically relevant to understanding agency in EAP. I conclude by highlighting that change in the theory and practice of EAP is possible at the micro- and meso-levels on condition that scholars and practitioners are engaged at the macro-level. What motivates these aims is the sense of collective endeavour, implicitly or explicitly stated in this volume, to theoretically ground and explain transformation and change in the field of EAP.

Historical overview, or why history matters

Like all human domains, EAP has history. Several critical theorists and philosophers take the view that history is contingent, in the sense that it could have been and can continue to be different (Said, 1994; Vico, 1959 (1725, 1730, 1744, 1928)). For the purpose of understanding critical realist theory and how it can help us make sense of transformations in the field of EAP, history is understood as non-deterministic. What this means within the philosophy of critical realism is that history is made up of a series of events that emerge from the interconnections and interactions of stratified (or layered) phenomena that together constitute all aspects of reality, including individual choices in relation to structural opportunities and constraints. Within this emergent and layered system, social reality, which includes educational practices, is understood as an 'open system' (Collier, 1994: 34–5; Molinari, 2021) that can be transformed and acted upon via rational judgements (or judgemental rationality) that presuppose a deep knowledge of how social practices come about (Mirzaei Rafe et al., 2020). Because of the stratified nature of these multiple interconnections and interactions, no single variable within a complex historical social reality can explain, determine or predict any given outcome. Rather, what allows humans to make inferences and thereby advance knowledge is a strategy referred to as 'retroduction' (Fletcher, 2017). Simply put, retroduction is a way of explaining, in hindsight, why something rather than something else happened. In critical realist terms, it is a way of providing a rich historical account – based on deep knowledge, informed understanding and judgement – of the structures and mechanisms that enabled a social phenomenon to emerge. Because these structures and mechanisms are stratified and interconnected within complex systems (Kuhn, 2008; Mason, 2008a, b), events are said to 'emerge' (Chalmers, 2006; Sawyer, 2001) rather than 'result' (Ablowitz, 1939; Brown et al., 2001: 76). Retroduction thus affords an *explanatory* rather than *causal* account of social phenomena by avoiding recourse to the more problematic deductive and inductive methods of scientific positivism (Daston and Galison, 2007) which rely on fixed axioms, or assumptions, about what is being observed and which assume the discredited Humean ontology of a world made up of constant and predictable conjunctions of events.[1] Rather, because retroduction privileges an abductive explanatory approach to analysing cause and effect within the social world, it tends to be non-linear, reflective and open to accounting for a range of factors that might explain why something has happened (Brown et al., 2001: 61, 78; Fletcher, 2017: 184). By understanding social reality as non-linear, we are more likely to understand, and therefore identify, the levers of change (Mason, 2008b) that can help us transform it. This doesn't mean we can transform it, just that we stand a better chance of doing so (should we so wish).

---

[1] Humean causality is discredited within critical realist social theory because it is based on the assumption that the world is a 'closed system' whereby there is a constant conjunction of cause and effect. This constant conjunction is ineffective to explain the social phenomena that emerge in an open system.

To illustrate the affordances of an abductive and retroductive approach, the following, admittedly simplified but familiar, EAP scenario should suffice. If a student text is found to have been plagiarized, inductively, the explanation might be that the student hasn't sufficiently practised paraphrasing (because experience suggests that practice makes perfect). Deductively, the putative explanation might be that the student hasn't used synonyms (because 'writing in your own words' invariably 'results' in the avoidance of plagiarism). However, both of these explanations are incomplete because what they are assuming is a closed ontology of constant conjunctions that invests an isolated cause (copying) with the explanatory power to explain a complex effect (plagiarism). Rather, what these explanations are missing is what critical realists refer to as 'transfactual' accounts of the same event (Brown et al., 2001: 74; Price, 2014: 55; 59–61): transfactual accounts broaden the pool of possible interacting causes that create the conditions for a phenomenon to emerge. Transfactuals are *explanans* that are not usually mobilized to explain a phenomenon (*explanandum*) because, for example, they are not part of a particular disciplinary or methodological canon. However, transfactuals exist and can, therefore, be explanatory. What a retroductive explanation might now reveal is that what caused the student to plagiarize was a range of complex inter-related 'facts', such as misunderstandings about the concept of plagiarism itself (Pennycook, 1996); the struggle to find a voice (Scott, 2013); writer's block (Rose, 1984); or the challenge of linking one's readings to their own research questions (Kamler and Thomson, 2006), which, in turn, frames writing as a method of enquiry (Richardson and St. Pierre, 2005) rather than a mechanical skill of replacing one word with another. Retroduction seeks to provide the 'best' explanation for an event by widening the explanatory pool.

This abductive and non-deterministic (because it recognizes there are multiple interacting *explanans*) approach to phenomena needs disclosing from the outset because it has implications for understanding the role that human agency – which is central to critical realist theory – plays in social transformations. A humanist conception of history (Alderson and Spencer, 2017), one where it is assumed that human agents, rather than divine intervention, create their own destinies, can be understood as non-deterministic in the sense that it looks (Said, 1994: 45):

> at situations as contingent, not as inevitable, [but] as a result of a series of historical choices made by men and women, as facts of society made by human beings, and not as natural or god-given, therefore unchangeable, permanent, irreversible.

EAP history can be similarly explained in complex non-deterministic ways that view situations as 'contingent' on a 'series of choices and facts' as well as in terms of a range of variables that can be retroductively accounted for via abduction. So, for example, the purpose of EAP itself might be explained in at least three distinct ways, each of which has implications for practice and each of which does not exclude the other (but nor is it the only, or most fitting, explanation): (1) in linguistic or pedagogic terms, the function of EAP is to '[assist] learners' study or research in that language [English]' (Hyland, 2006: 1). We assume this to be the case because that is what the textbooks tell us; (2) in ideological terms, its purpose can be described as a 'market for international students' (Turner, 2010: 17). We know that this, too, is the case because of research in critical EAP and Academic Literacies (Lillis and Tuck, 2016) as well as research on internationalization (Mittelmeier and Lomer, 2021; Mulvey, 2021); and (3) in sociological terms, EAP is both a 'research-informed academic subject' and 'a peripheral support service' (Ding and Bruce, 2017: 3). For Ding and Bruce, an understanding of EAP's dual identity can explain the marginalization of its practitioners (Davis, 2019).

A retroductive method of analysis, which includes both deductive and inductive knowledge but boosts its explanatory power through abduction, can thus reveal a multitude of interconnected ways of understanding a seemingly single, yet highly complex, phenomenon such as EAP. Were we to rely solely on a deductive method to explain EAP, we might adopt only one of these ways of understanding it (e.g. taking it as read that EAP magnanimously exists to help students succeed at university as opposed to being a neoliberal cash-cow (Mittelmeier and Lomer, 2021; Mulvey, 2021)). Deduction would fundamentally misrepresent its complex nature. Such a misrepresentation can in turn have deleterious consequences because it might lead to decisions that are based on incomplete accounts of why some event rather than another took place. For example, if EAP genuinely existed to 'help students succeed', then why has this magnanimity historically extended to some students but not others (Lillis, 2001; Mulvey, 2021)? A retroductive and abductive explanation can provide the rich explanatory tools needed to qualify our assumptions and their effects, thus increasing the likelihood of identifying levers of agentic change that can, over time, potentially transform the structures that either enable or constrain human agencies.

Were we to rely instead on inductive explanatory methods that depend on our experiences, we may similarly misrepresent the nature of EAP because we may over-generalize the specifics of what we happen to be familiar with at the expense of others. For example, when we premise our analyses of complex phenomena with 'In my experience' and then go on to generalize our limited, albeit no less significant, relative perspectives.

The reason all of this matters is that how we come to understand a phenomenon has implications for how we then act. Clearly, nobody can ever understand phenomena in their entirety but we stand a greater chance of making sense of complexity by recognizing that there exists an ongoing dialectic of both procedural and propositional knowledge (*knowing how* and *knowing that* (Knorr Cetina et al., 2001) and of what Michael Gibbons (1994) in Baber (1995) refers to as Mode 1 and Mode 2 knowledge (*disciplinary* and *interdisciplinary* knowledge). To understand EAP as a complex social phenomenon requires this degree of deep dialectical (and transfactual) knowledge because without it, EAP will fail to understand and transform itself in relation not only to academia but also to its own visions, missions and values: that these are varied and competing within and across the EAP sector is already evident. For example, some see EAP, and education, more generally as a harbinger of social justice (McArthur, 2020), whilst others highlight that it remains a free rider on the bandwagons of capitalism, which, according to O'Regan (2021), is the foundational economic ontology that allows the English language to dominate. Such deep knowledge is within the reach of EAP when personal and institutional investment in scholarship occurs (see, for example, Bond, 2020 on the 'accidental' and 'engaged' scholar; Davis, 2019).

We already know that universities' visions, missions and values change over time (Ashwin, 2020; Barnett, 2012; Besley and Peters, 2013; Collini, 2012; Connell, 2019; de Sousa Santos, 2017; Macfarlane, 2021a; Mulvey, 2021; Peters, 2017; Sperlinger et al., 2018; Warnock, 1989) and that during its fifty-year life span, EAP has struggled to establish its identities, accordingly. Increasingly, I have found myself capturing this struggle through the metaphor of EAP as a 'hermit crab', to further index its troubled and nomadic identities, in the UK context, at least: hermit crabs have no shell, they are exposed to and at the behest of the elements, to having no fixed abode and to being vulnerable as a consequence. Their survival strategy is to crawl under whichever container will have them, regardless of fit. Similarly, myriad elements – socio-economic expediencies, institutional ideologies, degree of academic status – dictate whether the EAP crab crawls under the shell of a 'service' offered by university libraries, of 'support' provided by student services or designated private and public EAP units. Even the ways in which EAP accredits itself mirrors ambiguous identities. For example, Nottingham University's designated EAP provider, CELE, aligns its professional identity with the British Council, a self-declared 'global soft-power' (British Council, 2018). This sends a clear ideological signal that it is the 'English' in EAP, as well as a certain variety of English, that is being foregrounded. Compare this to institutions who more readily identify with the EAP-specific BALEAP community and its framework of accreditation. Such a fragmentation of identities has significant sociological, and therefore practical, implications because it leads to professional and ideological differences that are incommensurable within and across the EAP sector.

It is because of the chameleonic accommodationist and 'socializing' (Turner, 2018) propensity to serve the university and shape itself to whichever shell will house it, that EAP becomes a prime candidate for a complex retroductive and abductive sociological analysis. Such an analysis might highlight, for example, that socializing students into the mores and conventions of higher education (whatever these may be and for whom (Thesen and Cooper, 2013) is not the purpose of EAP, or at least not the sole purpose. Moreover, when EAP is understood as a research-informed academic discipline rather than a marketplace for recruiting international students, more critical, nuanced and reflexive dispositions are likely to highlight the ways in which socialization is problematic because it presupposes, inter alia, an a priori acceptance that all students wish to or can converge (Boughey and McKenna, 2021; Thesen and Cooper, 2013: 18; Turner, 2010).

The role and purpose of EAP within the academy thus become an issue of *critical* sociological, theoretical and practical concern because they have consequences for the agency and flourishing (Fitzmaurice, 2010) of both practitioners and students. Critical realism thus affords both a conceptual and practical methodological space for locating where change may be possible.

What is critical realism?

> Critical realism is a philosophy of being that accommodates both the relativism of individual experience and practice as well as the existence of an ultimate reality independent of human thought and action.
>
> (Foreword by Chrissie Boughey in Molinari, 2022)

Like all theories and their under-labouring philosophies, critical realism (CR) is one of several ways of making sense of (our knowledge of) the world.[2] It is a

---

[2] An earlier version of this account is published in Molinari (2022).

philosophical and sociological theory that addresses the complex 'structure and agency' discourses that have characterized contemporary sociology. Although originally advanced by Roy Bhaskar (1979, 1989), it has subsequently been mobilized by a wide range of theorists and practitioners to explain the nature, the tensions and the implications emerging from the complex ways in which social structures and human agencies interact in their specific disciplinary fields.

CR attempts to articulate the extent to which we are determined by the structures we are born into (which are ontologically real) and to what extent and how we become critical agents able and willing to change these structures in accordance with our values and concerns (which are epistemologically real, but relative). For example, critical realists ask what powers do we, as human agents, have to enact social change and what must the world be like for these powers (such as our theories and practices) to be correct (Archer, 2000; Bhaskar, 1998). Critical realists acknowledge that we are constrained by history and the social structures we are born into because these are real. This is why it can be difficult, if not impossible, for individuals to enact change: for example, an international student wishing to study at a UK university is obliged, whether willingly or not, to sit an IELTS test because university admission policies and the commercial agreements they abide by are real and too powerful for any single individual to oppose. But, equally, CR posits that social structures are stratified 'open systems' and that, as such, they are permeable: what this means is that they are shaped by events that occur both within the system and outside of it, just as living organisms are part of a wider ecology that shapes them into different beings. Their openness allows them to be transformed even though their ontological status as 'systems' grants them stability. So, that same student who at a particular point in their academic trajectory is obliged to take the IELTS test may, having accessed the knowledge to make informed choices about other options, either wish to look and pay for an alternative entry exam or go along with whatever is their immediate path of least resistance, nonetheless biding their time until they are in a position, or have the capabilities (Robeyns, 2016), to have both a critical voice and a platform through which to challenge the system (Carmichael-Murphy, 2021; Nguyen, 2019) by exposing its 'cracks' (Lillis et al., 2015: 389).

CR distinguishes itself within the established canon of sociology by disambiguating the structure–agency binary and by introducing an explicit analytical construct referred to as 'analytical dualism'. The reason critical realism opts for this disambiguation is to counter the tendency of previous sociological theories (Archer, 2000; Collier, 1994; Sawyer, 2001) to explain social phenomena either by reducing the ontology of the structures of society to the level of individuals, thus denying the existence and influence of 'society' all together (as in Margaret Thatcher's infamous claim,[3] which can be understood with reference to a sociological position known as 'methodological individualism'[4]) or by reifying the structures of society to such an extent that the agency and powers of individuals to enact change are denied because their choices are entirely determined by society (a position known as 'methodological collectivism'). Instead, critical realists attempt to give structure and agency their own independent, albeit stratified, realities so that they can be studied separately with the intention of making non-reductive claims about each other. This avoids the conflation of structure with agency, even though they are interconnected and influence each other. For example, within a CR ontology, individuals have characteristics that structures do not. These characteristics can be explained structurally, but they are ontologically distinct from the structures that generated them: this distinction is important because it recognizes the experiences of individuals as diverse and real, regardless of whether any given structure was designed to inflict pain. Economic structures of casualized labour are a case in point: whilst they may not have been created with an intent to harm individuals, their effects can be harmful. The dialectic relationship between structure and agency is established via a 'stratified ontology' that links them via reflexive, knowledge-informed and emergent relations rather than via relative, deterministic or reductive claims. This allows critical realists to 'reclaim' (Bhaskar, 1989) the reality of agents as actors who have human 'rational judgement' (understood as values, emotions and wisdom) and therefore 'powers' to intervene and change social structures that are equally real and exist independently of individuals (i.e. the structures exist even if we do not experience them, meaning that knowledge of the world extends beyond our relative experience of it).

It is for this reason that CR theory is seen as generative and transformative by those who wish to change the inequalities and injustices of their contexts. Specifically, educationalists who are active where inequality of access and social injustice are prevalent, such as Jennifer Case (2013), Chrissie Boughey (2013) and Boughey and McKenna (2021), have turned their attention to critical realist theory because it affords a generative heuristic for mobilizing change in educational practices and policies. By retroductively explaining complex events, CR seeks to locate the levers of change needed in systems that are

---

[3] Former Conservative UK prime minister made the following claim in an interview on 23 September 1987 for *Woman's Own*: 'There is no such thing as society....... There are individual men and women and there are families' (https://www.margaretthatcher.org/document/106689)

[4] See Sawyer, R. K. (2001).

unjust (Boughey and McKenna, 2021; Judd, 2003; Mirzaei Rafe et al., 2020). CR is also an interdisciplinary philosophy of social science (Judd, 2003; Price, 2014). Since a humanistic research paradigm and a transfactual methodology, as described above, are at the core of CR, its appeal can be explained in terms of its pursuit to reveal the deep complex causes that enable injustices to emerge. An understanding of such deep causes allows CR to avoid reductionistic and monovalent[5] explanations, which can obscure the causes that maintain structures of oppression (Price, 2014: 59). By showing that the social and natural worlds we inhabit are 'stratified' according to what powers human agents have to modify their complex environments (for example, we can't change the natural force of gravity or the deep socio-economic infrastructures of capitalism, but we can choose the extent to which we adapt to, adopt or resist these), CR's appeal is that it articulates where we might create and locate the 'levers of change' (Mason, 2008b) that will enable us to transform reality in accordance with our rational judgement (which is composed of knowledge and values).

In the field of sociology, Margaret Archer (1998) has been prominent in extending Bhaskarian CR to provide a systematic analysis of the nature of the relationship between human agents and the structures they are born into. She articulates this relationship by showing how individuals, despite being born into pre-existing structures they have limited control of, over time (morphogenetically) can and do shape, maintain, re-generate and transform these structures through their values, knowledge, reflexivity and decision-making (Archer, 2000). In particular, her critical realist lens magnifies the role that human interactions, or relations, play in bringing about change to and within the social structures (Donati and Archer, 2015). The appeal of this position is that it can be seen as generating a fertile sociological imagination (Mills, 1959) in which practitioners across the (inter)disciplinary spectrum adopt and adapt a CR lens to transform reality collectively.

Within the field of writing studies, critical realism has provided academic writing scholars in the United States (Bernard-Donals, 1998; Judd, 2003), South Africa (Pratt, 2011) and UK (Molinari, 2022) with the theoretical foundations and practical vision to argue for knowledge-oriented writing pedagogies that are committed to authentic academic research practices aimed at eliminating the hollow display (Helms-Park and Stapleton, 2003) or 'performativity' (Macfarlane,

---

[5] In CR theory, monovalence refers to an ontological position whereby only things that exist have causal powers. For critical realists, this leads to the denial of the causal relevance of absences which commits us to denying the effects of 'events that did not happen'. See Price (2014) for a detailed discussion on how a monovalent ontology can elide the causes of sexual inequality and violence.

2021b) of academic writing templates, or 'straightjackets' (Hamilton and Pitt, 2009). And closer still, in the field of EAP, Ding and Bruce (2017: 158–61) have drawn on Margaret Archer to suggest ways in which practitioners might harness the agencies they need to push back against the commodification, casualization and marginalization of EAP within UK academia. Specifically, they have identified scholarship as a 'lever of change' that can mitigate the marginalization of EAP within the academy and enable practitioner agency to flourish. In keeping with the CR paradigm, identifying these 'levers' becomes a necessary step in the process of locating the conditions that ensure EAP practitioners – understood as human agents who care (Dall'Alba, 2012) and have free will and values – accrue the knowledge base to understand, and therefore stand a better chance of influencing and transforming, the socio-economic structures that both maintain and threaten the EAP industry.

Theories matter because endorsing their tenets, whether explicitly, implicitly, knowingly or unknowingly, has practical consequences for how we live, what ideologies we subscribe to and to what extent we are aware of the logical consequences of these ideologies (Arendt, 1953). Theories do not arise and evolve in isolation. All are historically situated and are responses to the theories that came before them and to the need to re-imagine how else practice could be: Aristotle's was a practical and empirical response to Plato's idealism; Kant's was a rational idealist response to Hume's scepticism; Bourdieu pushed back against the segregationist structural linguistics of Saussure and Chomsky (Bourdieu and Thompson, 1991) and Archer objected to what she perceived to be Bourdieu's social determinism, whereby subject and object (agency and structure) become 'conflated' (Archer, 2000: 172). Similarly, in the field of EAP, different theoretical approaches to literacy and language development can be understood as responses to and extensions of an ecology of approaches (Canagarajah, 2018, 2021) that have practical outcomes because they can benefit some students but not others at different points in time. For example, a student wishing to pass an IELTS test is unlikely to do so if they have been encouraged to think about academic writing as a social and transformative practice (Lea and Street, 1998; Scott and Lillis, 2007) underpinned by myriad threshold concepts (Adler-Kassner and Wardle, 2015) as opposed to becoming skilled in a particular genre, such as a five-paragraph essay (Warner, 2018). Conversely, an academic writer wishing to publish their research for an interdisciplinary and knowledgeable audience may indeed wish to engage with the broader threshold concepts that underpin academic writing rather than follow the more prescriptive advice of cognitive and skills-based approaches to writing that have influenced EAP (Flower and

Hayes, 1981; Hyland, 2016) and that can become more performative than substantial (Judd, 2003; Macfarlane, 2021b). Again, an understanding of theory, in this case academic writing theory, has practical implications (Molinari, 2022).

Whilst 'approaches to literacy and language development' are not theories per se, understood as principled approaches to action that orient our decision-making and that commit us to knowledge claims that are value-laden (Daston and Galison, 2007), they are nonetheless underpinned either implicitly or explicitly by theories which in turn affect how and whose literacy, writing, communication skills and academic language, more generally, are taught in the classroom. As Bourdieu has claimed, it is a 'particular version of language or writing' (Bourdieu and Thompson, 1991: 45; 257) that gets taught, the official and standard one, and it is somebody, somewhere who is making the decision, which is ultimately a political and ideological decision. I have made similar claims in Molinari (2022), where I show how EAP has to a large extent cherry-picked, re-invented and then reified a particular version of academic writing, one that is referred to as 'essayist' (Lillis, 1999: 131),[6] 'objective' and 'linear', and one that foregrounds the scientific or 'experimental' genre (Bazerman, 1988, 2015) rather than other literacy canons (such as creative non-fiction or ethnographic prose). This labelling betrays epistemological and ontological values, also known as epistemic virtues and vices, and it comes at the expense of other ways of writing academically that do not conflate the form of writing with what that form is a proxy for. What I mean by this is that if writing is understood as a method of enquiry (Richardson and St. Pierre, 2005) rather than a skill (Turner, 2018: 159), it is essentially a proxy for the reality it is investigating (in the same way that a microscope or a questionnaire are methods for representing reality). As a method of enquiry, writing becomes a mediating and mediated conduit for the reality it is describing and as such, by definition, it can never be 'objective' (because it needs a writer, a subject) or 'linear' (because the reality it is describing is complex, 'messy' (Law, 2003, 2004) and 'recursive' (Palmeri, 2012; Richardson, 1997). Theory, in this sense, affects practice because it alters what and how we teach. My intention in singling out theories of academic writing is not to foreground one or other approach but to simply draw attention to a point of principle about the theory–practice dialectic: in writing theory and practice, one possible outcome of our theoretical approaches is a commitment, in the case outlined above, to the belief that the language we use to describe what we do or what things are is never 'neutral' or 'objective' (Bourdieu and Thompson,

---

[6] See also Tuck, Jackie in this volume.

1991: 40) and that what we do in the classroom is necessarily at the expense of an alternative. And crucially, alternatives can only be known and understood through scholarly engagement.

By being an explicitly knowledge-oriented theory, CR embraces complexity. It seeks to understand our agencies within this complexity and to adopt an open, arguably more humble and patient, disposition to the totality of knowledge that we both have and don't have but that we need to make sense of complex phenomena such as EAP.

Relevance of critical realism to EAP

I have alluded to the relevance of CR to EAP at several points in the above discussion. In particular, I mentioned that CR describes complex social phenomena, like EAP, in terms of a stratified ontology and that agency, whether individual or collective, operates by locating the levers of change that make it possible to transform the different strata of reality. I have also mentioned that CR's preferred method of enquiry is retroductive rather than predictive (because reality is non-linear (Molinari, 2021: 58–60) and that it favours abductive reasoning that requires judgemental rationality and a transfactual methodology. In this final section I attempt to exemplify how it helps understand EAP as a complex open system whose identity can change.

Introductions to Roy Bhaskar's stratified ontology that seem to me accessible and relevant to the EAP context can be found in Fryer (2020), in Mirzaei Rafe et al. (2020), throughout Boughey and McKenna (2021) and in Chapter 4 of Molinari (2022). In short, a stratified ontology in CR is composed of three domains of reality. This tiered classification is designed to capture the fact that some things are ontologically real and others are epistemologically real (Fryer, 2020):

1. The EMPIRICAL[7] is epistemologically and transitively real. It is the domain where things happen, where we observe events and experience life as it appears to us. My own personal experience of EAP takes place here as do my values, preferred methods of enquiry, understandings of academic writing, etc. These are all real, but they are subjectively and relatively real. This domain can be understood as the micro-level.

---

[7] I have capitalized technical nomenclature (EMPIRICAL, ACTUAL and REAL) to signal that these are used in critical realism to explain stratified ontology and to distinguish them from everyday use.

2. The ACTUAL is also epistemologically and transitively real. It is the domain where events may or may not take place. Different approaches to EAP are located in this domain, ones that I may or may not have experienced but that are nonetheless real as well as possible. They may not exist, yet, but could. The actual is also relatively real because it is where events are manifest, whether we are aware of them or not. For example, the entire range of theories of academic writing are located at this level, including those that still don't exist, but are possible. This domain can be understood as the meso-level.
3. The REAL is ontologically and intransitively real. It is the domain of deep structures and mechanisms that explain the ACTUAL and the EMPIRICAL. These structures and mechanisms are often invisible and always enduring. They include policies and laws that explain why students pay university fees, why there is a gender and ethnic pay gap or a glass ceiling preventing social mobility. The REAL affects the other two domains and can be understood as the macro-level.

Hopefully, this rendering of what is meant by a CR-stratified ontology suffices to now understand where agency – understood as the judgemental rationality that all humans have – might locate the levers of change to transform reality. Based on the above (admittedly oversimplified rendering of a highly complex theory), transformative agency is far more likely to have impact at the levels of the ACTUAL and EMPIRICAL where reality is transitive, namely where it can change. However, it is only through deep knowledge of the structures and mechanisms at the level of the REAL, that agents can retroductively make sense of both their own experiences (EMPIRICAL) and those of others (ACTUAL). In the context of EAP, such deep knowledge comes through engagement in the scholarship of teaching and learning (Braxton et al., 2002; Hutchings and Shulman, 1999) which, as Ding and Bruce (2017: 111) argue 'involves activities relating to developing and refining one's overall knowledge of practice in EAP'. In a stratified ontology, that 'overall knowledge' is dialectically located across all three domains but ontologically situated in the REAL. What this means is that nobody can have access to all knowledge (this is located in the REAL and includes the totality of past, present and future interdisciplinary reality), but all agents can, within their contexts and the affordances of their structures, potentially interact with this knowledge.

To highlight why an understanding of critical realist theory matters to the transformations of the field of EAP, I return to the fractured identities of the field broached earlier in this chapter and exposed more fully in Ding and Bruce (2017) and Davis (2019). Essentially, what these scholars have foregrounded is the field's reluctance to engage with deep knowledge and that this reluctance is leading to its academic marginalization (Ding and Bruce 2017: 107). This reluctance is aptly captured by Davis' Practitioner F, who claims (Davis, 2019: 78):

> All EAP professionals would like to say we are a profession, but you are not encouraged […]. I find that contradictory really. The message from the department is 'it isn't your job to research, this isn't what you are employed to do … this does not benefit the ELC so you're not getting any time for that.

Interestingly, the claim that publishing 'does not benefit' EAP is spectacularly contradicted in the marketing of EAP, whereby some EAP units explicitly arrogate and derive their academic status from the scholarship of others whilst simultaneously not investing in their own of (see, for example, claims by EAP managers, who themselves don't contribute to scholarship, that '84% of *our* research is world-leading' (emphasis added)).[8]

A critical realist retroductive analysis – from the macro to the micro – can provide a transfactual explanatory account of these fractious contradictions by highlighting the stratified ontologies from which they emerge as well as their potential levers of change:

1. At the REAL macro-level of analysis, engaging with the purpose and remit of EAP (as outlined earlier) might reveal that, historically, EAP remains associated with ELT (Campion, 2016) and the ideology of English as a capitalist economic imperative of 'soft power' (British Council, 2018; O'Regan, 2021). This knowledge has implications for change at the meso- and micro-level rather than at this macro-level.
2. What emerges at the ACTUAL and manifest meso-level is that, on the whole, EAP is not seen as nor does it see itself as anything other than a service industry (Davis, 2019; Ding and Bruce, 2017). This doesn't mean it can't become Other, such as an emerging field of research, simply that the deep structures that spawned it remain real for many in the sector. The fact that there is a growing community of EAP scholars affords the potential levers of change needed to transform EAP at the micro-level.
3. At the EMPRICAL micro-level, EAP, and its cognate field of internationalization of higher education, is experienced as a 'cash-cow' (Mittelmeier and Lomer, 2021). The implications of this for pedagogy include knowledge-poor writing pedagogies that remain focused on

---

[8] Source: https://www.elgazette.com/university-meets-the-challenge/.

grammatical accuracy and transferable skills (Hyland, 2016: 146–7; 151) whereby 'what's going on in practice in the many EAP pre-sessional and in-sessional classes around the world' (Jenkins, 2016: 122) discords with what is touted in publications that claim to be moving beyond 'narrow templates of academic writing' (Jenkins, 2016). Knowledge of and access to the ACTUAL meso-level provides levers of change needed to transform the micro-level.

Transformative agencies operate dialectically across the three domains but change is more likely to occur at the micro- and meso-level.

Concluding implications for theory and practice

By introducing critical realism to the field of EAP, my aim has been to contribute to a collective understanding of the transformative and generative affordances of theories of social change. Critical realism distinguishes itself from other theories because it disambiguates structure and agency within an explicit realist ontology that nevertheless acknowledges relative and subjective epistemologies. It achieves this by advancing a retroductive and non-deterministic view of history that seeks to explain events as emerging phenomena whose multiple causes cannot be understood in isolation from the human choices that generate the macro (REAL), meso (ACTUAL) and micro (EMPIRICAL) levels of reality. It is for this reason that CR can provide a conceptual and practical toolkit to counter deterministic and anti-humanist refrains that tend to defer to 'the powers that be' rather than adopt more agentic dispositions (Litzenberg, 2020) that can transform EAP across its three domains, including the micro-level, where we experience the day-to-dayness of our practices.

Specifically, I have suggested that an interdisciplinary approach to EAP, one that through scholarship can draw on the deep knowledge base of cognate and non-cognate fields at the macro-level (such as philosophies of social science), can foster such critical dispositions.

References

Ablowitz, R. (1939), 'The Theory of Emergence', *Philosophy of Science*, 6 (1): 1–16. Retrieved from http://www.jstor.org/stable/184327.

Adler-Kassner, L. and E. A. Wardle, eds (2015), *Naming What We Know: Threshold Concepts of Writing Studies*, Colorado: Utah State University Press.

Alderson, D. and R. Spencer, eds (2017), *For Humanism: Explorations in Theory and Politics*, London: Pluto Press.
Archer, M. (1998), *Critical Realism: Essential Readings*, London: Routledge.
Archer, M. (2000), *Being Human: The Problem of Agency*, New York: Cambridge University Press.
Arendt, H. (1953), 'Ideology and Terror: A Novel Form of Government', *The Review of Politics*, 15 (3): 303–27. Available online: http://www.jstor.org/stable/1405171.
Ashwin, P. (2020), *Transforming University Education: A Manifesto*, London: Bloomsbury.
Baber, Z. (1995), 'The New Production of Knowledge: The Dynamics of Science and Research in Contemporary Societies., Michael Gibbons, Camille Limoges, Helga Nowotny, Simon Schwartzman, Peter Scott, Martin Trow', *Contemporary Sociology*, 24 (6): 751–2. DOI: 10.2307/2076669.
Barnett, R. (2012), *The Future University: Ideas and Possibilities*, New York: Routledge.
Bazerman, C. (1988), *Shaping Written Knowledge: The Genre and Activity of the Experimental Article in Science*, Madison, WI: University of Wisconsin Press.
Bazerman, C. (2015), 'Social Changes in Science Communication: Rattling the Information Chain', in A. G. Gross and J. Ruehl (eds), *Science and the Internet: Communicating Knowledge in a Digital Age*, 267–81, Amityville, USA: Baywood Publishing Company Inc.
Bernard-Donals, M. F. (1998), *The Practice of Theory: Rhetoric, Knowledge, and Pedagogy in the Academy*, Cambridge: Cambridge University Press.
Besley, T. A. and M. A. Peters (2013), *Re-imagining the Creative University for the 21st Century*, ed. T. A. Besley and M. Peters, Rotterdam: Sense Publishing.
Bhaskar, R. (1979), *The Possibility of Naturalism: A Philosophical Critique of the Contemporary Human Sciences*, Atlantic Highlands, NJ: Humanities Press.
Bhaskar, R. (1989), *Reclaiming Reality: A Critical Introduction to Contemporary Philosophy*, London: Verso.
Bhaskar, R. (1998), *The Possibility of Naturalism: A Philosophical Critique of the Contemporary Human Sciences*, 3rd edn, London; New York: Routledge.
Bond, B. (2020), *Making Language Visible in the University: English for Academic Purposes and Internationalisation*, Bristol, UK: Channel View Publications.
Boughey, C. (2013). 'The Significance of Structure, Culture and Agency in Efforts to Support and Develop Student Learning at South African Universities', in R. Dunpath and R. Vithal (eds), *Access and Success in Higher Education*, 41–9, Cape Town: Pearson Educational.
Boughey, C. and S. McKenna (2021), *Understanding Higher Education: Alternative Perspectives*, Cape Town: African Minds.
Bourdieu, P. and J. B. Thompson (1991), *Language and Symbolic Power*, Cambridge: Polity.
Braxton, J., W. Luckey, and P. Helland (2002), *Institutionalizing a Broader View of Scholarship through Boyer's Four Domains. ASHE-ERIC Higher Education Report. Jossey-Bass Higher and Adult Education Series*, Washington, DC: ERIC

Clearinghouse on Higher Education. https://eric.ed.gov/?q=digest&pg=234&id=ED469447

British Council, B. (2018), *The Future Demand for English in Europe: 2025 and beyond*. Available online: https://www.britishcouncil.org/sites/default/files/future_demand_for_english_in_europe_2025_and_beyond_british_council_2018.pdf.

Brown, A., S. Fleetwood, and J. M. Roberts (2001), *Critical Realism and Marxism*, New York: Routledge.

Campion, G. (2016), '"The Learning Never Ends": Exploring Teachers' Views on the Transition from General English to EAP', *Journal of English for Academic Purposes*, 23: 59–70. DOI: https://doi.org/10.1016/j.jeap.2016.06.003.

Canagarajah, S. (2018), 'Materializing "Competence": Perspectives from International STEM Scholars', *The Modern Language Journal*, 102 (2): 268–91. DOI: https://doi.org/10.1111/modl.12464.

Canagarajah, S. (2021), *Negotiating Norms in Academic Writing [Lecture]*. Stockholm University (online).

Carmichael-Murphy, P. (2021), 'It's Time to Decolonise the Doctoral Degree'. Available online: https://wonkhe.com/blogs/its-time-to-decolonise-the-doctoral-degree/.

Case, J. M. (2013), *Researching Student Learning in Higher Education: A Social Realist Approach*, London: Routledge.

Chalmers, D. J. (2006), 'Strong and Weak Emergence', in P. Clayton and P. Davies (eds), *The Re-emergence of Emergence: The Emergentist Hypothesis from Science to Religion*, 244–54, Oxford: Oxford University Press.

Collier, A. (1994), *Critical Realism: An Introduction to Roy Bhaskar's Philosophy*, London: Verso.

Collini, S. (2012), *What Are Universities for?* London: Penguin.

Connell, R. (2019), *The Good University: What Universities Actually Do and Why Its Time for Radical Change*, 1st edn, London: Zed Books.

Dall'Alba, G. (2012), 'Re-imagining the University: Developing a Capacity to Care', in R. Barnett (ed.), *The Future University: Ideas and Possibilities*, 112–22, New York: Routledge.

Daston, L. and P. Galison (2007), *Objectivity*, New York: Zone Books.

Davis, M. (2019), 'Publishing Research as an EAP Practitioner: Opportunities and Threats', *Journal of English for Academic Purposes*, 39: 72–86. DOI: https://doi.org/10.1016/j.jeap.2019.04.001.

de Sousa Santos, B. (2017), *Decolonising the University: The Challenge of Deep Cognitive Justice*, Newcastle-upon-Tyne: Cambridge Scholars Publishing.

Ding, A. and I. Bruce (2017), *The English for Academic Purposes Practitioner: Operating on the Edge of Academia*, in P. Macmillan (ed.), Palgrave Macmillan.

Donati, P. and M. Archer (2015), *The Relational Subject*, Cambridge: Cambridge University Press.

Fitzmaurice, M. (2010), 'Considering Teaching in Higher Education as a Practice', *Teaching in Higher Education*, 15 (1): 45–55. DOI: 10.1080/13562510903487941.

Fletcher, A. J. (2017), 'Applying Critical Realism in Qualitative Research: Methodology Meets Method', *International Journal of Social Research Methodology*, 20 (2): 181–94. DOI:10.1080/13645579.2016.1144401.

Flower, L. and J. R. Hayes (1981), 'A Cognitive Process Theory of Writing', *College Composition and Communication*, 32 (4): 365–87.

Fryer, T. (2020), 'A Short Guide to Ontology and Epistmeology: Why Everyone Should be a Critical Realist'. tryer.com/ontology-guide.

Hamilton, M. and K. Pitt (2009), 'Creativity in Academic Writing: Escaping from the Straightjacket of Genre', in A. Carter, T. Lillis, and S. Parkin (eds), *Why Writing Matters: Issues of Access and Identity in Writing Research and Pedagogy*, 61–79, Amsterdam: John Benjamins Publishing Company.

Helms-Park, R. and P. Stapleton (2003), 'Questioning the Importance of Individualised Voice in Undergraduate L2 Argumentative Writing: An Empirical Study with Pedagogical Implications', *Journal of Second Language Writing*, 12: 245–65.

Hutchings, P. and L. Shulman (1999), 'The Scholarship of Teaching: New Elaborations, New Developments. Change', *Change*, 31 (5): 10–15. Available online: http://www.jstor.org/stable/40165542.

Hyland, K. (2006), *English for Academic Purposes: An Advanced Resource Book*, Abingdon: Routledge.

Hyland, K. (2016), *Teaching and Researching Writing*, 3rd edn, Abingdon: Routledge.

Jenkins, J. (2016), 'Correspondence from Jennifer Jenkins', *English Language Teaching Journal*, 70 (1): 122. DOI: 10.1093/elt/ccv063.

Judd, D. (2003), *Critical Realism and Composition Theory*, London: Routledge.

Kamler, B. and P. Thomson (2006), *Helping Doctoral Students Write: Pedagogies for Supervision*, London: Routledge.

Knorr Cetina, K., T. R. Schatzki, and E. von Savigny, eds (2001), *The Practice Turn in Contemporary Theory*, London: Routledge.

Kuhn, L. (2008), 'Complexity and Educational Research: A Critical Reflection', *Educational Philosophy and Theory*, 40 (1): 177–89. DOI: 10.1111/j.1469-5812.2007.00398.x.

Law, J. (2003), 'Making a Mess with Method'. 1–12. Available online: https://www.lancaster.ac.uk/fass/resources/sociology-online-papers/papers/law-making-a-mess-with-method.pdf.

Law, J. (2004), *After Method: Mess in Social Science Research*, London: Routledge.

Lea, M. and B. Street (1998), 'Student Writing in Higher Education: An Academic Literacies Approach', *Studies in Higher Education*, 23 (2): 157–72.

Lillis, T. (1999), 'Whose "Common Sense"? Essayist Literacy and the Institutional Practice of Mystery', in C. Jones, J. Turner and B. V. Street (eds), *Students Writing in the University: Cultural and Epistemological Issues*, 127–47, Amsterdam; Philadelphia: John Benjamins Pub.

Lillis, T. (2001), *Student Writing: Access, Regulation, Desire*, London: Routledge.

Lillis, T., K. Harrington, M. R. Lea and S. Mitchell, eds (2015), *Working with Academic Literacies: Case Studies towards Transformative Practices*, Colorado/South Carolina: The WAC Clearinghouse/Parlor Press.

Lillis, T. and J. Tuck (2016), 'Academic Literacies: A Critical Lens on Writing and Reading in the Academy', in K. Hyland and P. Shaw (eds), *The Routledge Handbook of English for Academic Purposes*, 30–43, Abingdon: Routledge.

Litzenberg, J. (2020), '"If I Don't Do It, Somebody Else Will": Covert Neoliberal Policy Discourses in the Decision-making Processes of an Intensive English Program', *TESOL Quarterly*, 54 (4): 823–45. DOI: https://doi.org/10.1002/tesq.563.

Macfarlane, B. (2021a), 'The Conceit of Activism in the Illiberal University', *Policy Futures in Education*, 0 (0): 14782103211003422. DOI: 10.1177/14782103211003422.

Macfarlane, B. (2021b), 'Methodology, Fake Learning, and Emotional Performativity', *ECNU Review of Education*, 0 (0): 2096531120984786. DOI: 10.1177/2096531120984786.

Mason, M. (2008a), 'Complexity Theory and the Philosophy of Education', *Educational Philosophy and Theory*, 40 (1): 4–18. DOI: 10.1111/j.1469-5812.2007.00412.x.

Mason, M. (2008b), 'What Is Complexity Theory and What Are Its Implications for Educational Change?' *Educational Philosophy and Theory*, 40 (1): 35–49. DOI: 10.1111/j.1469-5812.2007.00413.x.

Mills, C. W. (1959), *The Sociological Imagination*, New York: Oxford University Press.

Mirzaei Rafe, M., K. B. Noaparast, A. S. Hosseini, and N. Sajadieh (2020), 'An Examination of Roy Bhaskar's Critical Realism as a Basis for Educational Practice', *Journal of Critical Realism*, 20 (1): 56–71. DOI: 10.1080/14767430.2020.1807799.

Mittelmeier, J. and S. Lomer (2021), 'The Problem of Positioning International Students as Cash Cows'. Available online: https://www.hepi.ac.uk/2021/11/04/the-problem-of-positioning-international-students-as-cash-cows/.

Molinari, J. (2021), 'Re-imagining Doctoral Writings as Emergent Open Systems', in C. Badenhorst, B. Amell and J. Burford (eds), *Re-imagining Doctoral Writing*, 49–69, Colorado: The WAC Clearinghouse; University Press of Colorado.

Molinari, J. (2022), *What Makes Writing Academic: Rethinking Theory for Practice*, London: Bloomsbury.

Mulvey, B. (2021), 'Pluralist Internationalism, Global Justice and International Student Recruitment in the UK', *Higher Education*. DOI: 10.1007/s10734-021-00750-3.

Nguyen, T. T. T. (2019), 'Doctoral Writing: Are You Ready to Unlearn What You Have Learnt? Available online: https://doctoralwriting.wordpress.com/2019/09/23/doctoral-writing-are-you-ready-to-unlearn-what-you-have-learnt/.

O'Regan, J. P. (2021), *Global English and Political Economy*, Abingdon: Routledge.

Palmeri, J. (2012), *Remixing Composition: A History of Multimodal Writing Pedagogy*, Carbondale: Southern Illinois University Press.

Pennycook, A. (1996), 'Borrowing Others' Words: Text, Ownership, Memory, and Plagiarism', *TESOL Quarterly*, 30 (2): 201–30.
Peters, M. (2017), 'Manifesto for the Postcolonial University', *Educational Philosophy and Theory*: 1–7. DOI: 10.1080/00131857.2017.1388660.
Pratt, D. (2011), *Modelling Written Communication: A New Systems Approach to Modelling in the Social Sciences*, Dordrecht: Springer.
Price, L. (2014), 'Critical Realist versus Mainstream Interdisciplinarity', *Journal of Critical Realism*, 13 (1): 52–76. DOI: 10.1179/1476743013Z.00000000019.
Richardson, L. (1997), *Fields of Play: Constructing an Academic Life*, New Brunswick, NJ: Rutgers University Press.
Richardson, L. and E. A. St. Pierre (2005), 'Writing: A Method of Inquiry', in N. K. Denzin and Y. S. Lincoln (eds), *The Sage Handbook of Qualitative Research*, 3rd edn, 959–78, Thousand Oaks, CA: Sage.
Robeyns, I. and Morten, F. L. (2016), 'The Capability Approach', in Edward N. Zalta (ed.), *The Stanford Encyclopedia of Philosophy* (Winter 2021 Edition), https://plato.stanford.edu/archives/win2021/entries/capability-approach/.
Rose, M. (1984), *Writer's Block: The Cognitive Dimension*, Carbondale: Southern Illinois University Press.
Said, E. W. (1994), *Representations of the Intellectual: The 1993 Reith Lectures*, London: Vintage.
Sawyer, R. K. (2001), 'Emergence in Sociology: Contemporary Philosophy of Mind and Some Implications for Sociological Theory', *American Journal of Sociology*, 107 (3): 551–85. Available online: http://iscte.pt/~jmal/mcc/Keith_Sawyer_Emergence_in_Sociology.pdf.
Scott, M. (2013), *A Chronicle of Learning: Voicing the Text*, Tilburg: University of Tilburg.
Scott, M. and T. Lillis (2007), 'Defining Academic Literacies Research: Issues of Epistemology, Ideology and Strategy', *Journal of Applied Linguistics*, 4 (1): 5–32.
Sperlinger, T., J. McLellan, and R. Pettigrew (2018), *Who Are Universities for?: Re-making Higher Education*, Bristol: Bristol University Press.
Thesen, L. and L. Cooper, eds (2013), *Risk in Academic Writing: Postgraduate Students, Their Teachers and the Making of Knowledge*, Bristol: Multilingual Matters.
Turner, J. (2010), *Language in the Academy: Cultural Reflexivity and Intercultural Dynamics*, Bristol: Multilingual Matters.
Turner, J. (2018), *On Writtenness: The Cultural Politics of Academic Writing*, 1st edn, London: Bloomsbury Academic.
Vico, G. (1959 (1725, 1730, 1744, 1928)), *La scienza nuova*, Rizzoli, Milano: Letteratura italiana Einaudi.
Warner, J. (2018), *Why They Can't Write: Killing the Five-paragraph Essay and Other Necessities*, Baltimore: Johns Hopkins University Press.
Warnock, M. (1989), *Universities: Knowing Our Minds: What the Government Should be Doing about Higher Education in*, London: Chatto & Windus Ltd.

7

Bourdieu and field analysis: EAP and its practitioners

Alex Ding

Introduction

The most fundamental underlying principle at work in Bourdieu's vast oeuvre is 'the quest to reveal the sacred as profane' (Maton, 2005: 102). Throughout his many books and articles, inter alia, *Homo Academicus* (1998a), *Distinction* (1984), *Pascalian Meditations* (2000) and *The State Nobility* (1996), there is, as Maton (2005) observes, a 'project [that] is a conscious drive to profanize' (Maton, 2005: 102) to bring the social and historical determinants to bear on knowledge, to place knowledge in a time and place, and to break with 'the enchanted circle of collective denial' (Bourdieu, 2000: 5) of ahistorical truths and doxas. To expose the hidden,

> sometimes leads you to 'twist the screw the other way' or to adopt a polemical or ironic tone, necessary to wake the reader from his doxic sleep.
>
> (Bourdieu, 1990: 53)

Twisting the screw the other way is 'to emphasise the truth very strongly' (Bourdieu, 2000: 173), a rhetorical strategy to wake the reader that also carries significant risks of being misunderstood. This misunderstanding is potentially compounded by translating Bourdieu across time and space without bearing in mind the national socio-political context in which Bourdieu was twisting the screw the other way. Wary of his publications becoming 'isolated asteroids' (Bourdieu, 1997: 450) torn 'from the constellation of which they are but elements' (Bourdieu, 1997) they risk becoming 'available for all manners of interpretation' (Bourdieu, 1997). Rather than twisting the screw the other way it may, at times, seem more appropriate to speak of twisting the knife.

His imposing erudition and rhetoric can hinder an engagement with Bourdieu because it can mask the central endeavour of Bourdieu; across a wide range of fields, he employs constantly modified but consistent thinking tools to reveal contingent and arbitrary symbolic forms in time and space (Maton, 2005; Webb et al., 2002). What we can take from Bourdieu, with precautions of translation from one national context to another, from one time to another, and acknowledging the risks of misunderstanding Bourdieu, is the central project of making the sacred profane and offering:

> A small chance of knowing what game we play and of minimizing the ways in which we are manipulated by the forces of the field in which we evolve ... [Sociology] allows us to discern the sites where we do indeed enjoy a degree of freedom and those where we do not.
>
> (Bourdieu and Wacquant, 1992: 198–9)

The purpose of this chapter is to provide a provisional sketch of a field analysis of English for Academic Purposes (EAP) using, primarily, Bourdieu's nexus of thinking tools: field, habitus and capital.

In considering EAP as a field, questions and issues arise requiring a writing structure that shuttles back and forth between an analytical exploration of Bourdieu's open concept of field and an investigation of the research within and beyond EAP to ascertain the specific features of the field of EAP. This shuttling back and forth will, I hope, lead to a rough mapping of the field of EAP and a clearer understanding and better deployment of the concept of field. My purpose is to focus on the field of EAP practitioners in the UK. I am not focusing on EAP globally nor EAP as a discipline, although the latter will feature in considerations of power and symbolic capital. Including the former would be difficult as any field analysis is *relational* (Bourdieu and Wacquant, 1992: 96–7) and this includes relations *within* the field as well as *beyond*, and the more *general* 'position of the field in relation to the field of power' (Bourdieu and Wacquant, 1992: 104–5), such as national economic and political fields, as well as other more *adjacent* but still *hierarchical* fields, such as higher education, and cognate disciplines and fields. The complexity of doing this on a global scale is too ambitious.

Parallel to this shuttling between field theory and relevant EAP research there is also a rhetorical purpose: to persuade practitioners that EAP needs much more reflexivity through field analysis and that this sociological gaze needs to be integral to the field and agents in EAP. The origins of this argument came from writing, with Ian Bruce, *The English for Academic Purposes Practitioner*

Operating on the Edge of Academia (Ding and Bruce, 2017). We emphasized the case throughout the book that practitioners 'need to understand the forces, theories, practices and ideologies that shape our work and lives' (Ding and Bruce, 2017: 207). We attempted to 'twist the screw the other way' to expose some of the structural forces and struggles shaping EAP practitioners' lives affecting their status, roles, positions and practices and, by doing so, provide a reflexive account of the field of EAP. And this chapter is a continuation of twisting the screw the other way.

The field of EAP

> EAP is 'a social field like any other, with its distribution of power and its monopolies, its struggles and strategies, interests and profits'.
> (Bourdieu, 1975: 19)

> To think in terms of field is to think relationally, one must see that the real is relational.
> (Bourdieu and Wacquant, 1992: 96–7)

From Bourdieu (1998b: 40–1), the characteristics of a field are: it is a structured social space; it contains agents (people and institutions) who dominate and who are dominated; the field is a permanent relationship of inequality; field agents struggle to transform or preserve the field; all agents harness the powers they have in this struggle; and power defines agents' positions in the field and their strategies.

If we start to think of EAP as a field in this way, a whole host of difficult and complex questions arise. Firstly, we must locate the field of EAP in relation to other fields, to locate the tensions *on* the field and then move to the struggles *within* the field, the latter of which 'are not pathologies that distort a field, but intrinsic to the dynamics of knowledge production and the autonomy of its fields' (Moore, 2009: 123). The question of autonomy of a field is crucial for Bourdieu (2001). A *scientific* field[1] is a 'world apart', having 'no link with social world than the social conditions that ensure their autonomy' (Bourdieu, 2001: 15) and become 'closed and separate microcosms' (Bourdieu, 2005: 7) The

---

[1] See Camic (2011) for these citations from Bourdieu and a very useful discussion of science and fields.

autonomy of fields is crucial to knowledge production and practices within a field because:

> the anarchic confrontation of individual investments and interests is transformed into rational dialogue only to the extent that the field is sufficiently autonomous (and therefore equipped with sufficiently high entry barriers) to exclude the importation of non-specific weapons, especially political or economic ones, into the internal struggles – to the extent that participants are constrained to use only instruments of discussion or proof corresponding to the scientific demands in the matter.
>
> (Bourdieu, 2000: 111–12)

However, this autonomy from external social fields is relative rather than absolute and in the case of EAP we can begin to understand that this field is lacking in autonomy, and this has profound consequences on the field, its practitioners and the struggles between agents within the field. EAP as a field has been and continues ever more intensely to be subjected to the economic and political fields where the doxa of neoliberalism, increasingly dominant in the UK and elsewhere since the 1980s, has exerted control over and transformed higher education. HE has been transformed over this period to comply with economic, political and social agendas demanded by various governments where education is seen a catalyst for economic growth and profit (Ding and Bruce, 2017: 24). Consequently, the historical (relative) autonomy of the field of HE has been reduced (decimated is perhaps nearer the truth), through the socio-political and economic fields restructuring the field of HE, by: *commercialization* of teaching, research and other activities to extract profit (Bok, 2003); *marketization* to enforce consumer choice and competition, through price and quality, to ensure innovations, cost-cutting, efficiency savings and profits (Ding, 2019; Ding and Bruce, 2017; Fosket, 2011), and to reconfigure students as consumers and education as a commodity; *managerialism*, through audits measuring and ranking institutions, disciplinary fields and academics, to regulate the HE field as a market (Radice, 2013). Universities values have been reduced to 'the values of business and industry' (Sauntson and Morrish, 2011: 83).

In turn, changes in the field of HE have structured the field of EAP. One way of constructing the history of EAP is through an internal reading of its intellectual development, focusing on key events, ideas and people; another is to focus on why EAP came about. The latter reading of the field of EAP reveals its origins and subsequent development as intertwined with the neoliberal transformation of HE. In short, the growth of EAP is due to the advent of neoliberalism in higher education and it is this that has shaped its problems within and beyond its own field. In brief, EAP in the UK emerged in the 1970s as a 'grass roots, practical response' (Hamp-Lyons, 2011a: 92) to meeting the needs of a relatively small number of 'international students'. From these modest origins in the 1970s we have witnessed an enormous expansion in the provision of EAP. This increase is entirely due to university strategies to increase the number of international students who pay significantly more for their education. EAP, for practitioners, would barely exist without neoliberal education policies and practices.

This uncomfortable truth highlights that EAP is essential to a neoliberal university but certainly not of its essence. And it means that EAP as a field has little autonomy which is vital to its establishment within HE. The field of HE, especially through the power of its agents such as senior leaders, disciplinary heads of schools, and the vast array of administrative officers and centres within universities who actively seek international students, including international offices, marketing and recruitment, constrain EAP to: be financially self-sufficient and profit-generating; attract increasing numbers of international students; operate efficiently (in business terms); and participate in marketization. This has led Hadley to describe EAP centres as 'student processing units' (Hadley, 2015: 39). As Turner puts it:

> [F]rom its outset, it [EAP] has accepted the role as an economic and intellectual short-cut .... [i]t seems that maximum throughput of students with minimum attainment levels in the language in the shortest possible time was the conceptual framework within which EAP was conceived.
> (Turner, 2004: 96–7)

While it may be true that '[t]he overt use of the international student "market" by governments to shore up the finances of universities is an embarrassment to many of us' (Hamp-Lyons, 2015: A2), it does nonetheless relegate the field of EAP to a highly dominated position within HE with consequent impacts on the various capitals its agents seek and leads to a significant number of struggles with other fields as well as struggles within the field to establish its autonomy. Autonomy, in any academic field, but especially EAP, is a quest of 'endlessly having to be undertaken anew' to achieve relative autonomy (Bourdieu, 2001: 47) as each and every field in never static with constant struggles for power and autonomy.

Readers might object at this point that the *discipline* of EAP has achieved autonomy for the field of EAP. After all, EAP 'has done a good job of consolidating a position at the forefront of language education' (Hyland, 2012: 30). *The Journal* of *English for Academic Purposes*, launched in 2002, 'was a clear indication that EAP had come of age as an independent academic field' (Hamp-Lyons, 2011a: 93). EAP is a bona fide discipline with all the 'paraphernalia of journals, monographs, conferences, and research centres: all the trappings, in fact, of a full-fledged educational practice' (Hyland, 2018: 389). However, this raises questions about whether there is complete overlap between EAP as a field of practice and EAP as a discipline, whether they are separate fields, or the fields are in the process of rupture. This will affect judgement as to what is at stake. Hamp-Lyons and Hyland both have very significant *symbolic capital* – roughly speaking a combination of other forms of capital (economic, cultural and social) – that is configured in field-specific ways to confer, by agents within the field, a legitimation, a recognition, a distinction and 'socially recognized authority to act' (Swartz, 2013: 102) upon agents in the field.

> Symbolic capital enables forms of domination which imply dependence on those who can be dominated by it, since it only exists through the esteem, recognition, belief, credit, confidence of others, and can only be perpetuated so long as it succeeds in obtaining belief in its existence.
>
> (Bourdieu, 2000: 166)

Symbolic capital provides 'a profit of distinction' and it is this symbolic capital that gives weight to pronouncements announcing the arrival of EAP as a discipline with attendant autonomy from other fields. Symbolic capital is the legitimate(d) authority to define situations.

What symbolic capital allows this pronouncement to hide or supress, in many subtle ways, through *skholè* and *epistemic doxa* is the relationship between discipline (and disciplinary practices) and practices (in the field). The positions occupied by Hamp-Lyons and Hyland at the apex of EAP, through their labours to accumulate valuable forms of cultural, social and economic capital, mean that they have skholè: they operate at a distance from the practices they are contemplating in 'time liberated from practical occupations and preoccupations' (Bourdieu, 2000: 13) of the field. Their relationship to practice modifies the *doxa* of the field:

> Each scientific universe has its specific doxa, a list of inseparably cognitive and evaluative presuppositions whose acceptance is implied in membership itself; these include the major obligatory pairs of opposites which ... unite those whom they divide, since agents have to share a common acceptance of them to be able to fight over them or through them, and so to produce [their] position takings.
>
> (Bourdieu, 2000: 100)

This modification of the *doxa* of the field calls into question the presuppositions of membership of the field and illuminates new struggles within the field. A widely accepted definition of EAP is 'the teaching of English with the specific aim of helping learners to study, conduct research or teach in that language' (Flowerdew and Peacock, 2001: 8). Three very recent large-scale, systematic historical reviews of the EAP research literature (Hyland and Jiang, 2020; Liu and Hu, 2021; Riazi et al., 2020) illuminate a shift away from this focus and emphasize a concern we articulated (Ding et al., 2022): the practitioner is 'poorly served by the EAP literature and especially by prestigious journals' (Ding et al., 2022: X); with an increasingly narrow foci within journals; an increasingly limiting/limited coverage of EAP (Bruce, 2021); and a rupture with practitioners, practice and pedagogy where claims of pedagogical implications are often unjustified (Bruce, 2021: 26), too vague (Cheng, 2019) or articles 'fade way before articulating well-articulated pedagogical applications' (Swales, 2019: 78). Practitioners and researchers in EAP are (generally) different agents in the field and researchers seek economic, cultural, social and symbolic capital through 'publishing prodigiously and prestigiously (they are often subject to the same neoliberal imperatives of performativity and metrics as in any other academic discipline)' (Ding, 2019: 73). It is researchers and those who compete for capital within the discipline of EAP who dominate those practitioners in the field who lack various capitals to compete. The doxa of the field is shaped by those with sufficient symbolic capital to define situations. This has been noted in different formulations such as: '[t]here is a danger that theory and research is outrunning practice' (Hamp-Lyons and Hyland, 2005: 30). It is less about research outrunning practice, however, and more about the *habitus* of those who occupy and compete in the field.

Before discussing agents' habitus shortly, we need to clarify what sort of field EAP might be as the two are intimately connected and reveal much about what is at stake. My first axiom is that EAP is an *ill-defined field* where the limits and boundaries of the field are very unclear. Bourdieu describes the ill-defined field as follows where

> the homology between the space of positions and the space of dispositions is never perfect and there are always some agents 'out on a limb' displaced, out of place, and ill at ease. The dissonance ..., may be the source of a disposition towards lucidity and critique which leads them to refuse as self-evident the expectations and demands of the post. The dialectic between dispositions and positions is seen most clearly in the case of positions situated in the zones of

uncertainty in social space, such as ill-defined occupations, as regards both the conditions of access and the conditions of exercise.

(Bourdieu, 2000: 157)

This encapsulates the field of EAP, not from the doxa of research(ers), but from the field of practice. Critique – or at least this sense of displacement – is visible in a number of publications that reveal uncertainty around an ill-defined occupation with consequences on practitioner habitus. Bruce (2021), Campion (2016), Davis (2019), Ding and Campion (2016), Ding and Bruce (2017), Ding (2019), Hadley (2015) and MacDonald (2016) are representative of a growing body of work that exemplifies, in different ways, the struggles to reflexivity break with 'the enchanted circle of collective denial'.

In terms of 'conditions of access' to the field EAP is unlike many academic fields where disciplinary autonomy from external fields is maintained with 'sufficiently high entry barriers' (Bourdieu, 2000: 111). Ding and Campion (2016), Ding (2019) and Ding and Bruce (2017) demonstrate that credentials to enter the field as practitioners are varied and vague and there is no specific prerequisite qualification. Many practitioners have an ELT qualification (CELTA, DELTA or MA in TESOL or Applied Linguistics) or postgraduate secondary school qualification. Relatively few have either an EAP specific qualification or a PhD. BALEAP, the UK association of EAP professionals, does not endorse the few EAP-specific qualifications that do exist. Compared to most, but not all, disciplines, EAP practitioners enter the field with little cultural capital in terms of both intellectual and academic capitals and this positions them in a highly dominated position within the larger HE field impacting their power, agency and symbolic capital.

Unlike EAP researchers, who operate in different disciplinary spaces as part of academic schools, practitioners' locations within the university reflect their dominated position within universities – 'in the zones of uncertainty in social space' (cf. MacDonald, 2016). In essence, EAP centres or units can be located in academic schools (including Business Schools), administration services such as external relations and marketing and, increasingly, externally through private providers. It is not only their location which reveals their lack of capital but also their nomenclature and contractual status (support workers, professional or teaching-only staff). Status and location of EAP practitioners reveal the most significant struggle within and with other fields, that of its purpose as that of a mercantile service serving university profit-seeking imperatives or engaging in a legitimate, recognized academic/educational endeavour (Ding and Bruce, 2017).

Heterodoxy of locations and titles extends to rewards (economic capital features here) in terms of remuneration, career development, promotions and professional stability. From without, lacking symbolic capital (recognition and legitimacy) practitioners struggle to define their practices as educational and academic against those agents in the HE field who dominate the social space in which EAP takes place and by doing so condemns EAP to the edge of academia. In response to being dominated and at the edge of academia, Ding and Bruce (2017) see engagement in scholarship and research as a means for practitioners to begin to accrue sufficient academic and intellectual capital to obtain power within EAP and the HE field.

In terms of 'the conditions of exercise' of practitioners, directors and managers of EAP, centres occupy an important if very complex position of power within HE, within EAP and over practitioners. Hadley's (2015) detailed research is an important study in which this complexity is revealed. Hadley states that managers and directors 'may present themselves as a bureaucratic entrepreneurial leader, unit protector or cutting edge academic' (Hadley, 2015: 126). Clearly, directors have greater symbolic capital than practitioners and therefore more power and status; however, the types of capital that combine to produce this symbolic capital they have vary. Because of constraints on EAP centres to be profit-generating the most significant capital they have in relation to other fields is economic as it is this which, in their subordinate position in university hierarchies, defines their success and distinction. Because directors have some symbolic power, which includes the power to define situations, economic imperatives can become overarching within EAP ensuring EAP is positioned as a service rather than academic endeavour as this is a means for directors (and others within EAP) to accrue economic capital. This struggle for economic capital also entails seeing other EAP centres as direct competitors for students and complicates relationships and exchange of information and ideas between centres and practitioners. Directors may have other types of capital, intellectual and academic, as well as social capital which can enhance their symbolic capital within HE as well as among practitioners. However, these other types of capital, especially intellectual and academic, appear no more or less present (accumulated) in directors than practitioners. They appear to contribute little to research and scholarship in EAP (Davis, 2019) and are as unlikely to have a PhD as practitioners. Their power, relative as it is dependent on their dominated position within HE, is reinforced as, unlike heads of academic schools and departments (although there are signs that this situation is changing), their role is permanent. They do not undertake this role for a fixed term and then return to the ranks; rather, they are in position permanently. This both reinforces their power over practitioners and may create conflicted loyalties, to those above them upon whom they are dependent to continue in their role, and to their colleagues and to the educational value of EAP. This symbolic power can have nefarious effects on practitioners' attempts to undertake scholarship in their pursuit of academic capital: 'lack of support or even opposition from managers and institutions is a barrier to development' (Davis, 2019: 82). Even when directors and managers are supportive, the contractual status of practitioners as 'teaching only' excludes or limits resources and time for scholarship. Whether by design, directors' fear of capital accumulation by practitioners, or constraints or combinations of these factors, practitioners are often thwarted in their pursuit of academic capital.

It is important to stress that the above is still a partial analysis of the struggles of practitioners within the field of EAP, especially in terms of accruing various forms of capital. What is needed now is an examination of the habitus of practitioners.

Practitioner habitus

Firstly, we need to return to Bourdieu's description of an ill-defined field:

> Because these posts ill-defined and ill-guaranteed but open and 'full of potential' as the phrase goes, leave their occupants the possibility of defining them by bringing the embodied necessity which is constitutive of their habitus, their future depends on what is made of them by their occupants, or at least those of them who, in the struggles with the 'profession' and in confrontations with neighbouring and rival professions, manage to impose the definition of the profession most favourable to what they are.
>
> (Bourdieu, 2000: 158)

The question of imposing definitions most favourable to practitioners reveals a further set of struggles within the field as well as questions around what exactly the habitus of practitioners is. This section will explore these questions and struggles.

Habitus is:

> a socialised body. A structured body, a body which has incorporated the immanent structures of a world or of a particular sector of that world – a field – and which structures the perception of that world as well as action in that world.
>
> (Bourdieu, 1998: 81)

Habitus is often understood as 'a principle of repetition and conservation' (Bourdieu, 2000: 159) in part because 'the responses habitus generates without calculation appear as adapted, coherent and immediately intelligible' within a field (Bourdieu, 2000). Habitus, 'perceived through categories already constructed by prior experiences' (Bourdieu and Wacquant, 1992: 133), promises a 'feel for the game', a generative principle where habitus and field align, practitioners achieve 'subjective expectations of objective probabilities' (Bourdieu, 1990: 59), and where practitioners can exercise practical mastery in their field. However, in such an ill-defined, porous and heterodox field where there is no prior socialization into the field (Ding and Campion, 2016; Ding and Bruce, 2017) and 'conditions of access' to the field are vague, habitus, on entry to the EAP field, is likely to be mismatched with the field ('between the objective structures and the incorporated structures', Bourdieu, 2000: 159).

This mismatch is likely to be compounded if practitioners were to read introductory texts to EAP (cf. Charles and Pecorari, 2015) which offer, at best, a doxa, a cracked mirror version of EAP as they all ignore the field struggles and say very little about the unwritten rules of the game. There is a small body of studies which explore transitions into EAP of which Campion's (2016) is significant. One way of reading her study, *the learning never ends*, is of a practitioner in search of apprehending the field and habitus, along with an important finding: 'There does not appear to be a magic moment where the 'novice', who is capable of very little, becomes an 'expert', with all the implied competencies and authority' (2016: 68). Alignment of field and habitus for practitioners is not a given. *Hysteresis* captures the lag and mismatch between field and habitus typical of entrants to EAP:

> The presence of the past in this kind of false anticipation of the future performed by the habitus is, paradoxically, most clearly seen when the sense of the probable future is belied and when dispositions ill-adjusted to the objective changes because of a hysteresis effect ... are negatively sanctioned because the environment they encounter is too different from the one to which they are objectively adjusted.
>
> (Bourdieu, 1990: 62)

Practitioners engage in defining the field in ways 'most favourable to what they are' and are likely to draw on their habitus as language educators (through their credentials, teaching qualifications, previous experience and as part of the definition of the field of EAP) with paradoxical consequences. Cultural capital and field boundaries are often claimed through practitioner linguistic capital (language experts) and pedagogical capital, expertise in teaching. However, the status/power of linguistic capital within the field of HE is ambiguous. In replying to a particularly virulent critique by Jenkins (1989), concerning his writing style, Bourdieu makes an important point:

> If ... Mr Jenkins had turned a reflexive gaze on his critique, he would have discovered the deeply anti-intellectual dispositions which hide themselves behind his eulogy of simplicity, and he would not have offered in such plain view the naively ethnocentric prejudices that are at the base of his denunciation of my stylistic particularism.
>
> (Bourdieu, 1992: 169)

Especially in terms of academic writing in HE, there is a fundamental *misrecognition* where 'writtenness is taken for granted' (Turner, 2018: 148) when 'expectations are met, the written materiality of the text does not count' (Turner, 2018: 147). By contrast in EAP and aligned fields, writing 'is seen as a complex amalgam of rhetorical, textual and linguistics functions, as well as a developmental process' (Turner, 2018: 149). Language in HE is invisible, taken for granted, ethnocentric prejudices abound, until there is a perceived infringement on writing doxa (clarity, 'grammar', referencing, etc.) in which case academics turn to EAP practitioners (or learning support), as the perception of EAP practitioners is of sub-academic language fixers, 'fixing up grammar in the language centre' (Hyland and Hamp-Lyons, 2002: 6), who can offer remedial support. This sustains the notion of domination – often cited as 'the butler's stance' (Raimes,1991) – and service to the disciplines as well as the notion that EAP is intellectually vacuous (Turner, 2004). Turner adds that EAP has 'colluded in its own marginalisation' (Turner, 2004: 96) through offering its 'quick fix attitude' (Turner, 2004: 92) to language development. Turner's assessment of collusion is partially true but undoing this collusion is hindered by the lack of symbolic capital of practitioners in the wider HE field to have the authority and legitimacy to redress this. This is just one reason why obtaining cultural capital, in the forms of academic and intellectual capitals through scholarship and research, is so important for practitioners.

The second example of defining the field in ways 'most favourable to what they are' is in terms of accruing cultural capital through pedagogic capital, expertise in teaching. Again, lacking in symbolic capital makes claiming this position and distinction difficult. In addition, the broader HE field has been subjected to students becoming consumers (see above) and through various metrics (such as the TEF) teaching has been under intense scrutiny where rankings in teaching are used in marketing to obtain economic capital. Because there is significant economic capital at play, there are greater rewards for agents in HE, opportunities for symbolic as well as economic capital. In investing in central services, acting as powerful institutional agents to enforce changes in teaching practices to satisfy student-customers, universities offer rewards, distinctions and power to those academic agents that undertake this mission. Therefore, these institutions attract those with greater cultural capital than practitioners to struggle over rewards and distinction. It is not unusual to have historians, chemists, engineers, or neurobiologists at the apex of power in teaching and pedagogy in HE.

Linguistic and pedagogical capital, claimed by practitioners, as part of their habitus adds to a sense of *hysteresis*. The dispositions that generate perceptions, appreciations and practices and which help constitute the field as meaningful for practitioners (and help constitute the field in turn) are complex. Habitus does not entail a rule but rather patterns or regularities and the patterns that can be seen in EAP. What is viable and visible as options within a field depends on the agents' current (objective) position within a field and the histories that practitioners bring to the field. This complexity can be seen in the relationship between practitioners and scholarship.

There has been, as we have already seen, a call for practitioners to engage in scholarship (cf. Ding et al., 2020; Davis, 2019) to accumulate greater cultural and symbolic capital both within EAP and in the field of HE. We have also seen those powerful agents within and beyond EAP, such as EAP directors or senior colleagues, do not always support and indeed can obstruct practitioner scholarship. Further, we have seen that the dominated and often service-orientated and mercantile positioning of EAP renders opportunities for scholarship difficult. Time, resources and recognition for scholarship are often in short supply. Yet, this cannot entirely explain lack of scholarship by practitioners. Some EAP centres do offer time, resources and encouragement, as well as rewards and recognition for scholarship (making this a very structured field where practitioners such as myself have considerable advantages in obtaining cultural and symbolic capital compared to colleagues working in less favourable conditions) and still many practitioners, even with favourable conditions, do not engage in scholarship at all. As the call for and opportunities for scholarship have become more insistent and available in some centres, they are nonetheless recent and one might explain the lack of scholarship through hysteresis (a lag between habitus and field changes) and perhaps we will see a *tendency,* where habitus adjusts to this field changes, for more practitioners to engage in scholarship. Although all this is highly plausible, my account may represent a *scholastic fallacy* (Bourdieu, 1990) that is this account has been developed in an *academic space* where understanding is *theoretical in nature,* 'made possible by the situation of skholè, of leisure' (Bourdieu, 1990: 381) in which we 'forbid ourselves to understand practice as such' (Bourdieu, 1990: 382). To understand practice as such, understanding the habitus of those who do not engage in scholarship is important.

Cultural capital through scholarship is not the only route to obtain relative power and distinction. A habitus formed through teaching, teaching credentials and through a field which 'prides itself on its applied nature' (Hamp-Lyons and Hyland, 2005: 30) – one could add, pragmatic nature – has a history, an orthodoxy, where economic capital in particular can be obtained through course leadership, marketing and attending to business activities, and developing a range of skills in, for example, digital technology, assessment and testing, and materials development. EAP, as a practice, is unusual in academic fields in that often practitioners work in teams, teaching to a standardized syllabus with materials, under the direction of a course leader. The practices of EAP often favour those who see opportunities in these areas. No demonstration of expertise through scholarship to undertake these roles is required. These opportunities for economic capital, because of the practitioners' position in the field and their attendant habitus in teaching, will predispose them to practices that seek/confer distinction in these areas and to 'impose the definition of the profession most favourable to what they are' (Bourdieu, 2000: 158) to conserve this doxa. The increasing emphasis on scholarship in EAP, at least in the ideational domain but also through practical effects such as promotion, can be viewed as an insertion of *heterodoxy* into the field, a challenge to historical practices in EAP and a potential redistribution of power, distinction, and economic and cultural capital. Practitioners that have a habitus attuned to a field that has afforded them some rewards in historical, orthodox ways will tend to feel ill-equipped to compete for cultural capital (their prior education and subsequent experience of teaching EAP have not prepared them for scholarship nor to make it visible to them as a viable option in the field) and some are likely to struggle against this heterodox insertion through asserting other values and practices that diminish scholarship. This may include a rejection of a more academic identity through asserting their pedagogical and linguistic capitals (defining themselves as expert language teachers), through aligning with business and neoliberal doxa (defining themselves as working in an 'industry' with all that this implies), and/or through a dismissal of scholarship (where theory is suspicious, research/scholarship irrelevant and experience priceless).

Final remarks: Limitations, criticisms and contributions

This chapter is an attempt, in a highly provisional way, to think *with* Bourdieu, to think with his nexus of thinking tools, to sketch a rough draft of a highly partial map of the field of EAP by paying particular attention to some of the struggles within EAP and upon EAP. It is partial and incomplete but will be extended and refined in further research. It can also be read as a provocation 'to emphasise the truth very strongly' (Bourdieu, 2000: 173) or less charitably but equally plausibly as an attempt 'to impose the definition of the profession most favourable to what [I am]' (Bourdieu, 2000: 158).

Bourdieu's 'work can now evoke an almost religious fervour in both support and denunciation' (Maton, 2005: 101). There is a formidable chorus (howl?) of critics of Bourdieu's work, and I do not intend to consider much of their varied criticisms in any detail. Instead, I would like to very briefly focus on two sets of critiques that practitioners reading this chapter might agree with.

The first is a knot of criticisms relating to Bourdieu's alleged determinism where field and habitus collude in social reproduction and his 'model of social practice remains fundamentally determinist' (Jenkins, 1989: 642). 'Bourdieu seems unable to keep himself from affirming determinism "in the last instance"' (Alexander, 1995: 140) where

> changes ... always come from outside of the actor (Jenkins, 1992: 83) who, as a prisoner of his own socially conditioned habitus (King, 2000: 427), is no more than a passive reflection of macro-scale social changes being pushed and pulled around as charged particles in a magnetic field.
>
> (Faber, 2017: 442)

It is true that Bourdieu does tend to focus on reproduction as a 'means of a deliberate (and provisional) reductionism' (Bourdieu, 1988: 1). Even so, I hope to have shown in discussions of habitus and field that there is nothing inherently *deterministic* in Bourdieu. It is a result, I think, of a misreading of habitus and field and to forget that Bourdieu searched for patterns, regularities and tendencies, not cast-iron rules. He is interested in probability and his writing is littered with caveats. For example, in *Outline of a Theory of Practice* there are 121 occurrences of the word stem and inflections of 'tend' and 217 occurrences in *Distinction*. Hardly, fatalist nor determinist. And Bourdieu is quite clear on this and why revealing tendencies can work to undo them:

> The fatalism of the probable, which is the principle of ideological use of statistics, makes it forget that the knowing of what is the most probable also contribute

to make less likely things happen. The science of tendencies inherent to the structure is a precondition of the success of the realisation of less likely political actions which have to play on the whole structure in order to make less likely scenarios happen.

(Bourdieu and Boltanski, 1976: 5)

The politics of Bourdieu, following a deterministic reading of habitus and field, is also under attack:

What we are left with is a theory of reproduction that displays little faith in subordinate classes and groups and little hope in their ability or willingness to reconstruct the conditions under which they live, work, and learn.

(Giroux, 1983: 274)

The eminent French philosopher, Rancière, has also undermined Bourdieu, as part of a collective, where they critique Bourdieu as follows: 'The orphaned fervour of denouncing the system with the disenchanted certitude of its perpetuity' (Collective, 1984: 7). Both Giroux and Rancière share (Rancière's arguments against Bourdieu are generally more sophisticated) the perspective that Bourdieu's work is politically useless. Rancière (cf. 2012) reads Bourdieu as the sociologist replacing Plato's philosopher king, the one who has wisdom over the 'presumed naivete or ignorance of its object of study' (Ross, 1991: xi) and the science of sociology, in Bourdieu, becomes 'the position of eternal denouncer of a system granted the ability to hide itself forever from its agents' (Ross, 1991: xii). We are all dupes. Bourdieu's concepts are difficult to grasp, and sociology offers a position and habitus to see the world in particular ways but, with effort, they are available to us too. As a practitioner, not a sociologist, I – however fallibly – have started to operate with a sociological eye.

As for Giroux's critique, this says more, I think, about critical pedagogies (and some adjacent movements such as social justice) that balk at an admittedly often disillusioned worldview where they tend to place too much hope and emphasis on a reductionist social theory 'that speaks of change only as an effect of socially transformative agendas' (Guillory, 1997: 370).

The final point I want to make regards reception of Bourdieu's writing style. Below are some illustrative comments:

What is really being communicated is the great man's distinction. It's a bit like an intellectual penis-sheath: it makes a point, but only concealing the true dimension of its contents.

(Jenkins, 1989: 642)

> The language of the book contains some of the worst excesses of academy-speak which continually prompt the desire ... to put the book down and turn to something more profitable.
>
> (Luntley, 1992: 448)

> it is written in language so obscurantist, so dense and so ugly that the effort of reading the damn thing will probably, for most readers ... heavily outweigh any benefit.
>
> (Jenkins, 1989: 643)

Not only is his style dire but he, apparently, commits other sins such as 'appropriating the ideas of opponents without recognition' (Burawoy, 2018: 21) and 'becomes the source of his own genius' (Burawoy, 2018).

Unsurprisingly, Bourdieu is fully aware of criticisms of his writing style (cf. 'the style of this book, whose long sentences may offend ...' (Bourdieu, 1984: xv)) and is fully in control of his writing. Bourdieu is not trying to make his writing 'clear and simple' (Bourdieu, 1990: 53) as this is dangerous because 'false clarity is often part and parcel of the dominant discourse' (Bourdieu, 1990) where '[c]onservative language always falls back on the authority of common sense' (Bourdieu, 1990). He has much more to say about his writing but his arguments for writing as he does rest on scientific and political justifications and largely in an attempt not to be misunderstood and to stop his texts from being 'deformed and simplifying things' (Bourdieu, 1990: 52). Simeoni (2000) offers a far more sympathetic account of Bourdieu's writing style employing Halliday to claim that, in Bourdieu, there is a 'formal correspondence between the *way* things are said and *what* is being said' (Simeoni, 2000: 75) and that to avoid misunderstandings and keeping his writing coherent has 'entailed a very personal, sophisticated, highly charged style of writing' (Simeoni, 2000: 79). With the somewhat startling conclusion that his style is 'uncannily informed with orality. He is best read aloud' (Simeoni, 2000). Perhaps less startling if you take into account that his whole oeuvre is about '... saying out loud to everyone what no one wants to know' (Bourdieu, 2008: 112).

These criticisms of Bourdieu's writing style and his explanation of why he wrote as he did provide the practitioner, as they read Bourdieu, an opportunity to confront many of the simplistic doxas that still prevail in teaching academic writing around, for example, clarity, referencing, complexity, form and content, the hidden aesthetic and ethno-centric assumptions around good writing, and the responsibility of the reader to make sense of a text among many others.

In writing about his writing, it seems fitting to conclude this chapter with a minimal hope of what this chapter has achieved:

> If people at least come away with the feeling that it *is* complicated, that's already a good lesson to have learnt.
>
> (Bourdieu, 1990: 52)

References

Alexander, J. C. (1995), *Fin de Siecle Social Theory: Relativism, Reduction, and the Problem of Reason*, London: Verso.

Bok, D. (2003), *Universities in the Marketplace: The Commercialization of Higher Education*, Princeton: Princeton University Press.

Bond, B. (2020), *Making Language Visible in the University*, Clevedon: Multilingual Matters.

Bourdieu, P. (1975), 'The Specificity of the Scientific Field and the Social Conditions of the Progress of Reason', *Social Science Information*, 14 (6): 19–47.

Bourdieu, P. (1977), *Outline of a Theory of Practice*, Cambridge: Cambridge University Press.

Bourdieu, P. (1984), *Distinction*, Abingdon: Routledge.

Bourdieu, P. (1988), 'On Interest and the Relative Autonomy of Symbolic Power', Working Papers and Proceedings of the Center for Psychosocial Studies No. 20, Chicago Center for Psychosocial Studies.

Bourdieu, P. (1988a), *Homo Academicus*, Cambridge: Polity Press.

Bourdieu, P. (1998b), *On Television and Journalism*, London: Pluto Press.

Bourdieu, P. (1990), *In Other Words: Essays towards a Reflexive Sociology*, Cambridge: Polity Press.

Bourdieu, P. (1996), *The State Nobility*, Cambridge: Polity Press.

Bourdieu, P. (1997), 'Passport to Duke', *Metaphilosophy*, 28 (1): 449–55.

Bourdieu, P. (1998), *Practical Reason*, Cambridge: Polity Press.

Bourdieu, P. (2000), *Pascalian Meditations*, Cambridge: Polity Press.

Bourdieu, P. (2001), *Science of Science and Reflexivity*, Cambridge: Polity Press.

Bourdieu, P. (2008), *Sketch for a Self-analysis*, Cambridge: Polity Press.

Bourdieu, P. (2005), *The Social Structures of the Economy*, Cambridge: Polity Press.

Bourdieu, P. and L. Boltanski (1976), 'La Production de l'idéologie Dominante', *Actes de la Recherche en Sciences Sociales*, 2 (2): 3–73.

Bourdieu, P. and L. J. D. Wacquant (1992), *An Invitation to Reflexive Sociology*, Cambridge: Polity Press.

Bruce, I. (2021), 'Towards an EAP without Borders: Developing Knowledge, Practitioners, and Communities', *International Journal of English for Academic Purposes*, Spring: 23–36.

Burawoy, M. (2018), 'Making Sense of Bourdieu: From Demolition to Recuperation and Critique', *Catalyst*, 2 (1): 51–87.
Camic, C. (2011), 'Bourdieu's Cleft Sociology of Science', *Minerva*, 49: 275–93.
Campion, G. C. (2016), 'The Learning Never Ends': Exploring Teachers' Views on the Transition from General English to EAP', *Journal of English for Academic Purposes*, 23: 59–70.
Charles, M. and D. Pecorari (2015), *Introducing English for Academic Purposes*, Abingdon: Routledge.
Cheng, A. (2019), 'Examining the "Applied Aspirations" in the ESP Genre Analysis of Published Journal Articles', *Journal of English for Academic Purposes*, 38: 36–47.
Collective (1984), 'L'Empire du Sociologue', *Révoltes Logiques*, 7.
Davis, M. (2019), 'Publishing Research as an EAP Practitioner: Opportunities and Threats', *Journal of English for Academic Purposes*, 39: 72–86.
Ding, A. (2019), 'EAP Practitioner Identity', in K. Hyland and L. L. C. Wong (eds), *Specialised English: New Directions in ESP and EAP Research and Practice*, 63–75, Abingdon: Routledge.
Ding, A. and G. Campion (2016), 'EAP Teacher Development', in K. Hyland and P. Shaw (eds), *The Routledge Handbook of English for Academic Purposes*, 547–59, Abingdon: Routledge.
Ding, A. and I. Bruce (2017), *The English for Academic Purposes Practitioner: Operating on the Edge of Academia*, Basingstoke: Palgrave.
Ding, A., B. Bond, and I. Bruce (2022), 'Clearly You Have Nothing Better to Do with Your Time than This: A Critical Historical Exploration of Practitioners', Discussions on the BALEAP Mailing List. *Journal of English for Academic Purposes*.
Faber, A. (2017), 'From False Premises to False Conclusions: On Pierre Bourdieu's Alleged Sociological Determinism', *The American Sociologist*, 48: 436–52.
Flowerdew, J. and M. Peacock (2001), *Research Perspectives on English for Academic Purposes*, Cambridge: Cambridge University Press.
Fosket, N. (2011), 'Markets, Government, Funding and the Marketisation of UK Higher Education', in M. Molesworth, R. Scullion and E. Nixon (eds), *The Marketisation of Higher Education and the Student as Consumer*, 25–38, Abingdon: Routledge.
Guillory, J. (1997), 'Bourdieu's Refusal', *Modern Language Quarterly*, 58 (4): 367–98.
Giroux, H. A. (1983), 'Theories of Reproduction and Resistance in the New Sociology of Education: A Critical Analysis', *Harvard Educational Review*, 53 (3): 257–93.
Hadley, G. (2015), *English for Academic Purposes in Neoliberal Universities: A Critical Grounded Theory*, Heidelberg: Springer.
Hamp-Lyons, L. (2011a), 'English for Academic Purposes', in E. Hinkel (ed.), *Handbook of Research in Second Language Teaching and Learning*, 89–105, vol. 2, New York: Routledge.
Hamp-Lyons, L. (2011b), 'English for Academic Purposes: 2011 and beyond', *Journal of English for Academic Purposes*, 10: 2–4.
Hamp-Lyons, L. (2015), 'The Future of Jeap and EAP', *Journal of English for Academic Purposes*, 20: A1–A4.

Hamp-Lyons, L. and K. Hyland (2005), 'Some Further Thoughts on EAP and JEAP', *Journal of English for Academic Purposes*, 4: 1–4.

Hyland, K. (2012), 'The Past Is the Future with the Lights On: Reflections on AELFE's 20th Birthday', *Iberica*, 42: 29–42.

Hyland, K. (2018), 'Sympathy for the Devil? A Defence of EAP', *Language Teaching*, 51 (3): 383–99.

Hyland, K. and F. K. Jiang (2020), 'A Bibliometric Study of EAP Research: Who Is Doing What, Where and When?' *Journal of English for Academic Purposes*, 49. DOI: https://doi.org/10.1016/j.jeap.2020.100929.

Hyland, K. and L. Hamp-Lyons (2002), 'EAP: Issues and Directions', *Journal of English for Academic Purposes*, 1: 1–12.

Jenkins, R. (1989), 'Language, Symbolic Power and Communication: Bourdieu's Homo Academicus', *Sociology*, 23 (4): 639–45.

Jenkins, R. (1992), *Pierre Bourdieu*, London: Routledge.

King, A. (2000), 'Thinking with Bourdieu against Bourdieu: A "Practical" Critique of the Habitus', *Sociological Theory*, 18: 417–43.

Liu, Y. and G. Hu (2021), 'Mapping the Field of English for Specific Purposes (1980–2018): A Co-citation Analysis', *English for Specific Purposes*, 61: 97–116.

Luntley, M. (1992), 'Practice Makes Knowledge?' *Inquiry*, 35: 447–61.

MacDonald, J. (2016), 'The Margins as Third Space: EAP Teacher Professionalism in Canadian Universities', *TESL Canada Journal*, 34 (1): 106–16.

Maton, K. (2005), 'The Sacred and the Profane: The Arbitrary Legacy of Pierre Bourdieu', *European Journal of Cultural Studies*, 8 (1): 101–12.

Moore, R. (2009), *Towards the Sociology of Truth*, London: Continuum.

Radice, H. (2013), 'How We Got Here: UK Higher Education under Neoliberalism', *ACME: An International E-Journal for Critical Geographies*, 12: 407–18.

Raimes, A. (1991), 'Instructional Balance: From Theories to Practices in the Teaching of Writing', in J. Alatis (ed.), *Georgetown University Round Table on Language and Linguistics*, 238–49, Washington, DC: Georgetown University Press.

Rancière, J. (2012), *The Intellectual and His People*, London: Verso.

Riazi, A. M., H. Ghanbar and I. Fazel (2020), 'The Contexts, Theoretical and Methodological Orientation of EAP Research: Evidence from Empirical Articles Published in the *Journal of English for Academic Purposes*', *Journal of English for Academic Purposes*, 48. DOI: https://doi.org/10.1016/j.jeap.2020.100925.

Ross, K. (1991), 'Translator's Introduction', in J. Rancière (ed.), *The Ignorant Schoolmaster: Five Lessons in Intellectual Emancipation*, vii–xxiii, Stanford: Stanford University Press.

Sauntson, H. and L. Morrish (2011), 'Vision, Values and International Excellence: The "Products" That University Mission Statements Sell to Students', in M. Molesworth, R. Scullion and N. Nixon (eds), *The Marketisation of Higher Education and the Student as Consumer*, 73–85, Abingdon: Routledge.

Simeoni, D. (2000), 'Anglicizing Bourdieu', in N. Brown and I. Szeman (eds), *Pierre Bourdieu Fieldwork in Culture*, 65–86, Oxford: Rowman & Littlefield.

Swales, J. M. (2009), *Incidents in an Educational Life: A Memoir (of sorts)*, Ann Arbor: University of Michigan Press.

Swales, J. M. (2019), 'The Futures of EAP Genre Studies: A Personal Viewpoint', *Journal of English for Academic Purposes*, 38: 75–82.

Swartz, D. L. (2013), *Symbolic Power, Politics, and Intellectuals: The Political Sociology of Pierre Bourdieu*, Chicago: Chicago University Press.

Turner, J. (2004), 'Language as Academic Purpose', *Journal of English for Academic Purposes*, 3: 95–109.

Turner, J. (2018), *On Writtenness*, London: Bloomsbury.

Webb, J., I. Schirato and G. Danaher (2002), *Understanding Bourdieu*, London: Sage Publications.

8

Ethnography: Expanding the boundaries in EAP

Haynes Collins and Adrian Holliday

In this chapter we will look at how ethnography helps both us to understand our students and our students to understand the nature of the University and of EAP. Furthermore, because of how ethnography has become a de-centring, postmodern methodology which defies common structures, it reveals a perhaps previously unrecognized knowledge and competence that students either bring with them or are able to discover. We will first look at the nature of ethnography and its potential contribution. Then, by means of the ethnographic method of creative non-fiction, we will demonstrate what we can learn about our students and the knowledge that they bring. In considering the possibilities of ethnography for EAP, we treat ethnography not as simply a data collection method, but as a social theory which offers 'a general programmatic *perspective* on social reality and how real subjects in real conditions of everyday life, possessed by real interests, make sense of it' (Blommaert, 2018: ix).

Ethnographic expansion in UK Higher Education

Since its historical colonial legacy, ethnography has undergone a thorough re-examination, for example, by Clifford (1988) and Fabian (1983), to the point where it can now be seen as operating within a counter-hegemonic paradigm (Blommaert and Jie, 2010) and no longer confined to the discipline of anthropology. This has entailed a disassociation from the image of the intrepid Western anthropologist sailing to faraway lands to study 'natives' and a distancing from the Greek origin of the prefix 'ethnos' meaning 'folk people', 'tribes' or 'natives' to a decolonial understanding which is arguably more resonant with the 'ethical' (Tyler, 1986: 122). Similarly, rather than the positivist position where the ethnographer is an objective observer and recorder of the so-imagined real world, ethnography now requires reflexivity where the ethnographer's stance and subjectivity are acknowledged and where there is a shift to an interest in how worlds are constructed rather than naïvely trying to describe them as objectively real things.

This reframing of ethnography has led to the recognition of the decolonial potential that it offers Higher Education (HE) with specific growth and salience across the social sciences and humanities. Wells et al. (2019: 1) argue that for Modern Languages, '[a]n ethnographic sensitivity encourages an openness to less hierarchical and hegemonic forms of knowledge, particularly when consciously seeking to invert the traditional colonial ethnographic project and envision instead more participatory and collaborative models of engagement'. This argument is similarly applicable to EAP where an ethnographically informed pedagogy can foster an active and critical approach.

There is a considerable history of critical ethnographically informed studies of specific universities and practices within HE (Thompson, 1970; Bourdieu, 1988; Edwards and Usher, 2000; Molesworth, et al., 2011; Cribb and Gewirtz, 2013; Collins, 2018; Bond, 2020). While these studies have the potential to inform academic debate and understanding of HE, they only feed rather indirectly into pedagogy. Ethnographic approaches in the field of linguistic ethnography have engaged more directly with pedagogy and specifically academic writing. Lillis (2008) classifies these approaches into three different degrees of depth. First, ethnography as 'method' generally makes analytical use of research participants' 'talk around text'. Second, more sustained engagement associated with ethnography as a 'methodology' draws on a wider set of data sources such as observed behaviour and a full range of cultural artefacts and may include repeated engagement with research participants in the form of cyclical talk around text. Third, ethnographic engagement can be pushed further by drawing on notions such as deep theorizing (Blommaert, 2007) and habitus (Bourdieu, 1991) and by considering how social structures and cultural and political dimensions affect how writing is produced and received. While these three approaches are valuable for EAP, they are largely from the perspective of researchers seeking to understand the academic writer, their writing process and how they are affected by the specific institutional context, and this is achieved through the analysis of the participants' texts and participant data about their texts.

A broader expansion of ethnographic possibilities emerges in the work of Paltridge, Starfield and Tardy (2016) who expand their focus from solely academic writing to also engage, with identity, socio-politics and power as well as considerable coverage of autoethnography. The emergence of autoethnography in HE is more recent and influenced by Canagarajah (1996, 1997, 2002, 2012) who draws on alternative narrative, autobiographical, dialogic and collaborative research methods. What stands out here is that student autoethnography is not limited to writing on behalf of or for the benefit of an academic researcher but serves as an outlet for voicing unrecognized lived experiences and perspectives that challenge institutional structures and academic demands. Stanley (2020: 10–11) argues that critical autoethnographies not only make use of deeply personal narratives which engage with power relations, but they have an 'overtly political agenda' which 'problematize[s] taken-for-granted canonical knowledges and empower[s] other ways of knowing'. Autoethnography often engages with academic writing and is thus particularly salient to EAP, but it also considers wider issues within the institutional context including identity (ex. Wang, 2020), native-speakerism (ex. Ahn and Delesclefs, 2020) and epistemological violence (ex. Bishop, 2020). This shift to student-led ethnographic engagement can open possibilities in EAP for a critical pedagogy and help students to make sense of the university and EAP practitioners to learn more about their students.

Critical language awareness for academic writing and university discourses

Raising critical language awareness is germane to EAP and an ethnographic lens can illuminate how, as noted by Fairclough nearly thirty years ago, language as discourse influences the shaping of society (1992: 9). Clark (1992: 118) highlights that '[t]he notion of an academic discourse community implies that there is a set of shared values and beliefs, of discoursal conventions', while also recognizing that 'like all communities' it 'is not monolithic'. Students therefore not only need to learn about academic discoursal conventions, but also need to strategically choose when to conform or when not conform to these. Ethnography can help inform these decisions as it provides a view of language away from a singular and static object of study to a focus on situated, fluid and embedded social practices which are context dependent. Ethnography also requires an active sense of engagement, with a greater sense of agency and ownership of both language and knowledge production – to promote dialogue, encourage a student-ethnographer to challenge previously held assumptions and provide a space for the sharing of knowledge and experiences. It is in this vein that through the creative non-fiction descriptions in this chapter we look at how students locate constructed aspects of writing within a wider discoursal setting.

While students face individual decisions regarding academic conventions in their own work, they also encounter wider discourses which permeate the university environment. These discourses mobilize a range of ideological agendas that exert the ontological and epistemological framing of global HE education. These agendas can seem to limit and exclude other possible ways of seeing and being in the world 'in attempting to make only certain meanings possible' (Edwards and Usher, 2000: 141). This is apparent in HE through the rise of increased 'neoliberal' transactional, managerial and marketized discourses. While 'neoliberal' may have become an overused and simplistic signifier for all that is wrong in HE, examples of neoliberal discourses remain evident – e.g. in how notions such as 'critical thinking' or the so-labelled 'native-speaker' are constructed to Other out-groups. Ethnography can be a tool for deconstructing such discourses and highlighting the stark differences between university discourse and the ways in which various social actors, including students and EAP practitioners, experience a university. A poignant example is Yamchi's (2015) study of Emirati women students appearing not to be able to apply the necessary criticality to 'correctly' perform writing tasks, when in fact they are applying their criticality, out of sight of the teacher because they find the tasks inauthentic. This then leads Yamchi to critique the established discourses of the writing syllabus and her own professionalism. Implicit here is the postmodern realization that the researcher is implicated as an actor in the intersubjective nature of ethnography and therefore needs to work hard to de-centre themselves from whatever structures they are working within (Clifford and Marcus, 1986).

Case study of three students

We illustrate ethnographic possibilities for EAP through a creative non-fictional study of three students who begin to develop an ethnographic eye and critical language awareness as they observe and explore their lives within a university and shared hall of residence roughly over the period of an academic year. Their observations are not always the result of having been given ethnographic assignments, but their EAP practitioner has taken the decision to not limit the learning focus to what may be historically associated with EAP. Thus, not all of the students' observations are about academic practices or academic writing per se, but also about observing phenomena and social interaction within the wider environment of their daily lives. This blurring of the boundary between daily life and academic work is intentional and is integral to debates about what EAP should be. The scenarios are also situated within the context of the Covid-19 pandemic which has given new perspectives to the students' lives and has amplified many of the issues that they are faced with.

As ethnographic attention has increasingly been turned inwards towards environments which might roughly be considered as 'close to home', this shift to a broader 'sociological imagination' carries ethical implications and often entails a need for ethnographers working as 'insiders' in known environments to adhere to the notion of making the familiar strange (Mills, 1959). Indeed, the pandemic has shown us that, as everyday routines have been severely disrupted, taken-for-granted social patterns have been thrown sideways to the point where the strange has become the everyday norm and has starkly exposed underlying structural issues and ideological positions and how they connect between the professional and the personal across many aspects of our lives. At the same time, some of the changes that are being framed in HE as a response to the pandemic may well become familiar fixtures for years to come.

Creative non-fiction

Creative non-fiction is just one example of ethnographic method. That we choose to use it here is because it seems appropriate to the scenario being studied. Part of the critical versatility of ethnography is that the choice of method is determined by the discovered exigencies of particular settings (Spradley, 1980: 29). In this instance, therefore, creative non-fiction enables us to synthesize our shared experience of engaging with students over a number of years, our knowledge of research about them plus our own experience of making sense of how to write. This is not however an ethnographic research paper. It is a glimpse of an example of ethnography and what it can teach us.

Our particular use of creative non-fiction is informed by Agar (1990). It involves ethnographic reconstructions in which composite events and characters are based upon multiple data sources which may or may not have been purposely collected. It therefore takes in unexpected, emergent data and themes as is central to the nature of ethnography. The fictional nature of the reconstructions also protects the identities of participants.

Creative non-fiction, as with all ethnographic methods, employs disciplines that underpin all ethnography – to combat the accusation that it is simply made up – (1) allowing meaning to emerge beyond the preoccupations of the researcher, (2) thick description, and (3) making the familiar strange. In creative non-fiction, these disciplines are further ensured through the construction of two or more composite characters each of whom have a different viewpoint so that a conversation is set up from which new meanings can emerge. Thick description implies that we are not looking for a triangulated average agreement of what each person thinks. Instead, a picture is developed from what is going on between all of them.

Throughout, we indent the reconstructions as would be the case with other forms of data to separate them from the authorial voice that then stands back and reflexively discusses them. That this data is clearly mediated by how it is authorially constructed as text draws attention to the fact that all data, including extracts from interviews, is similarly authorially mediated in how it has been selected for inclusion. Ethnography thus consciously manages the intersubjectivity implicit in all social research.

The students: George, Amira and Mani

We have constructed three students to represent a variety of background and orientation. They are all first-year undergraduates who are studying Politics & International Relations. They are all composites of a wide range of students that we have taught or met and they do not therefore represent any one particular student from whom permission needs to be obtained. The topics of their conversations are pertinent to their lives and their studies and these reflect current discussions which we have engaged in with students ourselves or that we are aware of (for example, see https://internationalstudentsvoices.com/2021/08/04/why-am-i-international-tuition-fees/). Interpretations of what they say or think are therefore entirely our own, though mediated by the ethnographic disciplines referred to above.

George is a British student:

> While there was an assumption in George's family that he would attend university, he remains anxious about the investment and the debt that he would incur during his studies and is therefore concerned about university ranking and graduate salaries. During Covid-19, the University assurances persuaded him to move into campus accommodation for a more protected 'student experience' with 'blended learning'. George is classified by the University as a 'home student' which determines the level of fees that he pays.

We therefore see that George is well-immersed in the marketing discourse of HE, and Covid-19 serves to exaggerate the service-provider dynamic that George later begins to question. This emphasizes that any 'learning experience' will be mediated by these factors.

Amira is from outside the UK and is thus classified as an 'international student' which determines the increased fees she pays for her degree programme in comparison with 'home students'. This does however mean that she gets more 'supportive' treatment:

> Amira, also hesitant because of Covid-19, received similar reassurances from the University regarding the support given to international students. After lengthy discussions with her parents, she travelled to the UK. Prior to starting her degree, she attended two terms of an EAP programme and during her studies she joined discipline-specific EAP support classes which were offered to all students on their course.

Amira thus shares George's exposure to HE discourses, but she is marked as different through the category of 'international student'. This both implies homogeneity for a diverse range of students and has the practical implication of much higher student fees. The 'international student' label also raises theoretical issues in the crossfire of multiple discourses and debates including: immigration, native-speakerism, the commercialization of internationalization agendas within HE, and cultural disbelief, in the sense that it is presumed that she needs more help. There can also be a high degree of ambivalence about the category of 'international student' felt by the students themselves (Margolis, 2016) as it can produce an uneven dynamic which comes with promise from the university of extra support and services that do not always materialize and it positions these students within a tacit deficit model which suggests that they lack qualities that 'home' students bring to their studies.

Mani is also subject to how the University classifies him:

> Mani's first language is English, but he has also joined EAP support classes as he finds them valuable for his academic work. He's lived in several different countries during his childhood as his parents were required to move frequently with their work and he has not lived in the UK for a sufficient time to qualify for home fees and is therefore also classified as an 'international student' and like Amira pays higher fees. Covid-19 has affected his plans because he isn't able to work and is struggling to make ends meet.

Mani's personal trajectory is therefore one which does not fit neatly into predetermined categories.

Over the years of living in different countries he has grown accustomed to the confusion that often arises when people try to place him within a particular nationality. Even though English is his first language, he often must answer questions about where he learned English, and he frequently receives comments noting how well he speaks English. Although he has been told that these questions and comments can be explained by his ethnicity, he sees these as micro-aggressions as there is no prescribed ethnicity for English language users. Mani finds self-introductions particularly challenging as his mobile adolescence is not easy to explain succinctly and he tends to avoid stating where he is from because it is never just one place. He has noticed as well that certain assumptions are made when his background is revealed such as an expectation that he is very wealthy. Mani believes he is fortunate to share accommodation with George and Amira as they both seem less judgemental about his background.

Amira is intrigued when Mani tells her about his problem with how he's labelled. She tells him that he's lucky because he has arguments for not being labelled as 'international' while she can't possibly escape from the label. Also, while she cannot possibly argue that English is her first language, she never forgets and always cites the experience she has had of helping a so-labelled 'native speaker' student with their grammar because they say they never learnt it at school.

The three students spend quite a lot of time exchanging stories that problematize their learning experience because the mixed messages during the pandemic mean that over much of the academic year, they are the only ones in their accommodation unit and depend on a shared kitchen.

Scenario 1: The ethnographic observation assignment

Amira is talking about the changes that she has noticed within the city and compares this new reality to the University prior to the Covid-19 pandemic.

She remembers one of the first tasks that she was asked to complete by her tutor when she joined her EAP course in pre-Covid times. She tells the others that it involved what was called an 'ethnographic observation' in which they had to bring to class what Agar (2006) calls a 'rich point' – an example of one significant observation or incident from on or around campus for discussion. The tutor said that it could be an observation of anything that resonated with them in corridors, offices or other spaces in and around the University. Amira told George and Mani about her own personal observation that was discussed in class.

She had stood at a road crossing just opposite the University and was looking at her phone and not paying much attention. She noticed a few other people had started to cross the road and assumed the pedestrian light had changed so she started to cross while still looking at her phone. When she stepped out into the road, she noticed a car heading right towards her, so she jumped back just in time. She was really shaken up and a couple of other students who saw what happened, came over and asked if she was OK. That helped, but she was embarrassed.

Amira said that this experience had generated a lot of discussion in the class. A few students started to make comparisons between different nationalities and their approach to pedestrian traffic lights. She said she initially made national comparisons between the approaches in her home country and here, but then she realized that this was too simplistic. Mani and George were surprised when she told them that the experience almost made her obsessed with watching people at road crossings. She told them that she even went to the city centre where there are busy crossings and almost everyone waited for the light there and then compared this to a less busy one where people were more likely to run across the road on a red light when there was no traffic. She said that she could begin to start seeing patterns in who was likely to cross on a red light and who tended to wait and that she started making notes and predictions.

Amira has made a crucial commitment to what Agar (2006) calls 'chasing the rich point'. Rather than simply letting the incident pass or explaining it through simplistic reference to 'cultural differences', Amira decided to dig deeply into this incident, and the rewards are apparent in what follows.

Despite George and Mani's bemusement that Amira spent hours watching people cross roads, they wanted to hear more and ask questions about the class discussion. Amira explained that, as other students recalled their own different approaches to road crossings, they began to agree that their approach to traffic lights really depended on different factors such as location, whether or not they were in a hurry and the type of crossing that was involved. Amira remembered there was a particularly long consideration of zebra crossings and that the tutor had become involved in the discussion and had pointed the students to the work of Blommaert (2018) who had written about the semiotics of zebra crossings. Everyone was taken by the fact that this was a subject which had been written about by an academic.

Amira then told George and Mani that she began to realise the degree of complexity around an apparently simple everyday action like crossing the road. She told them that there is a lot going on that they were unaware of and that it was also surprising but depressing that different orientations to such a simple practice could be used as a way of judging and Othering people.

Amira's willingness to 'chase the rich point' also allowed her and the other students to counter a culturalist explanation of her observations and to 'negotiate competing narratives for the purpose of overcoming essentialist blocks and finding non-essentialist threads' (Holliday and Amadasi, 2020: 18).

Amira's recounting of this experience led the three students to continue discussing different daily practices, particularly those that had been affected by Covid-19, and the ways of communicating that were outside their immediate awareness. Mani reported that he'd been on campus two or three times in the whole of the last six months and found it eerie how everyone walked around as though suspicious of each other.

They agree that this new reality combined with being confined in a very small flat for most of the day every week was not helping their mental state and that they would welcome the chance to be on a bustling university campus in comparison to an empty one. They then begin to discuss the politics of the University's statements about protecting their 'student experience'. Amira suggested that the student experience wasn't really about the parties, the nightclubs, the gym and all that, but about whether you actually received a reply to your email or feedback on your work in less than a month. She complained about all the unpleasant bureaucratic procedures you had to go through just to get here to do with visa applications. She questioned whether the University really had any duty of care whatsoever. George said he'd heard students from another university ironically saying that the 'student experience' means having a fence built around their accommodation which made them feel like a prisoner.

In this first scenario, the EAP practitioner's assignment follows a tradition of ethnographically observing and analysing the language and social interactions within university environments. An iconic example is Swales' (1998) *Other Floors, Other Voices* which he describes as a 'textography' of a small University of Michigan building. However, two key differences are that in the scenarios the students are ethnographers and the possibilities for what to observe have been expanded beyond textually mediated social interaction. Clearly, the results of a small-scale ethnographic assignment such as this will not yield anywhere near the same depth as the three-year study by Swales.

However, the limited ethnographic task assigned by the EAP practitioner opened a space in class for students to discuss their daily life and their observations, and this experience was retained by Amira well beyond the class.

With this acquiring of an ethnographic eye, Amira mentally returned to the discussion at different times as she believed it demonstrated the importance of reading an environment, analysing social interactions and seeing greater complexity.

Mentioning the assignment to Mani and George allowed for further reflection and comparison of some of the stark differences between their reality and the University's discourse of 'the student experience'. Amira, Mani and George challenge the commercialized positioning of the student experience as it does not reflect their own experiences over the year, and in refusing to conform they subsequently reconstruct their own meaning of the term, crucially drawing upon what has been excluded. Amira's comment which noted what she had learned through discussing the students' ethnographic observations challenges accepted notions of what, where, how, why and when learning occurs at university. It suggests the need for a more holistic understanding of what students experience at university and how that contributes to the learning process, as opposed to a positivist commodification of academic knowledge and student progress where learning is 'delivered' to students via online lectures through 'knowledge' that is separate from the students' lives and deposited in their minds in a 'banking model' of education (Freire, 2007).

Scenario 2: Deepening understanding of academic malpractice discourse and practice

George was sharing some feedback he had recently received on an essay. One of the comments that his subject lecturer made was that the work was not properly referenced and that he should consult his EAP tutor. George expected to get at least one EAP support appointment per semester, so he planned to find out where he was going wrong. Amira commented sarcastically that at least they didn't charge him with academic malpractice. Mani said that he knew someone who has been charged with plagiarism and they had to go before a committee and take an online course on academic malpractice and then redo the assessment but with the mark capped at the lowest pass mark.

Mani was also unhappy because he knew a few other people who referenced in almost the same way in their essay. In one case the lecturer hadn't even noticed, and they got a good grade. In another case the lecturer just wrote that they should be 'careful' with plagiarism. Amira said that she thought they just put the work through a programme like Turnitin so that everyone would follow the same rules and procedures, but that instead you could write something that one lecturer might call plagiarism and another might say is fine. She said she'd heard so much contradictory advice about paraphrasing, referencing and avoiding plagiarism that she'd just had to work it out for herself. She did value the discussions in the EAP support classes though.

Mani suggested that George should let Amira check his work because she seemed to understand about plagiarism. Amira then protested that they weren't even allowed to read each other's assessed work because of the University proofreading policy. George and Mani hadn't heard about this. They said that surely they were encouraged to read each other's work in the same way that academics do. Amira said the only place where you get to talk about these things and look at examples of good and bad referencing are in EAP classes. She said that they were not remedial classes as some people thought, but they provided a chance to think and talk about language, the decisions they made in their writing. Even the EAP tutor would talk about how the decision to send a student to an academic malpractice committee was difficult for them.

After some thought, Amira told them one reason why perhaps she seemed to 'know' things was because she'd got used to looking around to help her understand how to survive in a 'foreign' university. She said she made it her business to go to seminar presentations and notice how experienced researchers referred to each other, and how her lecturers referred to other research in their classes. Though Covid-19 didn't allow this now, her older sister had told her to really make the most of talking to lecturers in their offices just to see how they spoke and related to the books on their shelves. George said that this really made him think. After all, this university life might be just as 'foreign' to him as it was to her. He then remembered that in one of his classes, the lecturer had been talking about ethnography and how researchers should try and look through the eyes of strangers.

Amira said that she now understood more about the ethnographic skills she brought with her because of how her EAP tutor had drawn her attention to them.

In this scenario through actively comparing their own experiences and observations of University statements and policies, the students are building their own knowledge and coming to an understanding that the University approach to academic malpractice is not only uneven, but can be presented in legalistic terms which assumes universal understanding and does little to stimulate discussion or invite interpretation from those most affected by the policy. Similarly, policy documents avoid any mention of discrepancies in the interpretation and enforcement of academic malpractice. This contrasts with the students' experience and their feeling that these policies are difficult to navigate.

The positive to be drawn from this scenario is Amira's experience with the EAP classes and how they help her to understand the ethnographic skills she has brought with her. In explaining these she is keen to reposition the idea that these classes are remedial or for 'international students'. She sees these as a valuable way of encouraging critical language awareness (Fairclough, 1992) and making academic and language practices more visible (Bond, 2020). The discussions in these classes allow for a sharing of knowledge as the EAP practitioner learns which areas the students are finding difficult and by entering into dialogue with students, the students learn that academic malpractice decisions are difficult for staff as well. These positive exchanges can partially help to alleviate the underlining dynamic of the EAP practitioner being framed as a 'language fixer' as seen in the scenario where George is advised to consult the EAP teacher.

The students' developing personal ethnographic approach follows one of its main tenets, that of 'thick description' (Geertz, 1973). This enables them to interconnect instances about University malpractice policies from a variety of sources which include the experiences of other students in their classes, weighing that up against their own experience and also with what they are being told in different subject classes by different lecturers and then comparing these with a more centralized top-down policy document from the University. They are looking beyond the language of a policy document and are identifying discrepancies between what is stated and what they see happening. This allows students to be attuned to the hidden ideology within language as found in, for example, student-facing policy documents and how that language positions them. This active engagement and questioning, which the EAP practitioner recognizes as important, shares key features with ethnography, critical discourse analysis and experiential learning.

Scenario 3: The internationalization campaign

It should also be noted that in this and the previous scenario, the EAP practitioner is located within a specific subject area with the aim of helping students with discipline specific issues which they encounter. This is not a structure used consistently in EAP across UK HE.

Amira, Mani and George were discussing their online EAP support class which was designed to help students plan for an upcoming essay on basic concepts in international relations.

The EAP tutor had reiterated a point that the students' subject lecturer had made about not taking political statements at face value and the discussion quickly broadened out to how there are many types of statements encountered in daily life that need to be critically interrogated. One student in class had given the example of the University's 'internationalization' campaign which suddenly got a lot of discussion going. Rather than shut the discussion down and return immediately to international relations theory, the EAP tutor agreed that the process for critically analysing an organisation's use of a term such as internationalisation is not so different from analysing how a government might espouse a notion such as democracy or human rights. The tutor said the onus was on observers to consider 'actions versus rhetoric' and that identifying the discrepancies was part of a critical analytical process. The tutor went on to say that since the topic of the University's internationalization campaign generated so much discussion and was a well-known context, she proposed that students spend a couple of weeks ethnographically exploring where, when and how this term was used for further discussion in their next seminar and the students had agreed.

George reflected on what Amira had said about direct ethnographic observation and thought that what the three of them had already experienced was perhaps the best topic to investigate. Mani searched for an email which was relevant to the discussion in class. He remembered it was a perfect example because it was part of the university's internationalization campaign and it invited international students to record a message about where they were from and what it means to study at the University as global citizens.

Amira was getting quite agitated because she thought that it shouldn't just be so-labelled 'international students' who needed to think about being global citizens. She felt that she was already quite 'global' because of how far she'd had to travel in all sorts of ways. She also suspected that what the University was thinking about was to ask students to display something which superficially represented their 'home culture' or their national colours or flag. Mani said that this was why he'd deleted the email and that anyway he wouldn't be sure of what to display. He said the places where he felt most comfortable were airports and train stations, but he didn't think that made him a 'global citizen'. Amira was so angry. She said that the letter presumes that they were the walking embodiments of some sort of narrow image of their country's singular culture and that the University was just trying to create some kind of happy shiny image of itself through silly stereotypes. George followed her thinking and said that it was as though only international students 'have culture'. He said that the term Amira needed to use was 'essentialist', but she suggested that perhaps 'racist' was better.

Mani wondered what would happen if a student recorded some of the stuff that they'd really been going through this year, e.g. his thwarted plan to get a job to help pay his fees, and how many students had gone to the newly opened food bank. He felt that the email just felt like just another form of branding – of people and of their experience – asking them to commodify themselves for the University's benefit.

The students' discussion identifies the University's attempt to carefully manage an image of international students which can be used for further marketing purposes. This image jars with the students' realities partially because it constructs international students as reduced products of a 'national culture'. Although it does not require the uniquely mobile background of Mani to show how reductionist this message is, his personal trajectory clearly highlights its failings. Similarly, the students are also sceptical about the University's use of 'global citizenship', seeing it as a buzzword which does not reflect their own experiences and observations over the year. Although the students do not name discourses per se, for example, 'West as steward' (Holliday and Amadasi, 2020)', by taking issue with the ideology unpinning the notion of global citizenship and internationalization, they demonstrate an awareness of the very tangled discourses which are mobilized by the University. Amira's reference to race may have seemed extreme, but does resonate with literature that associates cultural profiling with racism (e.g. Spears, 1999).

Writing about these discourses, Pais and Costa (2020: 11) argue that the neoliberal discourse which emphasizes 'individual achievement' and 'self-investment' has overtaken the discourse of 'critical democracy' and that '[w]hat remains understated in the discourse around global citizenship education is the eminent subordination of education to the needs of the market'. Furthermore, what this particular pandemic year has revealed is that many students like Mani, Amira and George have experienced the harsher realities of the market and the historic shift to an economic model where universities are heavily dependent on student fees and particularly higher international fees has led to growing resentment.

After a fortnight the students returned to their online seminar class to discuss the task which they had been given. Other students had brought in various materials as data sources including photographs and the students had been discussing the genre of the examples and their resonance with advertising. Mani showed the email which he received from the internationalisation campaign and made what he felt to be quite a strong statement – about how insulting it was to be treated like cash cows and then to be asked to smile and present a silly image of 'our culture' for marketing purposes.

Not all students agreed with Mani's statement and one student remarked that she didn't mind having her picture on a University campaign because she could send it to her parents and they'd be proud that she was in the publicity.

What then surprised some of the students was that the EAP tutor joined the discussion and said that she sometimes felt complicit in this commercialised environment. She said that she knew colleagues who felt pressured to 'sell' their courses to prospective applicants and that she and other colleagues were on very short-term teaching contracts that were a form of casual labour. Some of the students were very surprised and the discussion continued until one student who was looking a bit disgruntled asked a question about what this had to do with academic writing.

Rather than answer directly, the tutor asked the students for their ideas about this question and Amira was first to reply. She said that everything that they were doing here was helping them to learn not just about the University, but about each other. She said that she knew more about the University and her teachers than she did two weeks before, and that hopefully her teacher knew more about her students.

Amira said that she'd also sharpened the critical eye that, and she emphasises, she already had, and learnt more about how she could apply it to her own work in analysing the type of writing that they were expected to produce and in making decisions about her own writing and her own voice. She laughed and noted for example that she wouldn't be using the style of writing in the internationalisation examples in her academic essays. She finished by saying there was a definite connection to academic writing and even beyond that as she had even begun to imagine changes to improve the University.

Three interconnected issues emerge from this scenario. First, the somewhat controversial decision of the EAP practitioner to reveal her contractual arrangement with the University and her stance towards what she sees as marketization in HE. This decision in many ways runs counter to trends in HE to depersonalize and depoliticize learning and to stick to a business-as-usual approach which emphasizes neatness and efficiency. 'Coming out' in this way in class can potentially place the EAP practitioner in a compromising position with respect to both her students and employer. The precarity that the EAP practitioner discloses also reflects increasing academic casualization which resonates with what Ding and Bruce (2017) see as the marginal position of EAP in HE. It should also be recognized, though, that not all students in this scenario object to the increasing commoditization of the University and see this as a system which they are committed to as it is expected to provide them a form of capital that ensures future prosperity.

The second issue concerns the student who thinks this critical discussion in class gets in the way of learning about 'nuts and bolts' of academic writing. This connects with the view that EAP practitioners are just 'language fixers' employed to teach and correct grammar. In this chapter we are very much arguing that, instead, it is only by taking an ethnographic approach to how academic writing is located within the wider discourses of the university and indeed society, that the EAP practitioner can narrow the gap between text and context (Lillis, 2008; James, 2018) and highlight the message that academic writing is about much more than grammar. This is a point which Amira clearly appreciates, even though it is not immediately accepted by all students.

Lastly, Amira's final statement which demonstrates a commitment to reshaping the University is salient. Critical examinations and ethnographic observations of institutions and social interactions do not always lend themselves to optimistic interpretations but can rather fall into cynicism. Yet, Amira retains a commitment to how things might be made better to reshape her environment and this is at the heart of criticality.

Conclusion: Ethnography as social theory for EAP

There are two overlapping layers in the creative non-fiction scenarios with respect to ethnography as a social theory for EAP. Firstly, the scenarios can be treated as part of an empirical study which allows us to make direct observations of what goes on between students and practitioners in terms of how they make sense of each other and what they are learning in the wider context of institutional and cultural environments. Interviews with students or practitioners or class evaluations would not do this because they would not get to the between-the-lines thinking or factors that might not be thought to be relevant.

In this chapter we have shown a facet of how this can work. It is thick description that allows us to look and make connections beyond the obvious.

The creative non-fiction we have provided only scratches the surface, however. In a more extensive study, we would need also to look at ourselves as researchers to de-centre the gaze that we bring to making sense of the people we portray by interrogating our prejudices, e.g. derived from our own positions within the neoliberal university. Also, the thick description would go on to connect with other times and other places. The scenarios allow us to point to emergent findings which include that the 'international student' label continues to be overly used in problematic ways and that within a neoliberal environment efforts aimed at helping international students can often make matters worse. We have nevertheless been able to demonstrate that students are critically aware of the discrepancies between marketized discourse and their own experience, even if they do not universally object to this framing of education.

The second layer is the suggestion of further ethnographic possibilities in EAP, not as a 'how to guide', but as specific examples which highlight the shift within the EAP pedagogy by the practitioner towards ethnography and where students were encouraged to develop an ethnographic eye.

We do not claim that this is easy, particularly given that the emphasis on greater 'efficiencies' in HE will render ethnographic engagement impractical primarily due to the time required to achieve sufficient depth of study. We also acknowledge the spatial and temporal changes which are ongoing across university campuses as a result of the Covid-19 pandemic. Thus, it is important to balance the degree of engagement which is necessary to 'count' as ethnography against the practicalities which students face during their studies.

In stating that 'true' ethnography is a rarity, Blommaert (2018: 1) rightly takes exception to ethnography being considered as simply a method for collecting data and he stresses that it is important that the epistemological and ontological principles of ethnography be adhered to. Following this lead, we suggest that ethnographically informed work in EAP is possible by adhering to these principles about ethnography:

a) a way of seeing which is not just another method, but which embodies an epistemology that is concerned with how *all* involved parties, including the university and other institutions, construct meanings;
b) allowing meanings and methods to emerge from the observed nature of settings rather than beginning with definitions – e.g. regarding the nature of writing and of learning how to write; and
c) noticing the emerging process of how all parties respond within and to the research event.

d) Employing thick description to interconnect meanings across subjective instances of action.

Finally, the starting point for retaining the value of an ethnographic approach on a smaller scale is recognizing that ethnography 'involves a perspective on language and communication, including ontology and epistemology, both of which are of significance for the study of language in society, or better, of language as well as of society' (Blommaert, 2018: 2).

With reference to social theory, an example of the unexpected that can emerge from the implicit de-centring of ethnography, where researchers, educators and students can be taken beyond their thinking-as-usual, is that especially Amira is bringing her own social theory about the politics of writing and the university. That the EAP tutor emerges as being able to recognize and respond positively to this is a tribute to the mediated positioning between institution and student that this role surely requires.

References

Agar, M. (1990), 'Text and Fieldwork: "Exploring the Excluded Middle"', *Journal of Contemporary Ethnography*, 19 (1): 73–88.

Agar, M. (2006), 'Culture: Can You Take It Anywhere?' *International Journal of Qualitative Methods*, 5 (2): 1–12.

Ahn, H. and D. Delesclefs (2020), 'Insecurities, Imposter Syndrome, and Native-speakeritis', in P. Stanley (ed.), *Critical Autoethnography and Intercultural Learning: Emerging Voices,* 95–99, London: Routledge.

Bishop, M. (2020), 'Epistemological Violence and Indigenous Autoethnographies', in P. Stanley (ed.), *Critical Autoethnography and Intercultural Learning: Emerging Voices,* 19–32, London: Routledge.

Blommaert, J. (2007), 'On Scope and Depth in Linguistic Ethnography', *Journal of Sociolinguistics*, 11 (5): 682–8.

Blommaert, J. (2018), *Dialogues with Ethnography*, Bristol: Multilingual Matters.

Blommaert, J. and D. Jie (2010), *Ethnographic Fieldwork: A Beginner's Guide*, Bristol: Multilingual Matters.

Bond, B. (2020), *Making Language Visible in the University*, Bristol: Multilingual Matters.

Bourdieu, P. (1988), *Homo Academicus*, Cambridge: Polity Press.

Bourdieu, P. (1991), *Language and Symbolic Power*, trans. G. Raymond and M. Adamson, Cambridge, MA: Polity.

Canagarajah, A. S. (1996), 'From Critical Research Practice to Critical Research Reporting', *TESOL Quarterly*, 30 (2): 321–30.

Canagarajah, A. S. (1997), 'Safe Houses in the Contact Zone: Coping Strategies of African-American Students in the Academy', *College Composition and Communication*, 48 (2): 173–96.

Canagarajah, A. S. (2002), *A Geopolitics of Academic Writing*, Pittsburgh, PA: University of Pittsburgh Press.

Canagarajah, A. S. (2012), 'Autoethnography in the Study of Multilingual Writers', in L. Nickolson and M. Sheridan (eds), *Writing Studies Research in Practice: Methods and Methodologies*, 113–24, Carbondale, IL: Southern Illinois University Press.

Clark, R. (1992), 'Principles and Practice of CLA in the Classroom', in N. Fairclough (ed.), *Critical Language Awareness*, 117–40, London; New York: Longman.

Clifford, J. (1988), *The Predicament of Culture: Twentieth-century Ethnography, Literature and Art*, Cambridge, MA: Harvard University Press.

Clifford, J. and G. E. Marcus (1986), *Writing Culture: The Poetica of Politics of Ethnography*, Berkeley: University of California Press.

Collins, H. (2018), 'Interculturality from above and below: Navigating Uneven Discourses in a Neoliberal University System', *Language and Intercultural Communication*, 18 (2): 167–83.

Cribb, A. and S. Gewirtz, (2013), 'The Hollowed-Out University? A Critical Analysis of Changing Institutional and Academic Norms in UK Higher Education', *Discourse: Studies in the Cultural Practices of Education*, 34 (2): 338–50.

Ding, A. and I. Bruce (2017), *The English for Academic Purposes Practitioner: Operating on the Edge of Academia*, London: Palgrave Macmillan.

Edwards, R. and R. Usher (2000), *Globalistion and Pedagogy: Space, Place and Identity*, London: Routledge.

Fabian, J. (1983), *Time and the Other: How Anthropology Makes Its Object*, New York: Columbia University Press.

Fairclough, N. (1992), 'Introduction', in Norman Fairclough (ed.), *Critical Language Awareness*, 1–30, London; New York: Longman.

Freire, P. (2007), *Pedagogy of the Oppressed*, New York: Continuum.

Geertz, C. (1973), *The Interpretation of Cultures: Selected Essays*, New York: Basic Books.

Holliday, A. and S. Amadasi (2020), *Making Sense of the Intercultural: Finding DeCentred Threads*, London: Routledge.

James, B. (2018), 'Closing the Gap between Text and Context in Academic Writing Research – An "Impossible" Task?' *Journal of English for Academic Purposes*, 36: 99–107.

Lillis, T. (2008), 'Ethnography as Method, Methodology and "Deep Theorising": Closing the Gap between Text and Context in Academic Writing Research', *Written Communication*, 25 (3): 353–88.

Margolis, R. (2016), 'Exploring Internationalisation and the International Student Identity', *The Language Scholar*, 0: 49–67.

Mills, C. W. (1959), *The Sociological Imagination*, Oxford: Oxford University Press.

Molesworth, M., R. Scullion, and E. Nixon, (eds), (2011), *The Marketisation of Higher Education and the Student as Consumer*, London: Routledge.

Pais, A. and M. Costa (2020), 'An Ideology Critique of Global Citizenship Education', *Critical Studies in Education*, 61 (1): 1–16.

Paltridge, B., S. Starfield, and C. M. Tardy (2016), *Ethnographic Perspectives on Academic Writing*, Oxford: Oxford University Press.

Spears, A. K., ed. (1999), *Race and Ideology; Language, Symbolism, and Popular Culture*, Detroit: Wayne State University Press.

Spradley, J. P. (1980), *Participant Observation*, Holt: Rinehart & Winston.

Stanley, P. (2020), *Critical Autoethnography and Intercultural Learning: Emerging Voices*, London: Routledge.

Swales, J. M. (1998), *Other Floors, Other Voices: Textography of a Small University Building*, Mahwah, NJ: Erlbaum.

Thompson, E. P. ed. (1970), *Warwick University Ltd.* Harmondsworth: Penguin.

Wang, Y. (2020), 'De-Chinese and Re-Chinese: Negotiating Identity', in P. Stanley (ed.), *Critical Autoethnography and Intercultural Learning: Emerging Voices*, 162–73, London: Routledge.

Wells, N., C. Forsdick, J. Bradley, D. Burdett, J. Burns, M. Demossier, M. Hills de Zarate, S. Huc-Hepher, S. Jordan, T. Pitman and G. Wall (2019), 'Ethnography and Modern Languages', *Modern Languages Open*, 1 (1): 1–16.

Yamchi, N. (2015), '"I Am Not What You Think I am": EFL Undergraduates' Experience of Academic Writing, Facing Discourses of Formulaic Writing', in A. Swan, P. J. Aboshiha and A. R. Holliday (eds), *(En)countering Native-speakerism: Global Perspectives*, 177–92, London: Palgrave.

Feminism: Affordances and applications for EAP

Yolanda Cerda

Introduction

The aim of this chapter is to advocate for the consideration of feminism(s) as a generative theoretical framework or lens for the analysis of English for Academic Purposes (EAP) and to consider the potential and myriad affordances of feminism for the EAP practitioner, the students we teach and the higher education contexts in which EAP labour and learning take place. In particular, I seek to highlight how the interest academic feminism has taken in the dialectical relationship between language, texts, the processes and agents of text production as well as pedagogies and praxis (in language education and in HE) point to a political concern with understanding power relations and their contingent inequalities. These power relations, inflected as they are by gender as well as other identities, are understood to be discursively reflected and construed, and feminist and critical linguists have sought to expose how such relations are operationalized ultimately in order to resist or destabilize the inequalities they perpetuate. This is a focus with a 'feminist imagination' (Lazar, 2017) and is entirely befitting a field which continues to be critiqued for its lack of engagement with the social world it inhabits as Hyland (2018) has recently affirmed:

> Nor have we distinguished ourselves in understanding how students experience their lives, their studies and their disciplines while privileging text above practice can sometimes lead us to treat language, and in particular writing, as primarily a linguistic, and perhaps even an autonomous, object rather than something which is socially embedded in particular lives, disciplines and contexts.
>
> (Hyland, 2018: 399)

As well as this, he claims that the 'problematization of pedagogy is still not a matter of regular communal discourse in the field' (Hyland, 2018: 399) suggesting that practitioners lack the time or opportunities to engage in meaningful and regular consideration of praxis. In this respect, feminist approaches may provide a suitable antidote to these criticisms of the field conceded by Hyland (2018), notwithstanding his defence of EAP or 'sympathy for the devil'. Nevertheless, although feminism has informed and infused studies and theoretical research within EAP in areas such as academic literacies and critical pedagogies, feminist (socio)linguistics or an overt espousal of feminist lenses remains fairly marginal. Given the relative proliferation of feminist literature on the relationship between language and gender (Cameron 1985; Ehrlich et al., 2017; Holmes and Meyerhoff, 2003; Litosseliti, 2006; Sunderland, 2006; Talbot 2020) and the role of gender in education (e.g. Mernard-Warwick et al., 2017), the attention to gender and feminism in EAP is surprisingly scant at least in mainstream considerations of what is or *should* be of interest in the field, what conditions impinge on the field and who and what define and determine the epistemologies we draw on.

The chapter begins with a conceptualization of feminism and some of the salient characteristics which might be variously applied to EAP contexts and are pertinent to my understanding of the possibilities that feminist approaches present. After addressing the relative dearth of relevant literature in EAP, some applications of feminist approaches from within EAP and related fields are presented briefly, particularly in respect of academic writing. It is not my intention to present a full review of feminist approaches to academic writing, feminist (linguistic) pedagogies or feminist scholarship as this would be beyond the scope of a single chapter. Rather I hope to highlight some of the avenues taken by researchers, educators and students which show how feminism has opened up new ways of thinking about, interpreting and performing academic practices, texts and cultures. Some of these (Danvers et al., 2019; Handforth and Taylor, 2016; Lillis et al., 2018) have also inspired my attempt at approaching the writing of this chapter in a (for me) slightly experimental way. Thus the chapter is interspersed with a reflective narrative thread in italic font which seeks to capture the writing process from a personal perspective, exposing the difficulties it has presented me with and the 'vulnerabilities' (Danvers et al., 2019) that belie the *argument* or the well-crafted persuasive rhetoric of academia. The chapter also includes an example of how a feminist critical discourse analysis (Lazar, 2005, 2017) might be applied to seemingly neutral and descriptive texts on specific genres by canonical authors (Swales and Feak, 2011) in the field as a potential means of critical enquiry about what we teach and how we induct students into our academic cultures. It ends with a range of questions which I contend either remain largely unexamined in EAP (though perhaps less so in some of its affiliate disciplines) or are avenues that are worthy of further exploration, which I hope will encourage others.

> *Writing this chapter in some ways involves a process of distillation from a vast body of research. There is too much to say or it is applicable in diverse and disparate ways. And Feminism seems a kind of orthodoxy in some academic circles and anathema or irrelevant in others. Writing about feminism feels daunting and in some ways at odds with the other chapters because unlike Bourdieu, critical realism, LCT or academic literacies I would predict that many readers (most) have at least some preconceptions about feminism and I imagine some will view it negatively or as 'for women' if public opinion is anything to go by. It is hard to write without anticipating criticism or indifference but this anticipation can be paralysing.*

Defining feminism

At the time of writing this, feminism as a social movement, in particular, is enjoying a popular renaissance in many contexts, though as Cameron (2019) has argued, its popularity has always periodically waxed and waned. Despite this, it seems important to specify what is meant by feminism or a feminist lens, not least because of the long history and evolution of feminist ideas and the 'varieties' of feminisms that co-exist, albeit sometimes uncomfortably. Indeed prominent sociolinguists and feminists often concur that 'there are many different types of feminism in circulation ...' (Mills and Mullany, 2011: 2) and, in Cameron's (2019) recent introduction to contemporary feminism, meant both for general and specialist readers, she points out how many of the central tenets of feminism (such as domination, rights, and so on) are matters of debate fraught with controversy.

> *Seems conventional, possibly pedestrian, to start with definitions. But in this case I suppose it's warranted given my beliefs about what readers already know and believe about feminism? I prefer the subtitle to include 'defining' rather than 'definitions' because it seems to better reflect active fluidity to offering or synthesising definitions of often abstract concepts.*

Notwithstanding this apparent confusion (an evaluation of feminism I return to below), Cameron (2019) offers a succinct representation of this polysemous concept. She views feminism as 'an idea [...] the belief that women are people;

[...] a collective movement which seeks to end sexism, exploitation and discrimination [and] an intellectual framework [...] a mode of analysis ... a way of asking questions and searching for answers' (Cameron, 2019: 2).

These three perspectives encapsulate the philosophical or ontological, the political and the critical senses of feminist meanings. It is primarily with the latter critical sense that this chapter is concerned, though in doing so its aims are also political (the second sense) and presuppose an acceptance of the first broader ontological sense. These aspects are also reflected in other sociolinguistic definitions of feminism. Mills and Mullany (2011: 2) argue that there are two unifying factors to all forms of feminism which are that it 'is a political movement which focuses on investigating gender' [...] and 'which has the overall emancipatory aim of redressing gender inequalities'. Similarly, within education scholarship (e.g. Weiner, 1994), feminism is recognized as 'an equality discourse' as well as 'an analytical framework for unpacking the micro-political – that is how power is exercised at local levels [...] how oppression works, is experienced and where resistances might be possible' (Weiner, 1994: 2). Therefore, from education and pedagogic perspectives, as well as political and critical dimensions, feminism is also praxis-oriented and especially 'concerned with more ethical forms of personal and professional practice' (Weiner, 1994: 7–8).

> *As a reader I find headings useful in terms of offering structural guidance through a stretch of written text, but as a writer, I find it really difficult to choose or craft appropriate headings. I always want to write in the style of newspaper headlines or longwinded questions – struggled with the next heading. Played with the following heading possibilities: pitfalls of feminism; the problem with feminism(s); the maligning of feminism, landscapes of feminism, plotting/navigating the landscapes of feminism.*

Representations of feminism

Despite the relative clarity and consensus suggested by the definitions above, feminism is commonly cast as confusing or embroiled in internal conflict by journalists and academics alike. The proliferation of types of feminism and indeed feminist labels (both academic and popular) compound perceptions of, at best, complexity and, at worst, confusion and conflict. Thus the academic literature (Arya, 2012; Bucholtz, 2017) discusses and explains the differences between forms of feminism: *Black feminism, radical feminism, cultural feminism, material feminism, liberal feminism, second-wave feminism, third wave feminism, fourth-wave feminism* while the media mentions, *angry feminists, bad feminists, femi-nazis, etc.*, among many others.

While it would be problematic to dismiss or minimize the nuances of understandings of the social world and its inequities which are intrinsic to these different types of feminism (and hence the use of feminism*s*), interpretations of this plurality can be more positive. I would argue that the various types of feminism which co-exist are indicative of a theoretical framework flexible enough to allow for multiple perspectives, many of which are locally and culturally bound. There is also a sense that different forms of feminism are in critical debate with each other (Bucholtz, 2019), and that elements and approaches from different perspectives have contributed to the evolution of feminism through metaphors of successive waves. However, it should also be noted that the 'wave' terminology has been considered potentially misleading (Cameron, 2005: 483) since it seems to suggest a linear evolution, whereas in reality, different feminist 'waves' co-exist and overlap.

It is also worth noting that not all current feminism(s) are politically engaged and much discussion around feminism focuses primarily on identity. Cameron (2005) regards this as a transition from the political to the personal (or from the 'What is to be done?' to the 'Who am I?' (Mills and Mullany, 2011: 4)) which in turn is an effect of postmodernist concerns with identity research and the 'theoretical shift to viewing identity as socially constructed'. Many researchers (e.g. Cameron, 2005, 2019; Lazar, 2009; Mills and Mullany, 2011) suggest that this is a move away from 'collective political action towards one of individualism and a focus on self-identification' (Mills and Mullany, 2011: 4), a move which might be viewed as detrimental to the achievement of collective goals or to the mobilization of structural changes. I would also argue that the representations of feminism as a confusing movement ultimately de-legitimizes its aims by focusing more on identities and feminist credentials than on matters of policy or politics. It is not difficult to see how this might ultimately serve the interests of the status quo or the hegemonies which support inequalities.

Definition of feminism

Despite the complexities of defining feminism(s) alluded to, below is an outline of the characteristics, which I consider most relevant from an analytical perspective in this chapter. Therefore, as well as the unifying perspectives delineated above, feminism(s) here is considered a theoretical framework which

- has social justice and liberation at its core (this is linked to, though not synonymous with, other equality discourses which are prevalent in education, such as decolonization and inclusivity) echoing the work of writers and theorists such as bell hooks (2000);
- is concerned with the collective and structural causes and effects of inequality (enacted through language, for example);
- regards intersectionality (coined by Kimberlé Crenshaw, 1989) as a key construct or 'paradigm' (Collins, 2002: 252);
- is questioning of distinctions between the private and public;
- encourages researcher and practitioner reflexivity;
- scrutinizes language as representative and discursively productive of the relative oppressions experienced by social groups, particularly though certainly not exclusively on the basis of gender;
- has a history of engagement with linguistics and language ideologies;
- has disruptive potential (to question or challenge the dominant discourses and hegemonies which shape the social world and communities of practice within it); and
- is versatile, allowing for differences of perspective and approach depending on contexts.

How do I move now from definitions to examples of how feminist approaches have informed approaches to pedagogies or academic writing or EAP. I ask myself also whether there is a difference between defining and characterising something? I find discursive shifts difficult and tedious though my doctoral writing experience showed me that I needed to guide the reader more.

The following section gives examples of how some researchers and practitioners have used feminist pedagogies and approaches to academic writing, in particular. The studies discussed, while not exhaustive, show how feminism has facilitated generic innovations or experimentation as well as radical critiques of normative practices.

Applications of feminism in EAP and Higher Education

As suggested in the introduction to this chapter, explicit reference to or espousal of feminism or feminist pedagogies within EAP seem surprisingly rare. Benesch (1998) has argued that this is partly the result of the predominance of an ideology of pragmatism in the profession, especially in English for academic purposes (EAP) (Benesch, 1998: 101). This is the notion that English language teaching should provide students with the grammar, vocabulary, and rhetorical forms of particular settings. The goal of pragmatic EAP is to fit students into existing academic and social structures, not to encourage them to question or revise those structures.

This absence is noted also by Belcher (1997: 9) within TESOL/TEFL literature, though she offers no explanation: 'In general, feminist ideology has so far played a minor role in the TESL/TEFL literature' (Belcher, 1997: 9).

Although not the only publication, a consideration of the published papers in JEAP, the well-established *Journal of English for Academic Purposes*, illustrates the gap. Since its inception in 2002, there have been fifty-four volumes of JEAP at the time this chapter was written, each volume with several issues. Since 2016 alone, over 250 articles have been published in JEAP. However, a search of *feminism* renders only five results and *feminist* renders only twenty-five articles which mention the term, and rather fewer which engage with feminist perspectives at all. For example, Hyland's (2015: 41-2) article features the term *feminist* but only to compare the academic linguistic styles of Debbie Cameron ('radical feminist' Hyland, 2015: 41) and John Swales with a view to exemplifying how the two applied linguists use genre conventions to construct a particular kind of academic identity and recognizable voice. Therefore, even when articles mention 'feminist' it is not always to engage with ideas or approaches, but rather to index particular academic identities. The journal has also produced seventeen special issues or collections, one of which was dedicated to *Gender and academic writing* in March 2018, edited by Theresa Lillis, Jennifer McMullan and Jackie Tuck. Most of the articles in the web search relating to or engaged with feminist frameworks were from this issue, as well as another issue on *Critical English for Academic Purposes* (Volume 8, Issue 2, June 2009) edited by Sarah Benesch, one of few EAP writers who explicitly reference feminist theory (e.g. Benesch, 1998).

Nevertheless, as mentioned, there has been some attention paid to the role of gender in EAP contexts and across language and gender studies more generally; many scholars and researchers focus on *gender and language in education* as well as *gender and language in the workplace* (e.g. Litosseliti, 2006 inter alia). Among the research articles reviewed for this chapter, including the JEAP *Gender and academic language* special issue, I attempted to identify some ways in which feminist theory had shaped the studies and articles in question, in order to draw out the affordances of feminism for an understanding of the field of EAP as well as for applications to our pedagogic and scholarship practices.

> One of the most satisfying aspects of reading and preparing to write for this chapter has been discovering the innovations to academic writing and very purposeful collaborative approaches which have influenced my thinking about the form of this chapter as well as the content. In the past, the form has often for me been a means to an end – a laborious working through of language and words, a jigsaw puzzle to build the points supporting the arguments. At times, though it also plagued me with self –doubt –exposing an interior monologue feels just as hard, if not harder. And then it can also seem self-indulgent and presumptuous – who cares about 'extraneous' thinking or innovations (deviations?) of form?

Feminist alternatives to academic writing and academic writing pedagogies

A key area that emerged was a critical questioning of the normative structures of academic writing, including the notions of argumentation, voice and genre which underpin many academic texts and would typically feature in EAP curricula, not to mention their prevalence in assessment criteria across many disciplines. Belcher's (1997) article aimed at 'L2 writing educators, both as teachers and as academic writers themselves' (Belcher, 1997: 1) provides an apposite case study, highlighted and endorsed by Canagarajah (2002) in the first issue of JEAP. In it Belcher (1997: 2) shows how two students succeed in resisting and reimagining an approach to academic writing influenced by 'our "agonistic heritage", the male ritual combat of Western academic discourse' (citing Walter Ong, 1981: 119). She goes on to elaborate that

> even at the undergraduate introductory level [...] polarization is encouraged, Sheree Meyer (1993) observes, through assignment of persuasive, argumentative writing tasks that ask students not just to inform their readers but to 're-form' them through a type of verbal assault that aims at defeating imagined opposing viewpoints (p. 48).
>
> (Belcher, 1997: 2)

In contrast, according to Belcher (1997: 3), feminists, alongside other critical researchers of composition, offer alternative approaches which may well appeal more to some non-Anglophone writers, some of whom, she argues, are cast as 'lack[ing] "high order thinking skills" that many Western academics refer to as "critical thinking"' (Belcher, 1997: 8) simply because they bring particular cultural sensibilities to their academic writing.

> By presenting a perspective on academic discourse that privileges cooperation over competition, and dialogue over debate (cf Meyer 1993), the feminist critique encourages development of a type of public academic voice that many already communally-minded ESL writers (Mao 1995) may find in harmony with their own (cf. Prior 1995).
>
> (Belcher, 1997: 3)

Belcher's illustrates this by describing how two students in her case study, Hiroko and Yi-Yin, resisted the advice of academic supervisors by taking a critical stance on dominant approaches to art criticism (in this instance) and indeed criticality, and thus exemplifying both critical *and* non-adversarial discourses. She concludes (Belcher, 1997: 16) that 'feminist critics of academic discourse remind us of some of these better ways [to approach areas of disagreement]; writers like Hiroko and Yi-Ying show us'. This case study is particularly relevant for EAP because it combines a consideration of feminist theoretical perspectives and resistance to the orthodoxies of academic writing and contingent notions of criticality with the work of students which shows how gender, cultural affiliations and educational backgrounds (among other aspects) can both challenge and contribute to approaches to academic writing.

Challenges to adversarial discourses have persisted and are often presented from linguistic perspectives in particular, as Lloyd (2014) highlights in his appeal to change the metaphorical representation of (academic) argument from that of conflict or 'war' to one of perception … [and] 'side-steps intentionally the persuasion/violence dichotomy by defining arguments as observations made because of and within specific personal, field-specific historical, and cultural lens interpretations' (Lloyd, 2014: 43). Similar feminist concerns with how academic conventions can be developed are interested in how linguistic resources might serve the critical and political agendas of feminist scholars. This involves a specific sensitivity to the linguistic straitjacketing of certain arguably masculinist academic genres by providing examples which are intended to be experimental and liberating (Belsey, 2000; Handforth and Taylor, 2016).

Similarly, Lillis, McMullan and Tuck (2018) in their persuasive introduction to the *Gender and academic writing* JEAP special issue exhort EAP practitioners and researchers to critically re-examine ways in which participation in academia may be 'mediated by gender' in order to fulfil a 'fundamental imperative' of EAP 'to enable people from a wide diversity of linguistic, cultural and social backgrounds to engage in English medium rhetorical practices' (Lillis et al., 2018: 1). The authors give an overview of four relevant strands of work reflected in the special issue. These strands include the consideration of gender and its relationship to academic writing per se across 'all discourses and genres'; gender as 'a key aspect of identity work in the production, reception and teaching of academic writing'; ways in which EAP or the teaching of student writing is gendered and how gender may affect 'the material conditions of academic work' (such as Appleby, 2018 in the same issue). They include helpful references to illustrative articles and studies in these areas which might serve as a useful starting point for interested practitioners. However, of particular interest, in my view, is the way in which these academic writers also model innovative, ethical and even pedagogic orientations to the academic research article by including their own reflections as well as 'snippets of notes' and comments on 'the pleasures and pains of academic work' (Lillis et al., 2018: 6). In doing so, the authors (particularly Tuck in this instance) address the critiques they raise about the ways in which 'the intellectual and emotional labour of authors and editors in crafting and re-crating texts' are 'occluded in textual practices' (Lillis et al., 2018: 3).

Despite this and the fact that these writers clearly draw on the work of feminist scholars and linguists (albeit not exclusively), they do not refer to their own approach specifically as feminist but rather leave readers to infer this. This was also true of (most) other articles in the collections which justified the attention which needed to be paid to gender (e.g. Lillis and Curry, 2018), though admittedly not all of them were explicitly informed by feminist theory or showed a 'feminist imagination' (Lazar, 2017: 182). Other sociolinguists have noted the importance of making specific reference to feminism (Mills and Mullany, 2011) and this seems significant given its persistent and perennial struggles for legitimacy both within and outwith the academy.

> *I ask myself whether this is a valid 'critique' I raise here. Do writers have to say they're being feminist when the influence of feminist theories are possibly self-evident? Perhaps that has been a purposeful decision, perhaps they are showing rather than telling or they don't see themselves as academic feminists. In adding this thought here, am I being cowardly in committing to this (albeit minor) critique? I am conscious of not wanting to offend or focus on identification, when in fact I think that identification is problematic in contemporary feminisms. After reading the article, I counted how many of the acknowledgements were to female (12) versus male (3) researchers (and nearly counted up the references). Does this even mean anything?*

Similar feminist approaches to writing practices and pedagogies are modelled by academics in fields such as education and sociology and there is much to be learned, in my view, from their engagement with academic writing and feminist praxis in teaching and researching. Handforth and Taylor's (2016: 627) 'feminist bricolage' is a rather beautifully crafted product of academic collaboration between 'two individuals at different stages of [their] academic careers'. The article is a text which self-consciously plays with form based on a metaphor of 'text-quilting' and through which the writers reflexively and purposefully foreground the writing and collaborative processes and problematize many of the notions which are subsumed into conceptualizations of academic writing. For example, they reflect critically on the complex concept of 'voice' by referring to how research subjects are represented. In the case of one of the students interviewed for her study (Lucy), Carol Taylor explores the power relations that belie the selective process of representation of research subjects. Her reflections effectively capture the ethical dilemmas involved and how they seek as researchers to (partially) resolve these. Thus they write:

> The problem remains: how to represent Lucy's voice? Given that this article is a writerly complicity that both distances 'us' from Lucy and her words, albeit in different ways, and intensifies the problem we were already acutely exercised by. Our temporary 'solution' is simply to highlight the fact that, in the glistening story Rachel and I are weaving, Lucy's voice is present but it is not 'her' voice you hear (or perhaps it is but only in brief moments). We take inspiration from Mazzei and Jackson (2012) to think not what a voice *is* but what it *does*. Thus, Lucy's voice is entangled with ours as we try to work up this diffractive text whose instability keeps meaning open (Hemmings 2007).
>
> (Handforth and Taylor, 2016: 632)

The innovations evident in this chapter (it comprises different fonts, narratives and colours), which the authors refer to as 'diffraction [...] an experimental practice to undo the normalised practices of academic writing', are underpinned by explicit feminist principles (they draw on Bhavnani, 1993) which interrogate accountability, difference and positioning in the enactment of academic research and writing.

Thus there is an ethical underpinning to feminist praxis which involves self-conscious attention to power relations in pedagogic encounters and contingent researcher and practitioner reflexivity. This is evident in other fields, and it is of particular interest to EAP, perhaps, when it is operationalized in areas such as the teaching of academic writing. Danvers, Hinton-Smith and Webb (2019), for example, discuss a collective approach to thesis writing through a doctoral writing group informed by feminist theorization and positioning. Of particular relevance to EAP practitioners is how these researchers conceptualize writing and the explicit consideration of what they refer to as 'the pedagogy of writing into meaning' (Danvers et al., 2019: 26). The authors see writing not as a product, but as a 'vehicle for learning' (citing Aitchison, 2009: 7) – a perspective that chimes with elements of the process approaches to teaching writing common within EAP and language pedagogies. As they elaborate:

> Academic writing becomes recognised as not merely a set of skills demonstrating achievements [...] not an add-on to research that simply happens instrumentally if we have the right recipe and materials; but rather a complex, contextual and highly personal process of construction, re/de-construction and nurture.
> (Danvers et al., 2019: 35–6).

Interestingly, the authors also confess to a self-questioning about labelling the writing group or the pedagogy as 'feminist' when they are directly asked the question by a colleague. They confess to an awkwardness in declaring a particular socio-political and ideological perspective: 'We were squeamish about a fixing of a pre-prescribed and particular valuing, that might deter some writers from joining. We had been wary of exclusivity and of setting up the group as an effete and self-congratulatory space unable to bear the noise of dissonant or contradictory contextual voices' (Danvers et al., 2019: 42). This reflection in my view is revealing because it highlights the 'double entanglement' (McRobbie, 2009) of espousing feminist positions, since they carry the baggage of perceived exclusivity while aiming to serve the interests of inclusivity.

The studies, scholarship and pedagogies touched on in this section offer much that might be of relevance to EAP practitioners in certain contexts with certain sensibilities and interests. However, there are many other fruitful avenues of exploration ranging from micro-linguistic considerations such as the use of epicene pronouns and gender-neutral language (e.g. Stornbom, 2019) to the political explorations of how EAP work may be gendered (Tuck, 2018) and indeed at macro-levels how access to disciplines and education policy is affected by gender (e.g. Ro, Fernandez and Ramon, 2022). It is worth reiterating, however, that it is not just feminist academics that have practised and demonstrated politically engaged, critical and reflexive approaches to academic language pedagogies, research practices and genre innovations. Indeed attention has also been paid to these by established EAP writers such as Swales (2019) and Tardy (2016), who provides an extensive justification for genre innovation and a case study of how to bring it effectively into the EAP classroom. Nevertheless, as Turner (2004) and others have highlighted, the constraints and practicalities of teaching EAP, what she refers to as the 'low economic and intellectual exchange value of language work' and the 'short-cut mentality' which persists in the field, may explain why often curricula and pedagogies, and even scholarship, remain necessarily expedient, and orientations to particular critical academic and ideological frameworks and resulting innovations are still rather exceptional.

Having reviewed some relevant feminist work, in the following section I give a short example of how a feminist critical discourse analytical approach (FCDA) can serve to highlight the affordances of a feminist critical approach to evaluating pedagogic EAP materials. The example may also suggest how similar methods deployed in the classroom can sensitize students to the ways in which power relations and particular symbolic and cultural capitals may be textually encoded and reproduced.

> *Again don't know what heading to give the next section. Have written it twice and I'm still not happy with it. Perhaps editorial or reviewer feedback will help. Am also wondering whether a snippet of analysis is enough?*

Revisiting genre teaching through FCDA

Although like any theoretical and interpretative approach to linguistic analysis critical discourse analysis (CDA) is not without its critics (cf Widdowson, 1996, 1998), it is a useful framework for textual analyses in the contexts of feminist theorization for two main reasons. The first is that (F)CDA considers texts in their contexts alongside the processes and social conditions of production (Fairclough, 2015), ultimately with a view to exposing and addressing social inequalities, and the second is that it requires a close and detailed *linguistic* examination and interpretation of texts. Both these characteristics suggest a broad affinity both with the ideological concerns of feminists to expose the unequal distribution of power in gender relations and an appeal to the linguistic interests and expertise of language educators and EAP practitioners. Similarly, like EAP, CDA has been significantly influenced by Halliday's (1994) seminal work on systemic functional linguistics (SFL) and, in particular, his view of transitivity, verb processes and modality. The latter are grammatical features which tend to encode relations of power between social actors or which at least allow for these interpretations, particularly in terms of SFL's understanding of language as 'social semiotic' (Halliday, 1978). Although CDA is not per se a feminist method, it has been convincingly affiliated to feminist perspectives by linguists and researchers such as Lazar (2005, 2017). There is not a single way to undertake or approach (F)CDA but the work of Fairclough (1995, 2001, 2015), Van Dijk (1989, 1998) and Wodak and Meyer (2009) is well-established and introductions such as Machin and Mayr's (2012) provide helpful guidance for researchers, practitioners and students.

As a short example of the affordances of this feminist and critical lens, below I subject a section of a straightforward short book, *Navigating Academia; Writing Supporting Genres* (Swales and Feak, 2011), to scrutiny through a brief analysis. The aim is to illustrate what might be occluded in this approach to genre instruction that can nevertheless have an effect on how individual writers successfully engage with the genres in question. While not wishing to suggest that the authors' traditional 'move' approach to representing genres is not useful, I contend that FCDA can help to highlight what may be occluded and worthy of further consideration when we induct students into the ways of academia. I chose this text in particular because it is aimed at supporting tutors and students with 'academic-related' genres. Therefore, it deals with genres which are relatively high stakes for students but are less likely to receive prolonged attention in EAP classrooms where the focus tends to be on the reading and writing required to navigate within the disciplines. More importantly, the genres in question are also more overtly transactional texts in that they aim to solicit positive responses and 'real' results (being awarded a grant, being offered a place, etc.). Therefore such texts could be regarded as documents which represent unequal relations of power, or at least which support the gatekeeping structures providing access to academia.

The second chapter in the Swales and Feak (2011: 9–18) text, *Getting into Graduate School*, explains the rhetorical moves that might typically be expected of a *personal statement* (in the UK) or *statement of purpose* (in the United States). After a brief preamble, the authors explain why this genre is problematic (Swales and Feak, 2011:10–11), why it is important, and then extracts from authentic successful examples of the genres are provided with a commentary, followed by longer model texts with a series of linguistic and evaluative tasks for students. After a list of the five rhetorical moves found in medical residency applications as identified by Bekins, Huckin and Kijak (2004 in Swales and Feak, 2011: 12), excerpts from opening moves or 'hooks' from two students' personal statements are provided (2011: 12-13):

Student 1 extract

> I remember hearing the loud snap resonating across the field and having no doubt it was broken. Looking down at my forearm during the high school

football game, the distal end dangling as both the left radius and ulna had been broken at midshaft. I felt certain I had experienced my last football event.

Student 2 extract

The moment came on Friday, June 23rd, 2006, at precisely 5:25PM. I was attending an XX conference ....
[...]
As the conference went on, I set a challenge for myself: I would ask a question of one of the speakers about their presentation. When the final speaker stepped up to the podium, I knew this was my last chance ... And so the moment arrived, that Friday afternoon; I stood up, took a deep breath, and crossed the line from observer to participant in the professional world of XX.

In the extracts presented, I have purposefully removed explicit references to the students' identities and field of study (marked XX). Is it possible for a reader of these extracts to make any assumptions about the students' identities based on the extracts alone and what linguistic elements would drive these assumptions? For either extract, is it possible to infer what subject or discipline the student might be applying to study? If so, a linguistic analysis is a useful way to decode how the identities in the texts are linguistically 'indexed'[1] (Bucholtz and Hall, 2004).

In the book itself, the gender and nationality of the writers are made evident from the outset and in the commentary, through the use of pronouns, and their respective subjects are also signalled. In fact, Extract 1 is by a male student from the United States applying for a medical residency and Extract 2 was from an application to a British university by a female student. It is striking that the selection of student examples is both stereotypical and gendered, with the male students describing a sports injury for an application to a STEM course and the female applicant describing how she had overcome her own diffidence in attending a conference in a social science or humanities discipline. This in itself is noteworthy in that it arguably shows how textbooks can uncritically reproduce the gendering of disciplines; underrepresentation of women in STEM subjects and overrepresentation in the Humanities and some Social Sciences are well documented in the higher education literature and persist notwithstanding sustained interventions to address these disparities. However, just as revealing are the linguistic particularities of each extract, as well as their

---

[1] Bucholtz and Hall (2005: 594) argue that identities are constructed discursively by means of a range of processes including linguistic indexing or 'indexicality' which 'involves the creation of semiotic links between linguistic form and social meanings' (Ochs, 1992; Silverstein, 1985).

similarities. As Swales and Feak (2011) highlight, both opening moves are effective (and thus ultimately successful) and discursively they share features such as a narrative structure with a sequencing of events in the past and rhetorical tropes such as creating suspense and the use of descriptive language. These linguistic elements conform to the story genre and serve to capture the reader's attention, conforming thus to rhetorical move 1 'hook' (Swales and Feak, 2011: 11).

However, there are also significant linguistic differences between the two extracts. Student 1 uses the following lexical items or noun phrases: *loud snap, the field, forearm, high school football game, distal end dangling, left radius, ulna broken, midshaft, football event*. These phrases denote two clear lexical sets – the football game and the sports injury. The injury in particular comprises a range of specialized technical lexis, which clearly signals the writer's anatomical knowledge. The noun phrases used by Student 2 are as follows: *moment, an applied linguistics conference, the conference, a challenge, a question, the speakers, their presentation, the final speaker the podium, my last chance, the moment, afternoon, deep breath, the line, observer, participant, professional world of applied linguistics.* These nominal phrases relate to the lexical field of academic conferences as well as to temporality and emotion and they reflect a focus on the writer herself rather than on her prospective academic subject. A consideration of the verb processes and clause structures is also revealing. In the second extract, Student 2 uses a string of simple clauses with verbs in the past tense of which she is the subject with the pronoun *I* used five times and elided twice. The verbal processes are material (describing her physical actions, *stood up, took a breath*) or mental processes or metaphorically represented mental processes (*set myself a challenge, crossed the line*). Conversely in the first extract by Student 1, the verbal processes associated with the writer are mental processes related to cognition and perception (*remember, hearing, looking down, felt certain, experience*) and the injury itself is also represented through passivization with agency or causation of the injury obscured: *the left radius and ulna had been broken*. Another feature of extract 1 is expressions of certainty: *having no doubt it was broken* and *I felt certain*. In contrast, the female student's narrative is about how she overcomes self-doubt.

Despite the similarities between the two extracts, then, a set of similar examples might show how genres, or at least how they are conformed to, can be gendered, and this in turn has implications for how gender structures and inequalities are socially reproduced. Within the same chapter, the authors explain that their experience of reading these types of statements of purpose

(SOP) is affected by students' cultural backgrounds: 'their drafts suggest that different parts of the world have different priorities and so emphasize different things ...' (Swales and Feak, 2012: 11), but 'cross-cultural differences', in this instance, do not relate to other elements of identity beyond nationality, including gender, class and ethnicity, which I would argue beleaguers the possibility of understanding how these aspects may affect the production and reception of texts. When the authors explain further that some SOPs have less positive effects because they 'contain appeals for sympathy and special consideration: "Despite my humble background ..."' or 'appear too modest or rely too much on the belief that "deeds speak louder than words"' (Swales and Feak, 2012: 11), it seems a significant oversight to disregard the impact of aspects of identity such as class, gender or ethnicity to be potentially as significant as cultural and educational provenance. Sensitivity to these in the pedagogic arena would not only model a deeper critical engagement with texts and their discourses, but could potentially lead to more meaningful and rewarding discussions in the classroom.

Conclusion

This chapter attempts to represent feminism as a theoretical framework accessible to both students and practitioners which can provide insights into ways of understanding texts and their implication in relations of power between social groups. The reflexive, enquiring, disruptive or innovative positions which feminist lenses can support from a variety of different perspectives have necessarily only be considered briefly, but I have sought to exemplify how a 'feminist imagination' (Lazar, 2017) might be fruitfully brought to bear on the texts that support EAP practices. I have argued that studies of EAP from feminist (socio)linguistic approaches and frameworks remain relatively peripheral, particularly considering the longstanding academic interest in the relationship between gender and language. I conclude then, perhaps rather unorthodoxly, with a range of questions and issues which would fit a broadly feminist perspective. These potential avenues of enquiry may not be entirely new nor exhaustive and they are also bound to be contextually variable, but they seem relatively under-researched and may ultimately contribute to us better understanding ourselves, our students, the discourses and theories which shape our pedagogic beliefs and practices, and the field.

EAP as praxis

- What education and language acquisition theories inform EAP practices, and how are gender and other identities considered in these theories?
- How might EAP classrooms reflect gendered approaches to or behaviours in education, as well as unequal power distributions? How do these intersect with other identity features?
- [How] do we focus on students' linguistic repertoires and needs *beyond* nationality or linguistic and educational background – can gender, class, sexuality and other identity markers affect these?
- How might we consider linguistic access from a perspective of power differences both within disciplines and more widely in institutional discourses?

EAP as theory

- What theoretical frameworks most influence EAP teaching and curricula, and (how) do they reflect power and consider the identities of text producers and 'consumers'?
- Who are the key authors and theorists in EAP, and where do other (applied/socio) linguistic and social theories fit and why?
- Is the production and consumption of knowledge and learning in EAP gendered?
- How do equality discourses in HE interact with EAP theoretically and practically?

EAP as a field of work in HEIs

- Is EAP labour gendered, and, if so, (how) is this reflected in terms of employment conditions?
- What is the proportion of male to female practitioners, and how does this compare in different subject disciplines? Are work practices affected in ways specifically pertinent to the field?
- Is the proportion represented in leadership and seniority?
- What academic fields/schools are they affiliated to institutionally, and why?
- What is the relative status of Language Centres or equivalent units or communities of practice in institutions?

References

Aitchison, C. (2009), 'Writing Groups for Doctoral Education', *Studies in Higher Education*, 23 (8): 905–16.

Appleby, R. (2018), 'Academic English and Elite Masculinities', *Journal of English for Academic Purposes*, 32: 42–52.

Arya, R. (2012), 'Black Feminism in the Academy: Equality, Diversity and Inclusion', *An International Journal*, 31 (5/6): 556–72.

Belcher, D. D. (1997), 'An Argument for Nonadversarial Argumentation: On the Relevance of the Feminist Critique of Academic Discourse to L2 Writing Pedagogy', *Journal of Second Language Writing*, 6 (1): 1–21. DOI: https://doi.org/10.1016/S1060-3743(97)90003-5.

Belsey, C. (2000), 'Writing as a Feminist', *Signs*, 25 (4): 1157–60.

Benesch, S. (1998), 'Anorexia: A Feminist EAP Curriculum', in T. Smoke (ed.), *Adult ESL: Politics, Pedagogy, and Participation in Classroom and Community Programs*, 101–14, Mahwah, NJ: Erlbaum.

Bhavnani, K. K. (1993), 'Tracing the Contours: Feminist Research and Feminist Objectivity', *Women's Studies International Forum*, 16 (2): 95–104

Bucholtz, M. (2017), 'The Feminist Foundations of Language, Gender, and Sexuality Research', in S. Ehrlich, M. Meyerhoff and J. Holmes (eds), *The Handbook of Language, Gender and Sexuality*, 2nd edn, 23–47, Oxford: Wiley Blackwell.

Bucholtz, M. and K. Hall (2004), 'Theorizing Identity in Language and Sexuality Research', *Language in Society*, 33: 469–515.

Bucholtz, M. and K. Hall (2005), 'Identity and Interaction: A Sociocultural Linguistic Approach', *Discourse Studies*, 7 (4–5): 585–614.

Cameron, D. (1985), *Feminism and Linguistic Theory*, 2nd edn. Hampshire; London: Macmillan.

Cameron, D. (2005), 'Language, Gender, and Sexuality: Current Issues and New Directions', *Applied Linguistics*, 26 (4): 482–502.

Cameron, D. (2019), *FEM.I.NISM: A Brief Introduction to the Ideas, Debates & Politics of the Movement*, Chicago: University of Chicago Press.

Canagarajah, S. (2002), 'Multilingual Writers and the Academic Community: Towards a Critical Relationship', *Journal of English for Academic Purposes*, I: 29–44.

Collins, P. H. (2002), *Black Feminist Thought: Knowledge, Consciousness, and the Politics of Empowerment*, ProQuest Ebook Central: Taylor & Francis Group.

Crenshaw, K. (1989), 'Demarginalizing the Intersection of Race and Sex: A Black Feminist Critique of Antidiscrimination Doctrine, Feminist Theory and Antiracist Politics'. *University of Chicago Legal Forum*. 1989, Vol. 1.

Danvers, E., T. Hinton-Smith, and R. Webb (2019), 'Power, Pedagogy and the Personal: Feminist Ethics in Facilitating a Doctoral Writing Group', *Teaching in Higher Education*, 24 (1): 32–46.

Ehrlich, S., M. Meyerhoff, and J. Holmes, eds (2017), *The Handbook of Language, Gender and Sexuality*, 2nd edn, Oxford: Wiley Blackwell.

Fairclough, N. (1995), *Critical Discourse Analysis*, London: Longman.

Fairclough, N. (2001), 'The Discourse of New Labour: Critical Discourse Analysis', in M. Wetherell, S. Taylor and S. J. Yates (eds), *Discourse as Data: A Guide for Analysis*, 229–64, London: Sage Publications.

Fairclough, N. (2015), *Language and Power*, 3rd edn, London: Routledge.

Handforth, R. and C. A. Taylor (2016), 'Doing Academic Writing Differently: A Feminist Bricolage', *Gender and Education*, 28 (5): 627–43.

Holmes, J. and M. Meyerhoff, eds (2003), *The Handbook of Language and Gender*, Oxford: Blackwell Publishing.

hooks, b. (2000), *Feminism Is for Everybody*, London: Pluto Press.

Hyland, K. (2015), 'Genre, Discipline and Identity', *Journal of English for Academic Purposes*, 19: 32–43.

Hyland, K. (2018), 'Sympathy for the Devil? A Defence of EAP', *Language Teaching*, 51 (3): 383–99.

Lazar, M. M., ed. (2005), *Feminist Critical Discourse Analysis: Gender, Power and Ideology in Discourse*, Basingstoke: Palgrave Macmillan.

Lazar, M. M. (2009), 'Entitled to Consume: Postfeminist Femininity and a Culture of Post-critique', *Discourse & Communication*, 3 (4): 371–400.

Lazar, M. (2017), 'Feminist Critical Discourse Analysis: Relevance for Current Gender and Language Research', in S. Ehrlich, M. Meyerhoff and J. Holmes (eds), *The Handbook of Language, Gender and Sexuality*, 2nd edn, 180–99, Oxford: Wiley Blackwell.

Lillis, T., J. McMullan and J. Tuck (2018), 'Gender and Academic Writing', *Journal of English for Academic Purposes*, 32: 1–8.

Lillis, T. and M. J. Curry (2018), 'Trajectories of Knowledge and Desire: Multilingual Women Scholars Researching and Writing in Academia', *Journal of English for Academic Purposes*, 32: 53–66.

Litosseliti (2006), *Gender & Language: Theory and Practice*, London: Hodder Education.

Lloyd, K. (2014), 'Feminist Challenges to "Academic Writing" Writ Large: Changing the Argumentative Metaphor from War to Perception to Address the Problem of Argument Culture', *Intertexts*, 18: 29–46.

Machin, D. and A. Mayr (2012), *How to Do Critical Discourse Analysis*, London: Sage Publications.

McRobbie, A. (2009), *The Aftermath of Feminism: Gender, Culture and Social Change*, London: Sage Publications.

Menard-Warwick, J., M. Mori and S. Williams (2017), 'Language and Gender in Educational Contexts', in S. Ehrlich, M. Meyerhoff, and J. Holmes (eds), *The Handbook of Language, Gender and Sexuality*, 2nd edn, 471–90, Oxford: Wiley Blackwell.

Mills, S. and L. Mullany (2011), *Language, Gender and Feminism: Theory, Methodology and Practice*, Abingdon: Routledge.

Mitchell, K. M. (2017), 'Academic Voice: On Feminism, Presence, and Objectivity in Writing', *Nursing Inquiry*, 24 (4). DOI: https://doi.org/10.1111/nin.12200.

Ochs, E. (1992). 'Indexing Gender', in A. Duranti and C. Goodwin (eds), *Rethinking Context: Language as an Interactive Phenomenon*, 335–58. Cambridge: Cambridge University Press.

Ong, W. (1981), *Fighting for Life: Contest, Sexuality, and Consciousness*, Ithaca, NY: Cornell University Press.

Ro, H. K., F. Fernandez and E. J. Ramon, eds (2022), *Gender Equity in STEM in Higher Education: International Perspectives on Policy, Institutional Culture, and Individual Choice*, Abingdon: Routledge.

Silverstein, M. (1985), 'Language and the Culture of Gender: At the Intersection of Structure, Usage, and Ideology', in E. Mertz and R. J. Parmentier (eds), *Semiotic Mediation: Sociocultural and Psychological Perspectives*, 219–59, Orlando, FL: Academic Press.

Stormbom, C. (2019), 'Language Change in L2 Academic Writing: The Case of Epicene Pronouns', *Journal of English for Academic Purposes*, 38: 95–105.

Sunderland, J. (2006), *Language and Gender an Advanced Resource Book*, Abingdon: Routledge.

Swales, J. M. (2019), 'The Futures of EAP Genre Studies: A Personal Viewpoint', *Journal of English for Academic Purposes*, 38: 75–82.

Swales, J. M. and C. B. Feak (2011), *Navigating Academia: Writing Supporting Genres*, Michigan: University of Michigan Press.

Talbot, Mary (2020), *Language and Gender* 3rd Edition. Cambridge: Polity Press.

Tardy, C. M. (2016), *Beyond Convention Genre Innovation in Academic Writing*, Michigan: University of Michigan Press.

Tuck, J. (2018), '"I'm Nobody's Mum in This University": The Gendering of Work around Student Writing in UK Higher Education', *Journal of English for Academic Purposes*, 32: 32–41.

Turner, J. (2004), 'Language as Academic Purpose', *Journal of English for Academic Purposes*, 3 (2): 95–109.

Van Dijk, T. A. (1989), 'Structures of Discourse and Structures of Power', *Annals of the International Communication Association*, 12 (1): 18–59.

Van Dijk, T. A. (1998), *Ideology: A Multidisciplinary Approach*, London: Sage Publications.

Weiner, G. (1994), *Feminisms in Education*, Buckingham: Open University Press.

Widdowson, H. (1996), 'Reply to Fairclough. Discourse and Interpretation. Conjectures and Refutations', *Language and Literature*, 5 (1): 57–69.

Widdowson, H. (1998), 'The Theory and Practice of Critical Discourse Analysis', *Applied Linguistics*, 19 (1): 136–51.

Wodak, R. and M. Meyer, eds (2009), *Methods of Critical Discourse Analysis*, 2nd edn, London: Sage Publications.

Afterword

Michelle Evans

The introduction to this volume outlined the inspirations for it and acted as a manifesto in stating that social theory should be a key element of the knowledge-base of EAP practitioners and that we should develop a reflexive understanding of the field of EAP. A key purpose of the first three *Foundations* chapters was to show how social theories underpin genre theories, academic literacies and systemic functional linguistics. In the second *Perspectives* section authors were asked to make the case for the affordances of their social theory for EAP practitioners. Authors could approach these tasks in any way they chose.

As noted in the Acknowledgement section in this volume, authors were invited to take part in regular online discussions to share their thinking and progress. This allowed insights into the research and writing processes that often remain opaque for readers. These include not only the intentions and aims of the authors but the challenges and development of their thinking and writing throughout the process.

The volume editors wanted to take the opportunity to share some of these insights as a final contribution to the volume. There are a few good reasons for wanting to do so. The first reason was an attempt to capture and present a more transparent account of the research and writing processes as experienced by the authors, including the challenges and inward-facing questions or dilemmas they managed as their ideas or work developed. Linked to this, we imagined some unveiling of issues or considerations that readers of the volume could relate to in some way – possibly in their own reading of social theory or use of social theory for teaching, scholarship and other discussions of EAP knowledge and practice. Finally, this was also an opportunity to gauge the extent to which the dialogic approach taken in this volume played a role in thinking about and development of individual chapters.

In addition to these online discussions between many of the authors, each contributor was asked to reflect on any initial uncertainties or trepidation about the process or the content of their chapter in the volume. Together with the volume editors, many authors considered what was learnt or realized along the way. These realizations were possibly related to the processes involved in the development of chapters or were related perhaps to further insights or understanding of the theory authors were exploring. As a follow-on, authors considered whether they would change anything or approach their project differently. Most authors responded in writing or discussion. A light-touch thematic analysis of their insights is shared below.

The first theme relates to those reflections about the transitions made between initial conceptions for chapters and the final outcome. These are encompassed within a general sense of 'finding our way'. The second theme relates to some key aspirations and principles noted by many authors – that is an endeavour to be authentic or true to themselves, to the theory or to EAP in different ways. 'Doing what we preach' encapsulates these principles in many ways. A final thread of reflection related to some of the risks and rewards of engaging in the project. These insights linked to thoughts about challenges that were overcome and what was learnt along the way.

To conclude the volume, this afterword briefly summarizes some of the discussion points that have been highlighted in chapters and encourages EAP practitioners to take forward the contributions shared here in ways that are most useful to them.

Finding our way

Feeling overwhelmed by the scope of (even one) social theory was a recurring concern for many authors. Appreciating the fullness of each theory required a depth and breadth of understanding and a considerable amount of scholarship. Authors carefully considered how best to present this wholeness while recognizing the need to take a particular focus or to select certain features or concepts to address them in a meaningful way within the word limit of one chapter. Familiarity with each theory was thus essential but did not necessarily help with the process on its own, for various reasons. For those with extensive knowledge of theory or those continuing to extend their knowledge of the theory, finding a focus or deciding on the scope of their chapter was difficult. As the scholarship developed, the richness of the theories or frameworks led some authors to change their focus many times. Others with well-established theoretical knowledge had a sense of 'wading into' some less familiar EAP discussions and debates, especially those most recent in the field. In one case, this provided an opportunity to approach the familiar theory itself in a new way – a way informed by language and linguistic discourse rather drawing entirely anthropological and humanities-based perspectives. So, as well as outlining what social theory can do for EAP, this could be an indication of at least one way in which EAP-related discourse and practice have the potential to make contributions to existing social theory and methodology.

In the process of moving from being overwhelmed to something else, two processes were reported to be helpful. One involved a re-reading of literature using a new lens, the second involved discussion with the other authors and mentors. For most authors, the discussions did not directly influence the content of their chapter, but individuals enjoyed being part of a community. For some, the community discussions offered different insights into current EAP issues and debates. For others, the sharing of decision-making and dilemmas was reassuring, as noted by one author below:

> The Editors' efforts to gather us periodically to share work in progress seemed like an opportunity to check-in with each other and to assuage some of these hesitations. Personally, these encounters served to reassure me that others were similarly trying to find their 'way in' to the task. Rather than provide me with an anchor or platform for my own chapter, meeting up with the other contributors afforded me respite from having to have a clear-cut, resolved, predictable template. [...] I gradually felt I had a license to remain tentative and explorative.

Similarly, others described the opportunity to explore the theory as 'liberating', and they wanted to be authentic in their writing and show the genuinely transformative processes involved in their pursuits. These aspirations for chapters were then negotiated in different ways in consideration of some recurring factors – one of these being anticipation of the readers. Some thoughts on these two considerations are highlighted below.

Doing what we preach

Many authors referred to the importance of being authentic in different ways. One way was the decision to base discussions in chapters on genuine EAP work or practice – so drawing on one's experiences of 'trying things out'. Some authors endeavoured to introduce concepts and tools that had helped them to 'think more sociologically about EAP'. Many of these concepts had helped to transform their thinking and to make connections between things. As stated by one author,

'I wanted to do something that would strike the balance between the theory and its enactment in practice'. Another contributor felt as they had 'been forced to think about the application and relevance of theory, more generally, to practice' and reflected on the apparent lack of discussion of theory in many EAP circles, in the UK at least. This however led to the dilemma of how far to go in presenting these connections or relations – not only between concepts and EAP practice but in how key concepts reach across many of the social theories discussed in the volume. The authors were mindful of the connections between or the intertextuality of their own chapter and the contribution of others in the volume, as well as preceding published texts and those forthcoming (which may or may not be their own work). Some authors found it useful to read one another's working drafts to consider these relations but also to recognize the directions individuals had chosen to take.

Another way in which many authors engaged authentically was in the way they aimed to show not only how the theories were enacted in EAP practice but also in the scholarship and writing process itself. This relates closely to those aspirations that aimed to demonstrate the transformative possibilities when working with social theories in this way. This also required however a further negotiation of how to show this enactment (e.g. of approaches to writing about/within feminism or conceiving a chapter as a semantic wave) for a rather diverse audience, in a style or approach to the genre, that would fulfil the authors' aim of enacting while meeting expectations and questions that readers might have. One author reflected on some key questions about the readers.

> Thinking about the audience was hard. Who is the chapter for? Who might read it? How might my decisions shape who reads it?

Some considered their relationships with colleagues in their own institution as well as the international community, whereas others reflected on the influence on their writing at the prospect of their chapter being read (and scrutinised) by luminaries in EAP, linguistics and sociology. It was challenging to decide how much detail to give, which assumptions could be deemed prerequisite knowledge and how best to tailor the discussion to the range of EAP practices those potential readers could be invested in. The uniqueness of these negotiations and balancing acts is evident in all chapters in the volume. Consequently, it is likely that each of the contributions will not satisfy all of the possible expectations and questions of all readers. In one case, an author felt that the final version of the chapter is 'something of a hybrid, in terms of the forms of writing'; it combines elements of the theory including parts of its heritage and examples of enactment in practice, but the author still questioned whether the balance between these elements was right. More than one author echoed the sentiments below:

> I don't think the chapter ended up being what I imagined it would be. It feels uncomfortable still to let it out into the wild – but I think many people probably feel like that about their writing. It helped to remember seeing writing as a form of development in itself and this chapter as just one opportunity to think through ideas and their articulation for a particular audience.

Hence, the anticipated readership of the volume and individual chapters did influence fundamental decisions in many chapters in terms of content and genre. Understandably, there were conscious attempts to ensure that one's work would not be 'dismissed as inaccessible'. The perceived risks taken when creating hybrid or otherwise atypical texts were also noted. Other related risks and rewards are outlined in the next section.

On risks and rewards

Most authors indicated a sense of putting themselves 'out there' in this project. Some questioned their authority to write about such social theory and to do so in a way that attempted to live or enact concepts in the writing process. Anticipation of and uncertainty about how the volume and individual chapters might be received was also inevitable for many authors.

The 'community approach' to writing taken may have introduced the risk of authors feeling overly steered or their scholarly autonomy undermined in some way, but reflections indicated the contrary as one author explained:

> We were all busy, all had multiple projects on the go and our chapters were all at different stages of (in)completion, so it was audacious of the Editors to ask us to commit to meeting up beyond the writing. But we did, which suggests the format was welcoming, promising and generative.

It is worth noting here that the discussions were voluntary, and, as indicated in the quote above, the community recognized that individuals were at different stages in the process. Other authors did note however that, although they were not obliged to share their work in progress (which may have been inhibiting for some for different reasons), participating in the discussions did encourage thinking, writing and keeping to agreed writing deadlines.

A further risk of taking on this project at this point in time (2020–21) related to the very difficult circumstances the authors were working in. As aptly put below:

> The chapter was also written under difficult circumstances, which reminds me of the materiality of writing and of the EAP practitioner experience. I had lots going on in my life and at work and this shaped the time and spaces I was able to write in.

The author above recognized the impact these difficult circumstances had had on their writing. Despite the risks associated with taking on what might be deemed additional workload and added commitment, the authors remained determined to complete the task. While they were all employed in relatively stable and non-precarious circumstances, the challenges in coping with very unusual and often demanding work–home balances were real. Authors were not asked directly to reflect on reasons why they chose to stick with the project, but a recurring theme may go some way in answering one part of this question. This theme resounds those reflections about the power of the process itself – that is, the first-hand learning and insights that authors gained by going through the reading, thinking and talking. While the community discussions were supportive in different ways, each author undertook their scholarship independently and worked through the various concepts and connections in a way that allowed them to offer their own interpretation and application of theory for EAP practitioners and practice. They have shared their insights for readers in this volume in the hope that others will have the opportunity to also engage with social theory and to extend discussions about the use of social theory across the EAP community. Each of the chapters in this volume, in their own way, has demonstrated how social theory can help us to make sense of and transform different aspects of the EAP knowledge-base and practice. Authors have strived to show the impact of ontological tensions as well as the affordances of working with conceptual frameworks to question and critique who we are, what we do and why we do it.

Each author has offered suggestions as to how their analysis might inform EAP thinking and practice. Jackie Tuck has explained how the pragmatic and principled Academic Literacies can continue to help us to be reflexive, to critique and 'open up empirical exploration of what it means to do academic writing and reading in specific contexts'. Similarly, Alex Ding calls for greater reflexivity in EAP through field analysis – this time drawing on Bourdieu to continue to 'twist the screw the other way'. In different ways, Ding's chapter and Julia Molinari's chapter on Critical Realism present a tailored and detailed exploration not only of 'everyday practices and experiences', not only of individuals' roles and positions, but also of the structures and mechanisms that shape EAP practices and experiences. With a particular focus on change and agency in EAP, Molinari encourages readers to consider how this theory of social change can 'counter deterministic and anti-humanist refrains' in favour of 'more agentic dispositions'. Both authors present interesting analyses regarding the role of scholarship; these alone could act as a discussion springboard and provide an ideal topic for further reflexive practice in EAP teams and wider communities.

Most chapters indicate a theoretical eclecticism of sorts and discuss this to differing degrees. Michelle Evans demonstrates aspects of the multi-paradigmatic nature of genre traditions and encourages readers to consider some of the implications of these within genre-based practices. Ian Bruce continues to explore the complexity of genre knowledge and addresses the 'lack of construct validity in defining and researching genres'. Using Social Realism to frame genre research, readers are encouraged to assess how this analysis helps to reconsider knowledge-building and operationalization in this area. Akin to arguments presented by Molinari and Ding, Bruce offers yet another opportunity to challenge binary divisions, this time between specialised theoretical knowledge and real-world everyday knowledge. In addition, Steve Kirk shows how Legitimation Code Theory (LCT) brings together influences from (social) realism, critical realism and Bourdieu (among others) to develop an approach that can be operationalized in both practice and research. In different places the volume also encourages readers to review the influence of sociolinguistics. Jim Martin's contribution on Systemic Functional Linguistics offers a series of tailored analyses for EAP practice. Yolanda Cerda shows how feminist (socio)linguistics can provide insightful and analyses of language and genres and Collins and Haynes demonstrate how ethnographic lenses and creative non-fiction case studies can enhance critical language awareness for academic writing and university discourses.

Hopefully, the uniqueness of each chapter and the insights shared go some way in encouraging EAP practitioners to extend their discussions and own explorations of social theory for EAP. We hope readers of the volume continue to consider the claims made in this volume regarding the transformative potential of reflexivity of and for the field. In our view as editors and authors, how these discussions are taken forward in the EAP community is the next exciting prospect.

Index

Abraham, M. 2
academic discourse 28, 68–9, 89, 93, 207
academic Literacies 39–58, 138
Agar, M. 181, 184–5
agency 3, 6–7, 48–9, 97, 106, 135, 137, 141–2, 144, 147, 162, 179
Aitchison, C. 210
Alblowitz, R. 136
Archer, M. 121, 141, 143–4
Archers, A. 53
Arendt, H. 144
Ashwin, P. 139
Askehave, I. 23, 27
Ávila Reyes, N. et al 53

Bakhtin, M.M. 15, 20
Barnett, R. 139
Bartholomae, D. 43
Barton, D. 43
Bastian, H. 18
Bawarshi, A. 15, 19, 20
Bazerman, C. 18, 20, 43, 145
Belcher, D.D. 205–7
Benesch, S. 18, 204–5
Berkenkotter, C. 19
Bernstein, B. 13, 49, 51, 77–8, 88, 90–1, 114, 116, 120
Bhagatt, D. 43
Bhambra, G. K. 2
Bhaskar, R. 89, 121–2, 141–2
Bhatia, V.K. 15, 20, 23, 26–7, 33, 118–19, 126
Biber, D. 126
Bitzer, L.F. 15, 23–4
Blommaert, J. 27, 41, 47, 50, 53, 177–8, 185, 194–5
Bloome, D., et al 45
Bond, B. 139, 178, 189
Boughey, C. 39, 41, 140, 13, 146
Bourdieu, P. 4–7, 49–50, 68, 87, 89, 144–5, 155–71, 178, 201, 225, 226
Bozalek, et al 48

Brereton, J., et al 43
Breuer, E. 53
Brezecry, C. E. 2
Brisk, M. 32
Brooke, M. 88, 94
Bruce, I. i, 3–4, 6, 8, 19–20, 29, 32, 40, 52, 92, 106, 113–15, 117, 123–5, 129, 138, 144, 147–8, 156–8, 161–3, 165, 193, 226
Bucholtz, M. 202–3, 213
Burger, T. 21
Burke, K. 15, 20, 23–4, 26, 30

Cadman, K. 52
Cain, K.S. 43
Callinicos, A. 2
Cameron, D. 200–3, 205
Campion, G. 148, 162, 165
Canagarajah, S. 144, 179, 206
Canton, U., et al 40
capital 6, 48, 51, 156, 160
Carlino, P. 43
Carrell, P.L. 119
Castanheira, M.L., et al 43
Christie, F. 20, 68, 120
Clarence, S. 88, 94, 101
Clifford, J. 177, 180
Coffin, A. 22, 32, 41, 44
cognitive/cognition 4, 13, 29, 123–4, 130, 144
Cohen, L. 117, 122, 130
Coleman, L. 49, 51–3
Collier, A. 136
communicative purpose(s) 23, 118, 123, 125
Connell, R. 2
context (in genre) 23–4, 26–31, 59–60, 67, 69–70, 119, 125
conventions 16, 26, 41, 44–6, 140, 179–80, 205, 207
Cope, B. 19–20
Cowley-Haselden, S. 88, 91, 94

Creme, P. 49
Crenshaw, K. 204
critical discourse analysis 49–50, 189, 200, 211
critical Realism. 4, 9, 121, 131–54, 226
Crombie, W. 125–6
culture(s) 4, 6, 21, 22, 26, 30–2, 60, 70, 77, 190–1, 201
Curry, J.M. 44, 49, 52

deficit model 41–2, 46, 183
determinism/tic 118–19, 135–7, 142, 144, 149, 169–70
Devitt, A. 15, 19, 27–8
Ding, A. I, 3, 6, 40, 52, 92, 115, 138, 144, 147–8, 151, 157–8, 161–3, 165, 167, 193, 225–6
discourse competence 120, 126
Donohue, J.P. 22, 32, 41, 44
doxa 131, 158, 160–12, 165–6, 168
Dudley-Evans, T. 118
Durkheim, E. 2, 17, 21, 24, 29, 123

Eckberg, D. 17
Eggins, S. 30, 119, 126
Ehrlich, S., et al 200
English, F. 46
epistemology/ical 3, 53, 77, 121–2, 125, 130, 144–5, 194
ethnography/ethnographic methods 9, 16, 20, 26, 42, 45, 47, 50–3, 98–9, 118–19, 177–98

Fairclough, N. 49, 50, 179, 189, 211, 212
Feak, C.B. 32, 92, 200, 212, 214–15
feminism 199–219
Ferguson, G. 3–4
field
    of Academic Literacies 39–40
    analysis (Bourdieu) 89, 156, 161
    of EAP 3–4, 114, 135, 147, 157–8, 216
    in SFL 28–30, 69, 118, 119
Firth, J.R. 15, 21, 26, 28029, 70
Fletcher, A.J. 136
Flowerdew, J. 26, 115, 161
Freadman, A. 19
Freire, P. 187
French, A. 43

Gardner, S. 26, 93, 116
Geertz, C. 189
genre(s)
    analysis 16, 18, 70, 124, 130
    definitions of 18, 23, 59, 70–1, 118, 121
    pedagogies 15–16, 21, 50, 113–17
    traditions/approaches 15–17, 20, 47, 118–99
Gibbons, M. 139
Gimenez, J. 43
Giroux, H.A. 170
Goffman, I. 13, 20

Haberle, V. 20
habitus 49–51,161, 164–5, 167–8
Hadley, G. 43, 106, 159, 162–3
Haggis, T. 43
Halliday, M.A.K. 15, 20–3, 26, 28–30, 47, 59, 60, 62, 64–5, 68, 71, 74, 78, 171, 211
Hamilton, M. 43, 46, 144
Hamp-Lyons, L. 19–20, 159–61, 166, 168
Handforth, R. 200, 207, 209
Harwood, N. 43, 44
Hasan, R. 29–30, 118, 125–6
Heath, S.B. 47
Henderson, J. 47
hierarchy/ical 17–18, 31, 64, 71–2, 128
Hill, L. 17
Hill, P., et al 43
Hilsdon, J., et al 43
Hoey, M. 119, 121, 125–6
Hollis, M. 17
Holmwood, J. 2
Hood, S. 59–60, 118
Huckin, P. 20
Huckin, T. 19
Hutchings, C. 42
Hutchings, P. 147
Hyland, K. 5–6, 15–16, 18–19, 26–8, 32, 57, 89, 93, 121, 125–6, 138, 145, 149, 159–61, 166, 168, 199–200, 205
Hymes, D.H. 28
Hyon, S. 15–16, 19, 26

identity 3, 6–8, 19, 40–1, 45, 51–3, 77, 138–9, 146, 168, 179, 203, 205, 208, 215–16

ideology/ical 6, 18, 30, 41–2, 46, 90, 138, 140, 145, 148, 180–1, 189, 191, 205, 210–11
inequality/ies 19, 46, 48, 50, 142–3, 157, 199, 204, 213–14
Ivanič, R. 39, 41–2, 44, 49–51

Jacobs, C. 43
Jenkins, R. 166, 169–71
Jiang, F. 5, 16, 161
Johns, A.M. 19
Johnson, M. 125–6, 128–9
Judd, D. 143
judgemental rationality 121–2, 130, 136, 146–7

Kalantzis, M. 29–20
Kaufhold, K. 43–4, 49
Kendal, A. 43
Kiteley, R. 52
Knorr Cetina, K. 122, 139
knowledge
    base/ of 1, 13, 3–7, 32, 45, 88, 92, 99, 107, 113–18, 125, 127, 128–9, 136, 139, 144, 147–9, 225
    building/ production/making 86, 88, 90, 94, 97, 113–14, 121–2, 127 179, 226
    claims 89, 122, 145
    structures 78, 116
    schematic 27–8, 125
Krausse, M. 1

Lakoff, G. 119
language
    learning/teaching 13, 116, 119, 145, 166, 168, 180, 189, 199, 205, 210, 216
    social semiotic/semiosis 22, 59–60, 70
    stratum/levels of 62, 64, 66, 116
    theories/models of 21–2, 28, 40, 42, 45–8, 59–60, 66, 166, 179, 195, 204, 211
Lazer, M.M. 199–200, 203, 208, 212, 215
Lea, M. 40–5, 47, 49–50, 125, 144
legitimation/legitimate(d) 89–90, 160
legitimation Code Theory 88–105
    development of 88
    knowledge-knowers 90
    semantic gravity 93–6, 102–5
Leibowitz, B. 42
Leung, C. 43–4, 52–3

(lexico) grammar/grammatical 26, 28–9, 59, 62, 65–6, 70, 101, 118–20, 149, 166, 211
Lilliedahl, J. 215
Lillis, T. 18, 26, 39, 41–6, 49–53, 138, 141, 144–5, 178, 193, 200, 205, 207–8
literacy 42, 45, 47, 89, 97, 99, 115, 120, 129, 144–5
Lyons, J. 26

MacDonald, J. 162
Macfarlane, B. 139, 154, 145
Macnaught, L. 92, 94, 96–7
macro, meso, micro (analyses) 17–18, 28, 31–2, 48, 106, 124, 135, 147–9, 169, 210
Malinowski, B. 15, 21–2, 25, 26, 29
Mann, S.J. 43
Martin, J.R. 8, 15, 20, 22, 28, 30–2, 44, 59–60, 3, 65–6, 68, 70, 72, 74–7, 79, 88, 105, 117–20, 226
Marton, F., et al 45
Mason, M. 136, 143
Maton, K. 68–9, 87–91, 93–7, 99, 102, 107, 114, 121–2, 128, 155–6, 169
McGrath, L. 39, 43–4
McKenna, S. 39, 41, 88, 140, 143, 146
Mead, G.H. 15, 18, 20, 24
Meghji, A. 2
metadiscourse 121, 126
Meyer, S. 206–7
Miller, C. 15, 20, 23–4, 26, 30–2, 124–5
Mills, C.W. 143, 181
Mills, S. 201–3, 208
Mitchell, S. 43, 49
Mitchell, T.R. 17
Mittlemeirer, J. 138, 148
Molesworth et al 178
Monbec, L. 68, 78, 88, 91, 94
Moore, R. 1, 113, 121–2, 157
Motta-Roth, D. 20
moves 20, 32, 62–3, 66, 70, 118–21, 126, 188–9, 212, 214
Murray, N. 44

Nash, J. 21
neoliberalism, 3–4, 158
Nesi, H. 26, 89, 93, 116
new Literacy Studies 47

new Rhetoric 15, 23–4, 32
norms 18, 41–2, 44–5, 48–9, 123

ontology/ical 10, 21, 24, 120–1, 137, 141–2, 145–7, 194, 202 225
O'Neill, P. 43
Outhwaite, W. 2, 11

Paltridge, B. 26–28, 116, 119, 178
paradigm(s) 17–18, 20, 53, 143–144, 177, 204
Parkin, S. 52
Parsons, T. 21
Peacock, M. 115, 161
Pennycook, A. 137
Peters, M. 139
positivism/positivist 136, 178, 187
postmodern 2–3, 17, 177, 180, 203
power relations 6, 8, 17–18, 41, 48–49, 89, 156, 163–164 45, 179, 199, 209, 211, 216
pragmatic/sm 19, 22, 30–1, 45, 50, 120, 121, 127, 168, 205
Preece, S. 44
Price, L. 137, 143

Quinn, J. 126

Rai, L. 43
Raimes, A. 166
Rancière, J. 170
recontextualization 51, 78, 113–14, 116
reductionism/ist 143, 169–70
Reiff, M.J. 15, 19–20
relativism/t 3, 122, 140
reflexivity 4, 6, 9, 52–3, 142–3, 156, 162, 178, 204, 209–10, 225–6
register 30, 59–60, 70–1, 118–19
rhetorical
  actions/interactions 24, 27
  functions 17, 166
  moves/ steps 188–9, 212, 214
  purpose(s) 16 124–6, 129
Riazi, A.M., et al 16, 161
Ritzer, G. 17–18
Roberts, C. 5
Roberts, J.M. 151
Rose, D. 32, 59, 63, 70, 75–6, 117–19
Rose, M. 137
Rosh, E.H. 124, 119

Said, E.W. 135, 137
Saint-Georges, I. 28
Scalone, P. 41
schemata 119, 125–6, 131
schematic structures 119, 121, 126, 128
Schmaus, W. 123
Schön, D. 52
Scott, D. 122
Scott, M. 18, 39, 42, 44–5, 49, 137, 144
semantic(s) 28–9, 31
  choice 62, 69
  discourse 62–3, 70
  gravity (waves) 93, 95–6, 128–9, 223
Shaw, P. 6, 15
Shay, S. 47–8
Shutz 18
Skinner, Q. 17
social action 17–18, 20, 32
social change 18–19, 141, 149, 169, 225
social purpose(s) 17, 21, 23–4, 124
social Realism 8, 113–34
social relations/hips 21, 29, 66, 69, 123
social semiotic(s)/semiosis 22, 52–3, 59–60, 70, 211
social structure (s) 18, 28, 48, 141–2, 178
social/socio linguistics 29, 53, 78, 226
social turn 1, 79
social system 21, 28–9
socialization 4, 24, 41–2, 140, 165
society 21, 27, 32, 48, 89, 115, 141–2, 179, 193, 195
sociological
  imagination/gaze/thinking 1, 4, 6, 13, 91, 143, 156, 170, 181, 222
  themes 19, 32
  theory/framework 3, 13, 15, 32, 53, 87–8, 90, 105, 113, 121, 140–2
Spradley, J.P. 181
Stierer, B. 42, 44
Street, B. 40–4, 47, 49–50, 52–3, 125
structure and agency 6–7, 48, 141–2
Swales, J. 5–6, 20–1, 23, 26–7, 92, 117–20, 125, 126, 162, 186 200, 205, 210, 212, 214–15
Systemic Functional Linguistics
  coupling 72
  individuation 59, 76
  metafunctions 29–30, 66–7
  nominalisation 65
  realization 29–30, 64–6, 120

(re)Instantiation 30, 59, 71–2, 75
semogenesis 74–5
stratification 63–4, 66, 68, 71

Tang, R. 43
Taylor, C.M. 178, 210
text(s)
    analysis/(of) 16, 23, 32, 41, 44, 46, 64, 70, 116, 118, 178, 211, 213
    multimodal 41, 60–1, 64, 72
    types 70, 126, 212
theoretical eclectism 6–7, 19, 53, 226
Thesen, L. 39, 42–44, 52–53, 140
Torres, C.A. 17
Tribble, C. 45
Tuck, J. xii, 8, 42, 44, 46, 48, 50, 138, 145, 205, 207–8, 210, 225
Turner, B.S. 2–3, 9

Turner, J. 39–40, 42–6, 49–50, 52, 106, 159, 166, 210
Tusting, K. et al 51

values 3–4, 6, 18, 48, 91, 99, 123, 139, 141–5, 158, 168, 179
Van Dijk, T.A. 27, 119, 212
Van Pletzen, E. 44
Vico, G. 135

Wacquant, L. J.D. 4, 7, 156, 157, 165
Wan Fakhruddin, W.F.W. 15
Weiner, G. 202
Wells, et al 178
Widdowson, H.G. 26–32, 125, 211
Wingate, U. 40, 43, 45, 49

Young, M. 113

www.ingramcontent.com/pod-product-compliance
Lightning Source LLC
Chambersburg PA
CBHW062142300426
44115CB00012BA/2012